• ROMAN MURADOV

to

Cover

CLASSIC PENGUIN

Cover

to

A VISUAL CELEBRATION *of* PENGUIN CLASSICS

Edited with an Introduction by

PAUL BUCKLEY

Foreword by

AUDREY NIFFENEGGER

Preface by

ELDA ROTOR

Book Design by

MATT VEE

Hi Paul
I was in the neighborhood
and decided to drop
this. it's just a
little reminder to
say I'm always up
for a collaboration!

Have a nice day

Simone

SM

Contents

CLASSIC  PENGUIN

• DADU SHIN

Foreword

by AUDREY NIFFENEGGER

THEY SAY YOU CAN'T JUDGE A BOOK BY ITS COVER. BUT WHEN THE BOOK IS A CLASSIC, you don't have to—that book has already been judged many times over whilst sporting wildly different covers. A classic book has survived and endured great and egregious designs; it carries its world in its title and the name of its author. It is more than the sum of its covers.

This leaves the designer and the artist free to play. When the potential reader thinks she or he already knows this book (whether it is a favorite, read repeatedly, or a book so famous and entrenched in the culture that it's impossible not to imagine we know it), then the artist can reach for less obvious ideas. We don't have to define the book or sell the book using only design: The book's reputation is a design element.

Hundreds of years ago, books were bound in leather and wood. Then books were sold without covers: Readers took the blocks of uncut pages to their favorite bookbinders and had them bound to suit their own tastes. Books were furniture. Then books were issued with modest cloth covers—shy, quiet covers that might flash a little gold stamping but mostly just sat around waiting to be noticed. Then there were dust jackets, and paperbacks, and things began to get livelier.

These days books are bound in ideas.

More than a million books were published on earth in the year 2013, according to UNESCO. Many of these were self-published; many were e-books; most of them sold a few hundred copies at best. In a world of extreme competition for the affections of readers, physical books have to be alluring. They have to be intellectually sexy, these flowers of culture; they have to be colorful, innovative, strange, and wonderful. In the Darwinian library jungle a book has to advertise its charms or be overlooked.

Classic books need to be reimagined every now and then, no matter how terrific their original covers might have been. The cover shapes the reader's desire. The book only lives in the minds of its readers. The book designer and the artist respond to the book itself, to the writer's biography, to the book's reputation, to the covers that have come before this one. They deploy typography, images, wit, history, sex, flattery, anything they can think of to give this book a future, to seduce the reader into picking up this book and no other. Then they go off and have lunch and come back and do it all again for the next book.

Paul Buckley has presided over the series of Penguin Classics Deluxe Editions since 1995. The series includes books by Franz Kafka, Fyodor Dostoyevsky, Mark Twain, Mary Shelley, Jack Kerouac, Jane Austen, Thomas Pynchon, Angela Carter, Roald Dahl, the Marquis de Sade, Erica Jong, and many others. Paul has been the instigator and matchmaker for merrily various pairings of books and artists such as Frank Miller, Jillian Tamaki, Noma Bar, Mike Mignola, Ivan Brunetti, Peter Sís, Chester Brown, Art Spiegelman, Jessica Hische, Tony Millionaire, Rachell Sumpter, and so many others. It seems a little promiscuous at first glance, but the results are spectacular.

In the friction and interaction among artist and designer and book, a new thing is born. The book is remade, its delights are refreshed, it becomes inviting again. The artists are at play; they offer the books the respect of not respecting them. The artists flirt with the books, tease them and love them and leave them, knowing that these books will live to see another artist remake them once again. It's the prerogative of classics to outlast everyone who loves them.

In the end the only question left is: Why this book? Penguin Books was founded in 1935 to publish inexpensive editions of classic books. From the very beginning, innovative design was used to attract and reassure readers: Here is quality; you'll like this. *Classic Penguin: Cover to Cover* is a quintessential Penguin book, a distillation of literary design wonders both old and new. Paul Buckley and his artists have responded to these books in surprising ways and here they all are, in their crazy classic splendor, to drive us all to distraction with book lust. It is impossible to ignore any of them, but here they are in one book, so for once, dear Reader, you can have them all.

—**AN**

• EDWARD KINSELLA III

Preface

by ELDA ROTOR

AT PENGUIN, THE THURSDAY PACKAGING MEETING IS A HIGH POINT OF THE WEEK. Publishers, editors, and marketers join our creative directors and designers to talk about how we want the books to look. As editors, we share what the book conveys and the major themes, and show any competitive covers that we admire or want to avoid. Occasionally we have specific requests, like "no bonnets!" on *Middlemarch*, or a cross-section of the *Titanic* wrapped around the book, or clues sprinkled across the London streetscape for *Sherlock Holmes*. But our designers are always up for the challenge of avoiding the obvious and reaching for something fresh and smart, maybe subversive, but always **PENGUIN**.

That is just the beginning. Paul Buckley, Roseanne Serra, and their talented team put all that feedback in some creative pot on the second floor of our New York office and let it marinate. A few weeks later, they present samples from the portfolios of potential cover artists, laid out across the boardroom table like maps for us to choose our adventure. In their own way, the members of the art department begin to storytell and point out what *could* be. That is, they see what that artist may potentially contribute to enrich our overall publication, based on aesthetics, a certain palette, or just a creative instinct for the right match. Above all, they trust that collaborative artistic process, beyond the portfolios and the rough drafts. For the editors, it can be a leap of faith we take, but usually what's created is something spectacular and so much better than what we could have envisioned.

Figuring out a cover for a book—what we think readers want and what they deserve—can be daunting for all parties, but figuring out the cover for a Penguin Classic holds especially exciting challenges. Many of our titles have long histories of cover art from previous editions, even previous Penguin Classics editions. Each book possesses the dual qualities of timelessness and modern relevance that draw in readers again and again. So what should such a book look like? And what should the Penguin Classic look like?

Since the inception of Penguin Classics in 1946, book design with distinction has been part of the Penguin DNA. Shelves once dotted with the mint green spines of Penguin Twentieth-Century Classics now find a home for the tuxedo crispness of the current black spine Penguin Classics, launched in 2003. This past decade has seen the flourishing of the award-winning Penguin Classics Deluxe Editions, with deckle edges and French flaps to extend the canvas for our artists and illustrators. With Paul Buckley's guidance and vision, we've delved into designing hardcovers, providing even more opportunities for designers to dream and readers to gasp.

Many of our editions become love songs to the physical book. In my office I sit with the full rainbow spectrum of Penguin Drop Caps at my back along with the Penguin Horror series, all together a welcome sign to colleagues and visitors who can't help but pick up a book and remember a favorite classic. I would argue that the key to that remembrance, and to your encounters with a book from first read to rediscovery, begins with the cover. A book cover demands our initial engagement with a work. You may not think a cover reflects your own thoughts of a book, but it evokes a response and inspires a reader's imagination to begin building the world within the pages created by the author. The first to play with those tools are the artist and the creative director, and their collaborative efforts signify some of the most satisfying elements of the publishing business—creative visual work to connect a reader to a book, to serve as an invitation to a great reading experience.

I have been fortunate to have the opportunity to collaborate with Paul Buckley and our great design team and to enjoy the process from early rough drafts to published books. We have shared handmade stitched crafts, beautiful letterforms from favorite websites, and, of course, favorite lines from classics, to add texture and flavor to the process. My office is adorned with preliminary sketches, half-finished proofs, and printouts from packaging meetings—all stages of creative work that inspire the same editorial sentiment when I get back to my desk: *I can't wait for this book to be published.*

That's the excitement a Penguin Classics cover evokes on this end. When it's out in the world, on tables and bookshelves, it is the reader's turn to respond, and she does when she first holds the book in her hands, and years later, when she pulls a finely battered, dog-eared, annotated, and beloved Penguin Classic from her shelf. These covers imprint our memories of reading, and with each encounter, spark our imagination. A book cover is a key with which we open a world of storytelling crafted by the author, by the artist, and by ourselves, one page at a time, cover to cover.

—ER

• WILLIAM SWEENEY

Introduction

by **PAUL BUCKLEY**

WITH GREAT LITERATURE COMES GREAT RESPONSIBILITY.

I KNOW, I SEE IT, MY FIRST LINE AND I'M ALREADY A CLICHÉ. But I do believe this, or maybe it's more like I worry about it. And I'm not just talking the you-must-do-great-work-alongside-it sort of responsibility—I do work extremely hard—I'm talking about the you-might-want-to-walk-the-walk sort of thing. But I cannot. Gravitas has knocked on my door and found me completely uninhabitable. Board this one up, she said, it's never gonna work, smells like a hundred cats in there. Maybe it's my own form of artist self-doubt, but I do worry pretty much daily that these books, these authors, these colleagues deserve a more sophisticated, more urbane, far better dressed art director, or at least a version of me that comes from Connecticut, not a brick row home in Northeast Philly.

How I got here is a long rambling journey that begins with "A long time ago" and finds us here now with "At some point we all decided to have fun with it" and never looked back. Designers are fond of saying that we are only as good as our best clients. This is monumentally true—look at the imprints doing beautiful work. Much of it is attributed to a certain art director or a celebrated designer, or a much-lauded design team. But behind those visual creatives are editorial powerhouses embracing and encouraging that work. For me and my team working on the Classics, Elda Rotor rides up front yelling, "Yes, let's try this!" followed by John Siciliano and young Sam Raim. They are flanked by the always-fearless Kathryn Court and the unflinching Patrick Nolan. Everyone simply has a good time and lets artists do what they do best: follow their vision. Not a stifler in the bunch.

Due to this brand of open-mindedness, my job is often quite easy. I reach out to an artist I love whose voice matches that of the material in some modern way. I write things like "Please go for it and please have fun." Maybe that sounds a bit trite—but that's what I write, because that's what I want. I want us to laugh, to be shocked, to maybe be a touch worried. I want us all to see the material in a way that we never would have otherwise. If it looks like a familiar classic, start again.

To me the beauty of packaging the Classics is often what others see as the curse—these books, these covers have each been done over a million times, and that is exactly what frees us up to go a bit out of left field with this very well-known material. For a designer and art director, there is no better client, no better material.

It amazes me how very easy it is to be so distinctive with material for which we all have built-in ideas. When Jimi Hendrix played "The Star-Spangled Banner," it was those two things coming together that made the world stand up and go, "YES." When you find a mashup that should be so wrong but it just comes out so right, that is what art can do with material you thought you knew.

Within these pages the artists and writers involved tell you what it was like for them to dive into this material and with their hands, their minds, give it a new continuity to propel these timeless themes and stories into the world you and I are now occupying. You will see what did not make it onto the covers, rough ideas, outtakes, the excellent and the my-god-man-what-were-you-thinking?

This book is a celebration of the marriage of beautiful Art & Design and powerful iconic Literature. There will always be ways to experience things anew—the fun is in finding those who want to help you do exactly that.

—PB

Penguin

GALAXY
SERIES INTRODUCTION BY
NEIL GAIMAN

Penguin GALAXY SERIES

TYPOGRAPHY BY ALEX TROCHUT

DUNE, 2001: A SPACE ODYSSEY, NEUROMANCER, THE LEFT HAND OF DARKNESS, THE ONCE AND FUTURE KING, STRANGER IN A STRANGE LAND

CREATIVE DIRECTOR: PAUL BUCKLEY **SERIES INTRODUCER:** NEIL GAIMAN **EDITOR:** JOHN SICILIANO

● **Alex Trochut,** DESIGNER / LETTERER

The brief for the covers of the **GALAXY** collection for Penguin Classics asked to create strictly typographical covers for each title with a unique concept for each book, and to bring consistency in style that could be present in all books, from the shortest title, **DUNE**, to the longest, **THE LEFT HAND OF DARKNESS**. It was the first time I'd worked on a book collection, and although this wasn't a designing system per se, it did demand that decisions not be made on a full custom context on each book, but thinking as a series, with all the variables between titles.

The first step was about finding a typographical concept for each title. Once that core idea was defined for each book, it was about defining the series style, which should work consistently to keep all covers together but be flexible enough to allow each title to have its own typographical personality. For example, **NEUROMANCER** has an '80s technological nostalgia look in the font style, while **DUNE** is more based on an art deco style, and **2001** is a basic modular geometric design.

DUNE: This novel revolves around Arrakis, a strategic and political key planet in the galaxy, seen from different points of view by different characters playing parts in the events.

DUNE, as a word, has a unique letter structure that allows you to have the same U shape rotated four times at ninety-degree angles so that it always reads as DUNE.

This letter puzzle connected well with the idea of Arrakis being such a calculated event in the galaxy. The design ended up being on the back cover because of readability issues. And the front cover focused on a futuristic take on a medieval epic type of mood. Egypt or art deco intersected well with the idea of future and desert.

-90°

+90°

FRANK HERBERT

SERIES INTRODUCTION BY

NEIL GAIMAN

• BOOK SERIES PHOTOS, ALEX TROCHUT

Alex Trochut, DESIGNER / LETTERER

2001, A SPACE ODYSSEY is a timeless enigma that escapes human understanding. The cover presents another game to us, which forces us to look at things from a different point of view in order to be able to read them. It's almost an incomplete puzzle, where it seems difficult to be able to complete the reading. The back cover is a previous sequence of this reconstruction, with even fewer pieces to be read. The first sketches were more abstract and pushing readability to the limit, making the game harder for the reader.

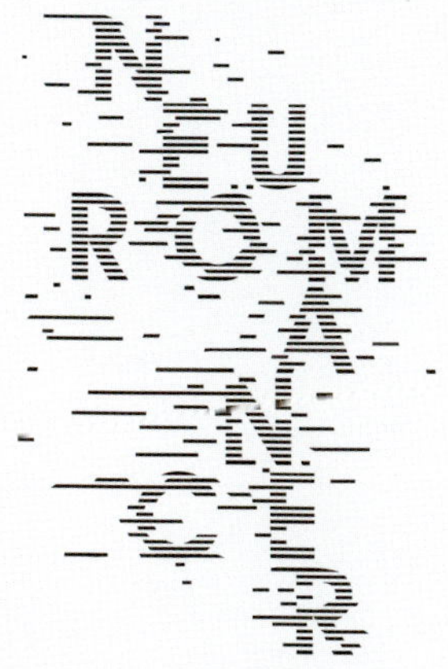

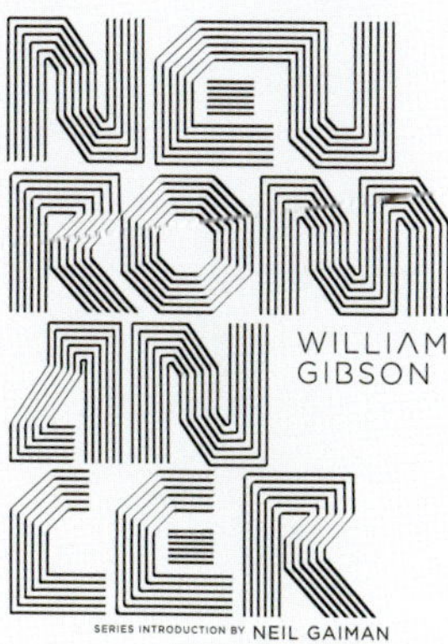

● **Alex Trochut, DESIGNER / LETTERER**

NEUROMANCER: William Gibson made the concept of cyberpunk famous. The world that **NEUROMANCER** portrays is chaotic and complex, within a more complex and intricate digital one. The future pictured in the book is not clean or sleek; it's low key and obscure, mutated into a hybrid of all kinds—cultural, racial, and even man/machine.

The glitch was a good way to capture this mix of human and machine, physical and digital, humanizing the machines and mechanizing humans, making a hybrid of both.

This is the very first idea.

● **Alex Trochut,** DESIGNER / LETTERER

The process of creating these covers was immersive and playful, and that's when good things happen—when you turn the project into an addictive game. But let's be honest, design depends on a collective acceptance and agreement between parts, and is never an act of personal freedom. This dialogue between client and designer in order to find the best way to introduce a product is key in the final result, and the process has to be an exchange of work on both sides so that they can overcome together the limitations that the process will be presenting. Limitations are what creates design. Design is about dealing with them with your own personality and style, but finding a common ground which you establish with your client. I think this series speaks to that, and it was a total privilege to be able to work along with the Penguin team, with these history gems.

• BACK COVERS, ALEX TROCHUT

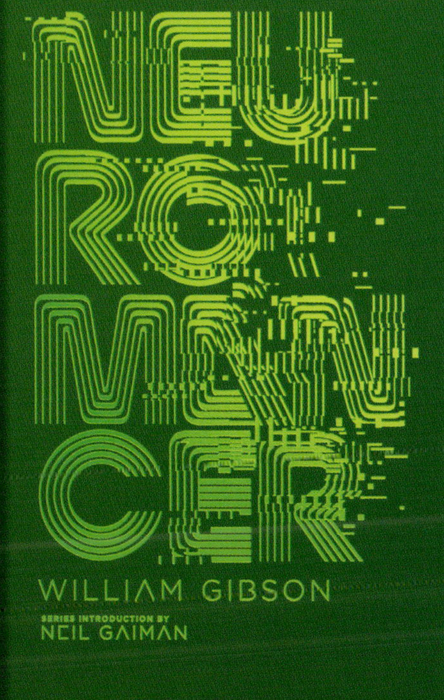

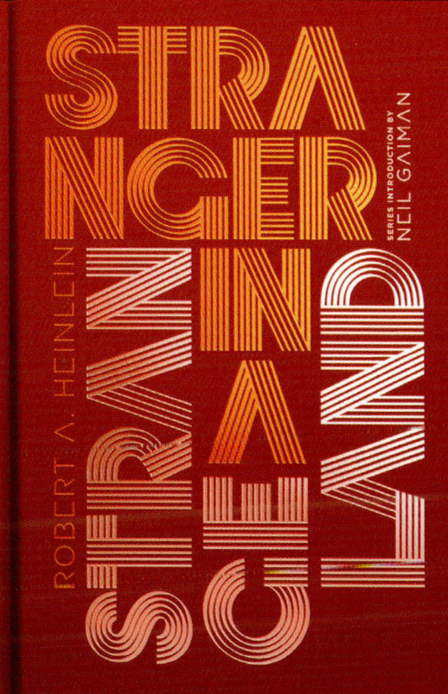

PENGUIN GALAXY

COLLECTION

Penguin Orange Collection

Penguin Orange Collection

Penguin ORANGE COLLECTION ILLUSTRATED BY ERIC NYQUIST

THE BROOM OF THE SYSTEM, THE SNOW LEOPARD, EAST OF EDEN, THE CALL OF CTHULHU

DESIGNER / CREATIVE DIRECTOR: PAUL BUCKLEY **EDITOR:** ELDA ROTOR

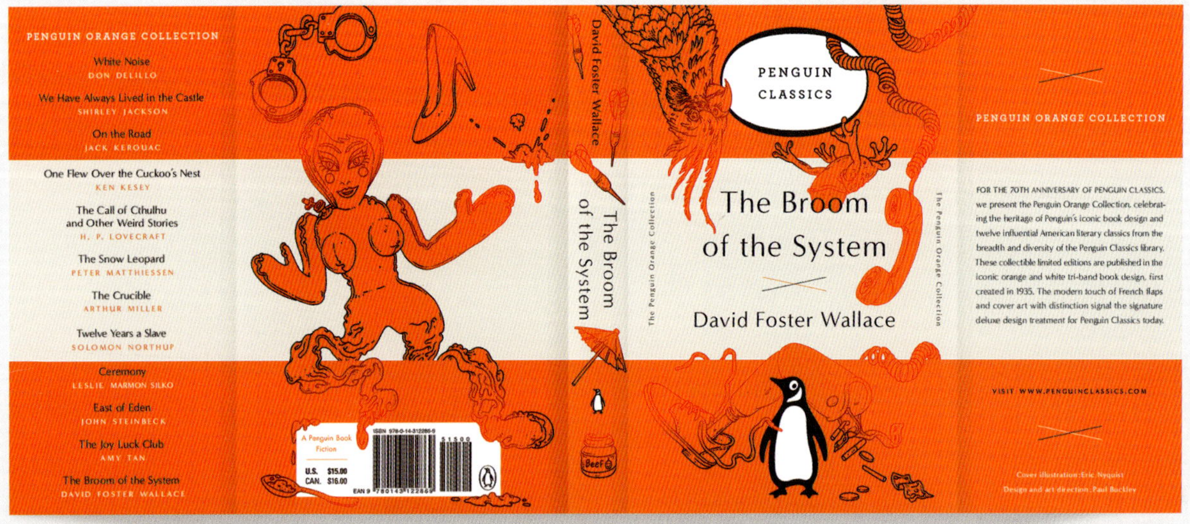

● **Eric Nyquist, ILLUSTRATOR**

The Penguin Classics' uniform design is a pillar of tradition in the publishing industry. So when Paul Buckley introduced the concept of interweaving my artwork in and around the crisp typography and stately looking orange blocks, I was thrilled. I would be visually assaulting not only the classic design, but the masterful works of Steinbeck, Wallace, Kerouac, and others. Though many of the works, like **ON THE ROAD**, **EAST OF EDEN**, and **ONE FLEW OVER THE CUCKOO'S NEST**, have become films, I chose to read each book to harvest imagery from the author's written words. One week, my fiancée became a bit curious when she discovered a Post-it on my desk with words like "Bambi's," "Vlad the Impaler," "handcuffs," and "Brenda the blow up doll" scribbled on it. I explained that they were my notes from David Foster Wallace's **THE BROOM OF THE SYSTEM**. I now look at the Penguin Classics cover differently. Not as a classical flat design, but as a rebellious 3-D landscape that displays the horrific, the absurd, and the taboo. I enjoy the fact that fluorescent splattered, dripping sludge beside a blow-up doll and handcuffs might suggest a storyline of an '80s porno, but upon further review is actually the remnants of Stonecipheco Corporation baby food (beef flavor) spit out by an unruly infant.

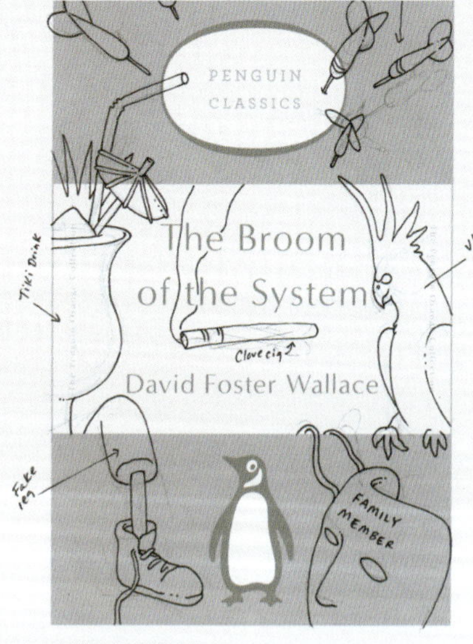

• SKETCH, ERIC NYQUIST

• BOOK SERIES PHOTOS, IN-HOUSE

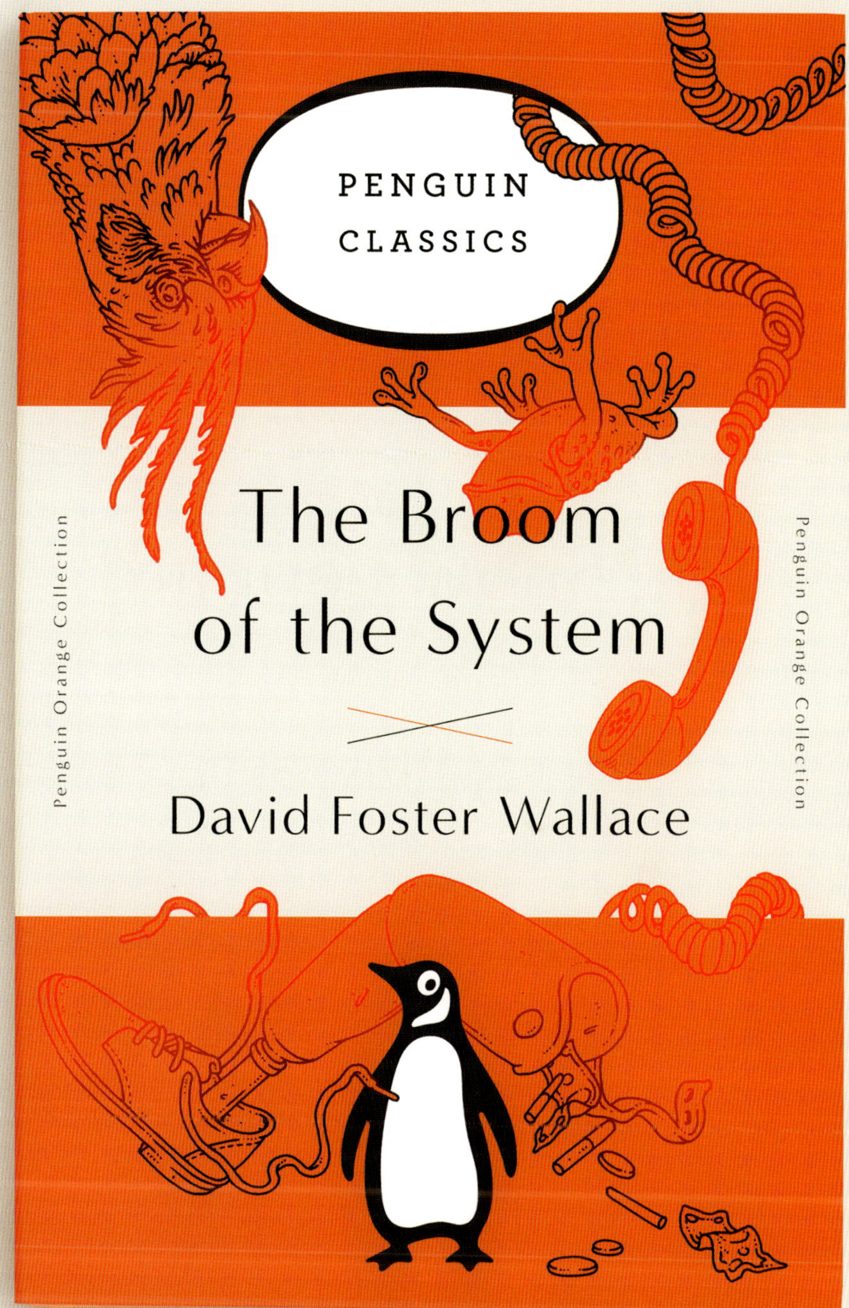
PENGUIN
CLASSICS
The Broom
of the System
David Foster Wallace
Penguin Orange Collection
Penguin Orange Collection

PENGUIN
CLASSICS
The Snow Leopard
Peter Matthiessen
Penguin Orange Collection
Penguin Orange Collection

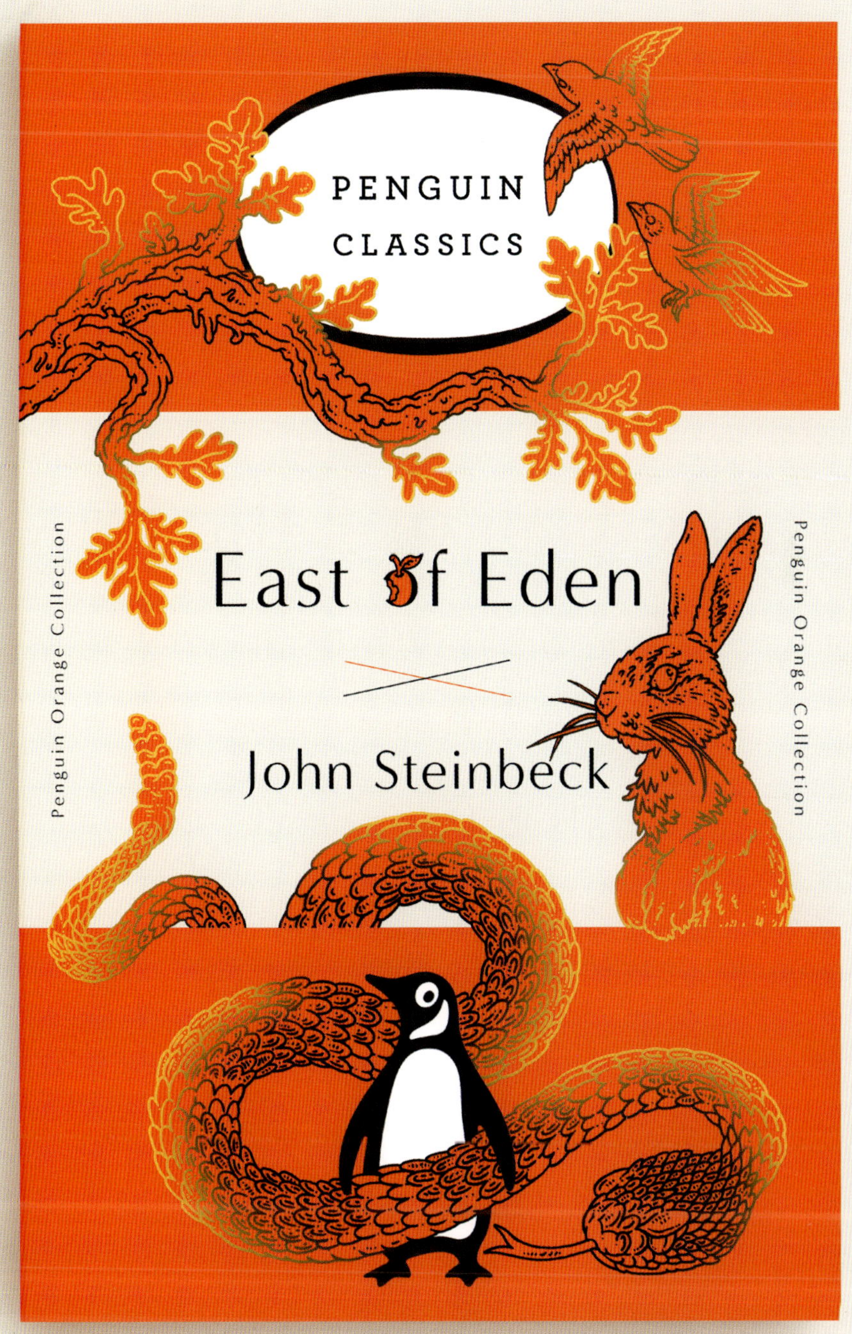
PENGUIN
CLASSICS
East of Eden
John Steinbeck
Penguin Orange Collection
Penguin Orange Collection

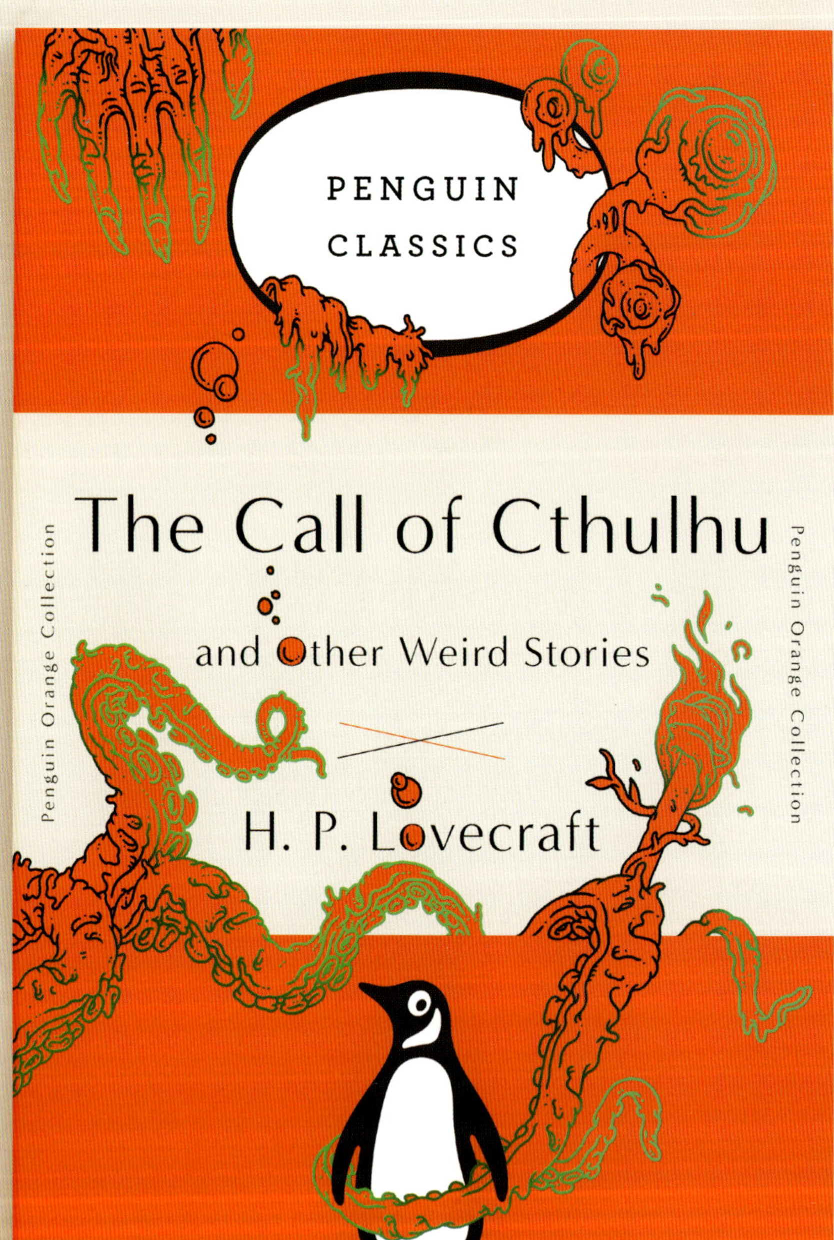
PENGUIN
CLASSICS
The Call of Cthulhu
and Other Weird Stories
H. P. Lovecraft
Penguin Orange Collection
Penguin Orange Collection

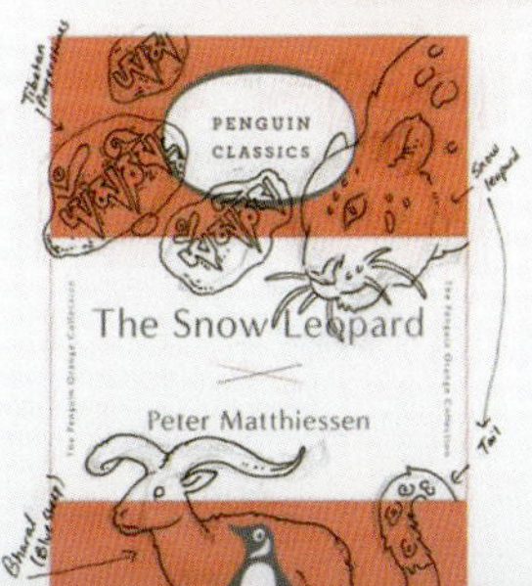

• SKETCHES, ERIC NYQUIST

Paul Buckley, DESIGNER / CREATIVE DIRECTOR

PENGUIN is one of the most iconic, most visual brands in the history of branding and this tri-stripe series is literally *the* most recognizable series in the history of book covers. If you were to google image the two words, *Penguin* and *covers*, 50 percent of all the images will pop up as this famously well-known group of books. What we are doing is taking this celebrated piece of Penguin history and playfully turning it on its head.

Elda has introduced new and often more contemporary titles, and I've updated the design to be more modern. Integral to that was the deconstruction of the Penguin logo to create a less wonky look—though, trust me, I do get that the inherent wonkiness is a big part of the charm of the original books. I wanted this offshoot to be immediately recognizable as belonging to this group while also letting the viewer know they were not exactly the same. Siblings going sleeker and more contemporary was the way I chose to convey that feeling. Integral to that was removing the penguin from its oval and keeping that oval exactly the size it would have been around the beloved bird, turning it sideways, and placing it up top where the original Penguin Books blobby shape was located (what should one call that shape?). Art-wise, there was our regular weekly art meeting, where the new series was introduced to me, and I immediately knew that I wanted to add imagery to all its shapes in an interactive three-dimensional way. A few days previously, I had just finished designing the initial cover of **CLASSIC PENGUIN**, and exploring how things can weave in and out of panels was fresh on my mind. I immediately made this little sketch during that meeting, and Elda, Kathryn Court, and Patrick Nolan liked the idea.

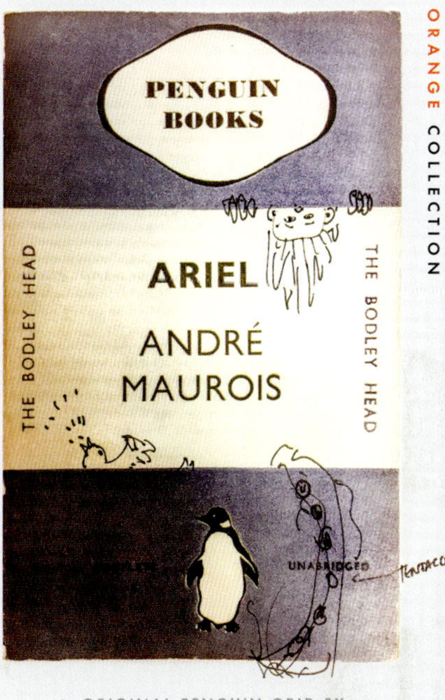

• ORIGINAL PENGUIN GRID BY JAN TSCHICHOLD WITH SKETCH BY PAUL BUCKLEY

The next step was finding the right artist and having them work in and out of the grid to highlight some of what the reader will encounter within each book. I'd been wanting to work with Eric for a very long time and his samples were on my work pile. Returning from my meeting, I knew immediately he'd be pure gold on this commission. What he has done with this series is what every art director dreams about: take this crappy ten-second sketch, and see the potential of it, and breathe amazing life into it.

Black

BLACK SPINES

SPINES

PENGUIN  CLASSICS

AUTHOR

Title

Introduction by ____________

The Case Against Satan RAY RUSSELL

ILLUSTRATOR: LOLA DUPRÉ **ART DIRECTOR:** MATT VEE **CREATIVE DIRECTOR:** PAUL BUCKLEY **EDITOR:** ELDA ROTOR

● Lola Dupré, ILLUSTRATOR

Every piece of paper is arranged by hand and dropped onto the surface using a fine brush. There can be hundreds of pieces of paper, sometimes thousands. By working with paper you run into obstacles you would not face if working digitally. There is no Ctrl+Z option when working in the paper-collage world—and a small smear of glue can be disastrous! But paper has its advantages too—not only can you observe small shadows and textures in the real physical piece, you are also only restricted by the dexterity of your hands. There was no eureka moment that made me work this way; it just always seemed to make perfect sense to me.

• UNTITLED, DETAIL WITH MATCH TO SHOW SCALE, LOLA DUPRÉ

● Matt Vee, ART DIRECTOR

During the process, it became clear that the more we added to the piece, the less evil it seemed to become. The then "bestial" and "demonic" horns now look like a silly idea in hindsight. They only served to detract from the focus of the piece—the unnerving detail always present in Lola's work. It turns out, as is usually the case, that all we needed was a simple concept, brilliantly executed. Horror, but elegant.

• SKETCHES, LOLA DUPRÉ

PENGUIN  CLASSICS

RAY RUSSELL

The Case Against Satan

Foreword by LAIRD BARRON

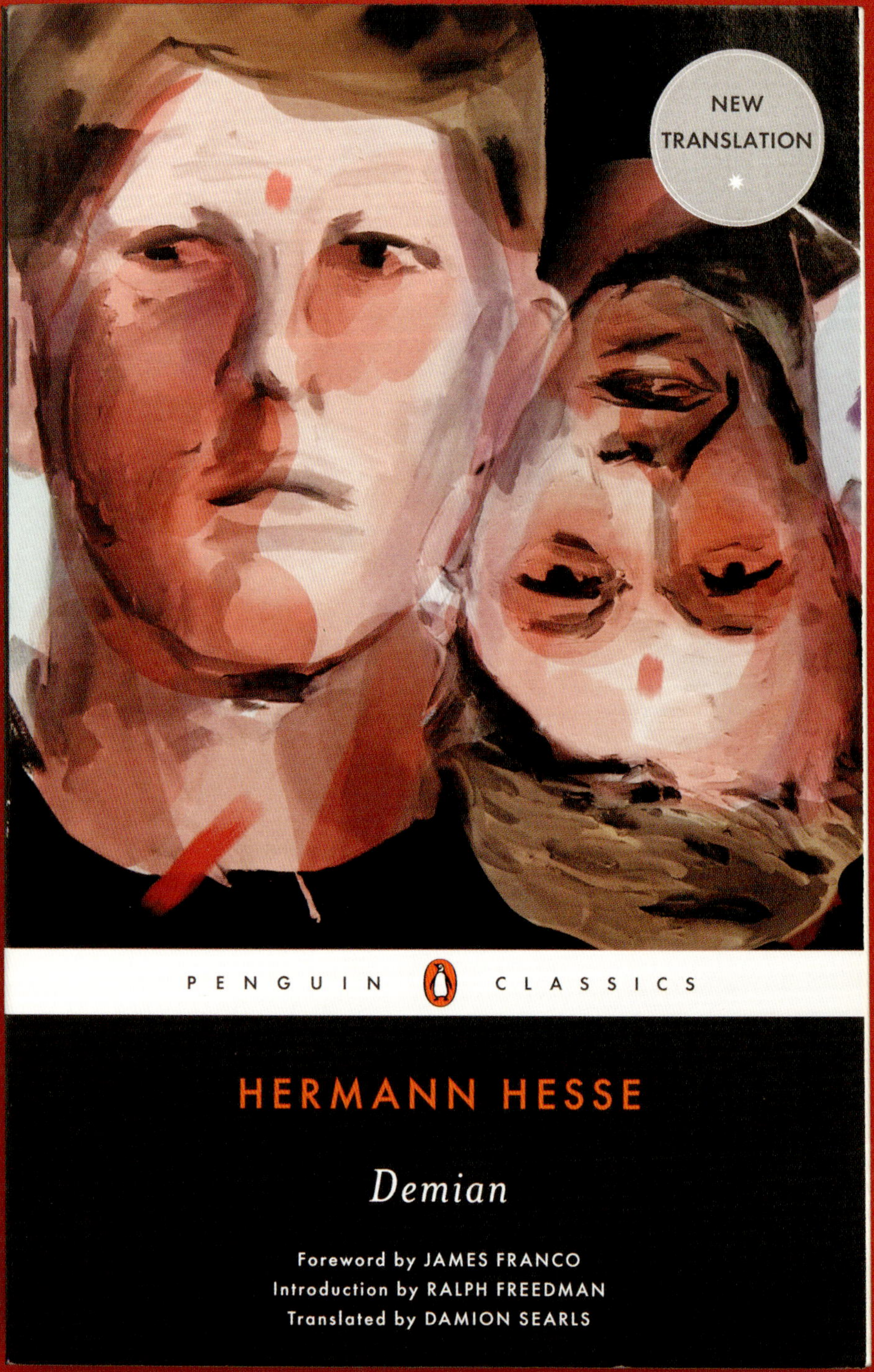

NEW TRANSLATION

PENGUIN  CLASSICS

HERMANN HESSE

Demian

Foreword by JAMES FRANCO
Introduction by RALPH FREEDMAN
Translated by DAMION SEARLS

Demian HERMANN HESSE

ILLUSTRATED BY JAMES FRANCO

ILLUSTRATOR: JAMES FRANCO **COLLAGE:** JOHN-PATRICK THOMAS **CREATIVE DIRECTOR:** PAUL BUCKLEY **EDITOR:** JOHN SICILIANO

● **James Franco,** ILLUSTRATOR

IVAN, MY DEMIAN

DEMIAN, the story of the strange artistic mentorship of one boy by his mysterious peer.

I had done a series of black and white paintings based on images from my high school yearbooks: students posing for awkward pictures, playing volleyball, playing water polo, performing on the school stage, etc.

The best painting of the series was a portrait of my troubled friend Ivan, a pale-skinned miscreant of Russian descent, with hair so fair it was white.

Ivan was not a positive mentor to me like Demian is to the hero of the book; Ivan had pulled me into the dark alleys of teen crime and debauchery. We drank malt liquor, shared Camel cigarettes, and smoked cheap weed.

Ivan would get into a fight every weekend.

He would always lose.

So every Monday he would come to school with black eyes, cuts on his cheeks, purple bruises like huge blueberry amoebas on his cream-white body.

Whenever things got bad for me, even when I was on probation, even when my license was revoked, even when my parents threatened to put me in a home for delinquent youths, I told myself that at least I wasn't as bad as Ivan.

After high school Ivan was diagnosed as a schizophrenic. He leapt from a building in San Francisco and killed himself.

I decided to use the image of Ivan matched with one of myself at age twelve. Me, innocent and unaware; he, knowing, jaded, and willful. The juxtaposition was the closest I would get to a **DEMIAN** relationship.

I had no mystical savior, but I had Ivan, the wild spirit who burned through his life, attacking everything that got in his way, and then exploded before he even had a chance.

Rest in peace, Ivan.

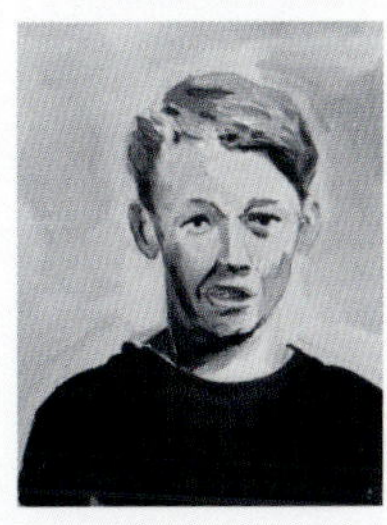

• PAINTINGS BY JAMES FRANCO

Perchance to Dream

CHARLES BEAUMONT

ILLUSTRATOR: WILLIAM SWEENEY ART DIRECTOR: COLIN WEBBER CREATIVE DIRECTOR: PAUL BUCKLEY EDITOR: SAM RAIM

● **William Sweeney**, ILLUSTRATOR

Working on the **PERCHANCE TO DREAM** artwork was something of a dream brief: The stories in the collection contain many surreal and nightmarish images, characters and scenarios which appeal to me very much. I also found Charles Beaumont's writing to have a garish, comic book–like quality, which I wanted to try and bring out with the coloring and drawing style of the artwork.

The composition of the road through a hellish landscape came to me pretty quickly and was one of two roughs that I sent to Colin Webber. The other idea was to take an image from the story "The Jungle" of a brooding figure, standing on a balcony and looking out at a futuristic landscape. This could have been interesting but I felt it didn't pack the punch of the ghost train–type journey through a land populated by various monsters from the stories, so I was glad when the latter was chosen.

The stippling technique was my attempt to evoke a bit of Virgil Finlay, one of the giants of sci-fi/fantasy illustration. I failed to come close to his masterful technique, but managed to arrive somewhere else in terms of feel, which I think sits well with Beaumont's writing. I was really happy to see the final cover design, and particularly excited for my artwork to share a book cover with the names William Shatner and Ray Bradbury.

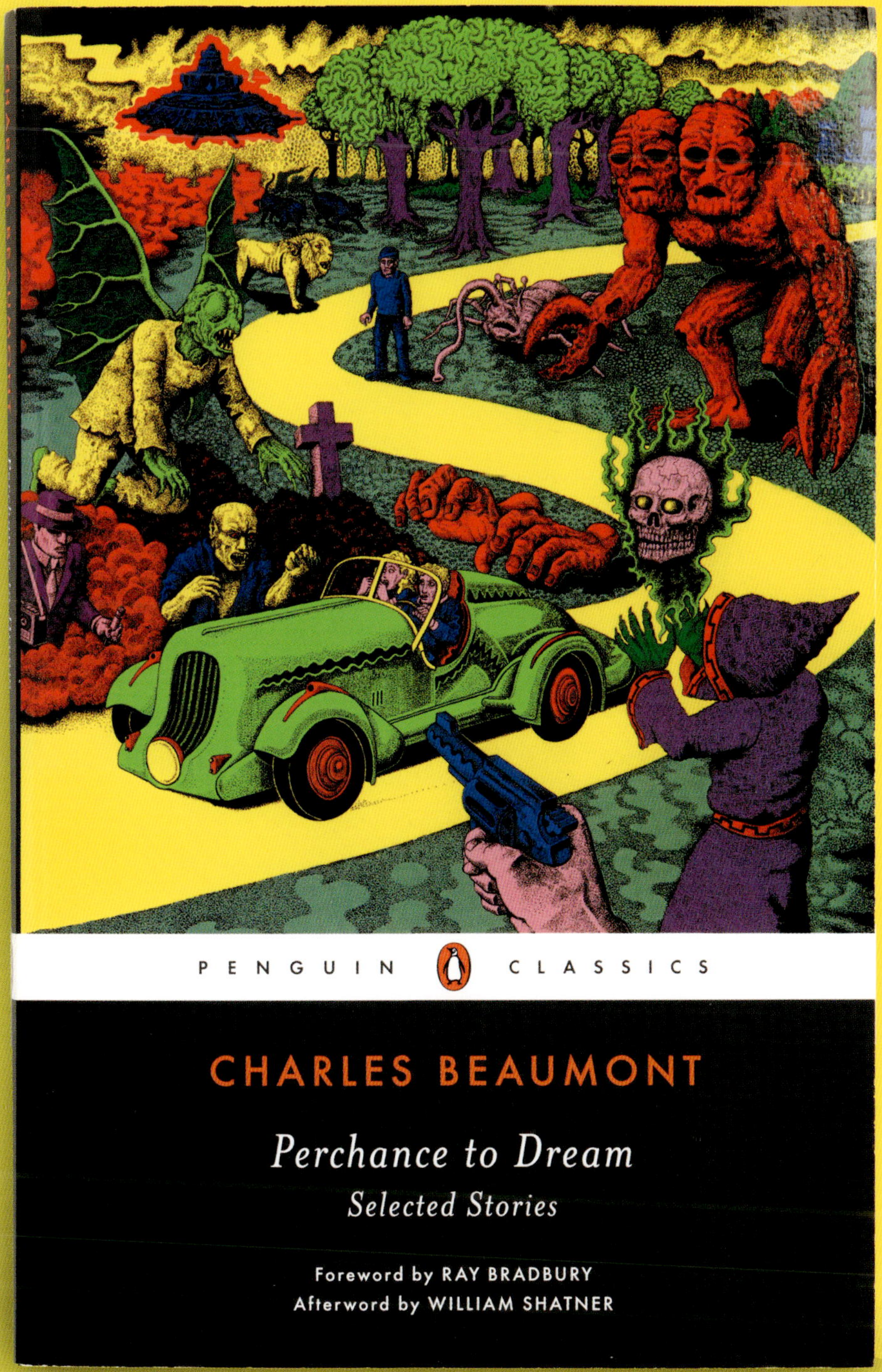

PENGUIN  CLASSICS

CHARLES BEAUMONT

Perchance to Dream

Selected Stories

Foreword by RAY BRADBURY

Afterword by WILLIAM SHATNER

• FACE BY ALEX MAJOLI, PAINT BY BON DUKE, COLLAGE BY ERIC WHITE

Black SPINES

ILLUSTRATED BY ERIC WHITE

THE TUNNEL, THE MARTYRED, IN CORNER B, DOWN SECOND AVENUE

CREATIVE DIRECTOR: PAUL BUCKLEY EDITORS: JOHN SICILIANO, ELDA ROTOR

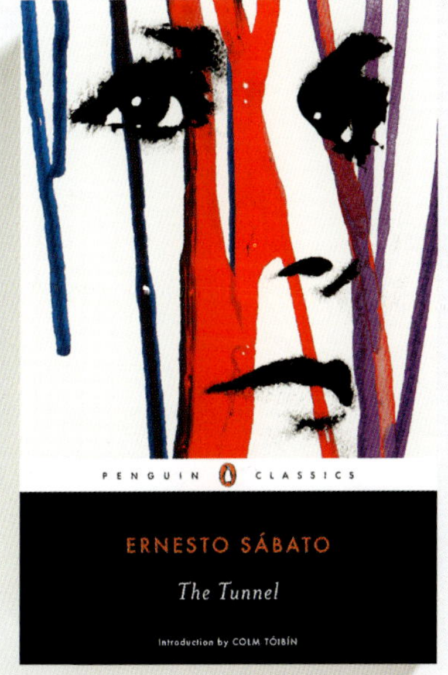

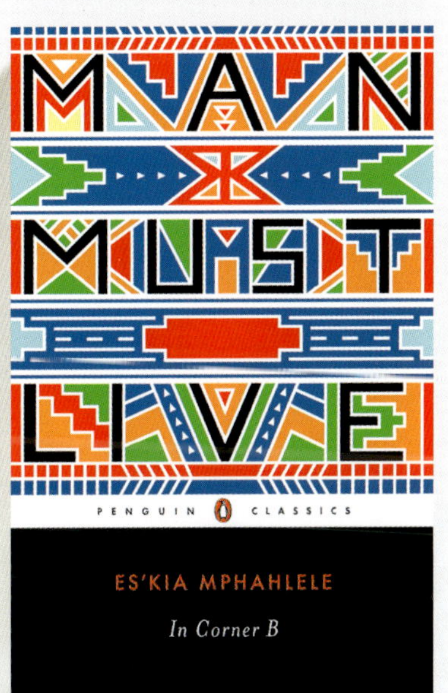

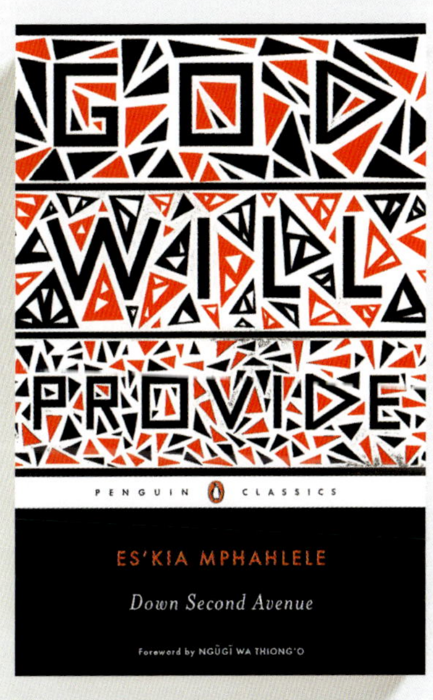

● **Eric White,** ILLUSTRATOR

THE TUNNEL – My original idea was paint pouring out of a sliced canvas. I went through the process of stabbing canvases, dripping paint all over the place, photographing drips—a big production, but the photos felt sterile. Minutes before the cover meeting I combined my paint photos with the woman's face and it clicked.

THE MARTYRED – I stayed up all night trying to solve this. Alvin Lustig's work and Robert Capa's photographs were scattered on my desk and somehow this illustration came together.

IN CORNER B – I saw this image in my mind while reading the story "Man Must Live." I then had to go through the terrible process of re-creating it.

DOWN SECOND AVENUE – The cousin of **IN CORNER B.**

Classic Crime

SERIES ILLUSTRATED BY JAYA MICELI

THE PENGUIN BOOK OF GASLIGHT CRIME, AN AFRICAN MILLIONAIRE, THE PENGUIN BOOK OF VICTORIAN WOMEN IN CRIME

ART DIRECTORS: JEN WANG, ELSA CHIAO **CREATIVE DIRECTOR:** PAUL BUCKLEY **EDITOR:** ELDA ROTOR

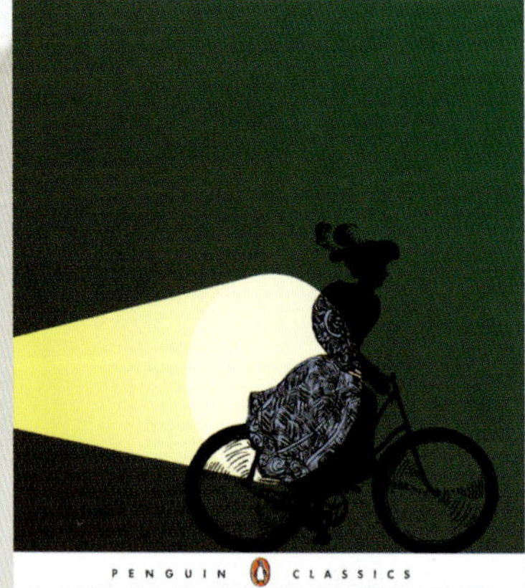

● **Michael Sims, EDITOR**

THE PENGUIN BOOK OF GASLIGHT CRIME – For this anthology I recommended a particular gaslight-era painting of London, which would have been attractive but not clever. I'm glad the designer ignored my recommendation. This cover is perfect. The book is a collection of clever stories about clever thieves—not murderers, not detectives, just thieves, from art forgers to burglars—so a clever image of theft is the best possible cover design.

Paul Buckley designed the cover for the hardback of my Viking book *Adam's Navel*, and Jaya Miceli designed the cover for my Viking book *Apollo's Fire*. I love how these books' histories connect.

THE PENGUIN BOOK OF VICTORIAN WOMEN IN CRIME – I love this cover in part because bicycles are a wonderful image of women's newfound freedom of movement in this era, and because one plays an important role in a story included. There was much consternation about the wild habits of the New Woman. The style of the drawing nicely matches the tone of the prose within. You can't tell whether the woman on the bicycle is a heroine or a villain.

● **Jaya Miceli, ILLUSTRATOR**

THE PENGUIN BOOK OF GASLIGHT CRIME was an illustration assignment given to me by Jennifer Wang. The Penguin logo theft idea was Paul Buckley's, and he had asked for a simple drawing of a hand stealing the small logo. It was a brilliant idea from Paul and a generous decision on Jen's part to ask me to illustrate the hand. Being that I was an in-house designer at the time and overly consumed by my own frantic design deadlines and projects, I kept forgetting to do the actual drawing and missed some deadlines. Jen kept pestering and I finally groggily remembered on a Thursday morning, our usual Penguin meeting day, and I drew the gloved hand while sitting on the train to work that morning, my own hand wobbling and rushing to finish the drawing before my stop came.

Black SPINES

ILLUSTRATED BY BRIANNA HARDEN

A PRINCE OF SWINDLERS, PITCHING IN A PINCH, TEN NORTH FREDERICK

CREATIVE DIRECTOR: PAUL BUCKLEY EDITORS: HENRY FREEDLAND, JOHN SICILIANO

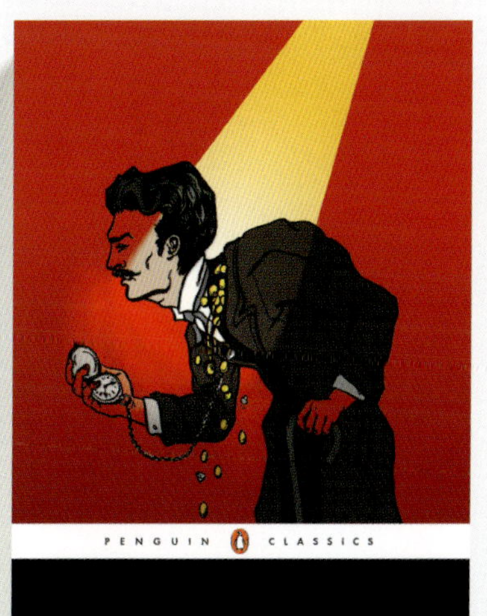

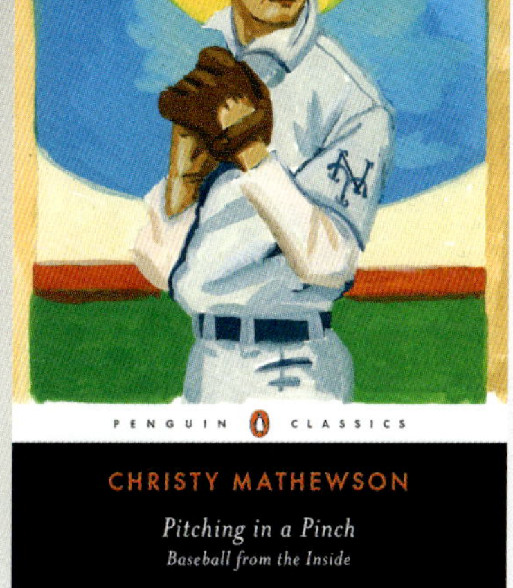

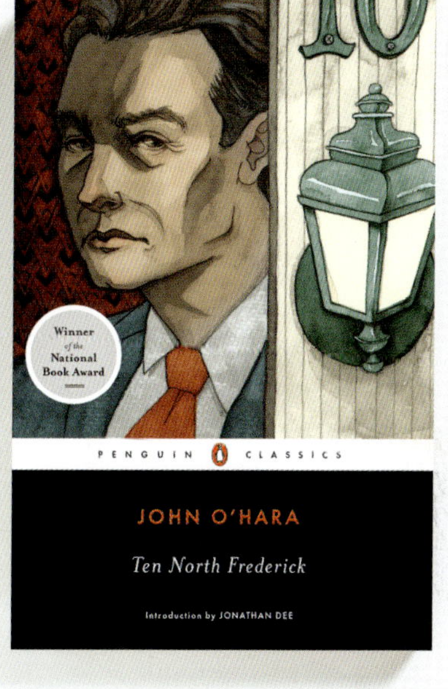

● **Brianna Harden**, ILLUSTRATOR

A PRINCE OF SWINDLERS – They say that artists tend to draw their own likeness into the people they depict. I have a slightly different affliction: When I draw men, I tend to inadvertently evoke the features of whoever I'm dating at the time. While I've long since scrubbed my social media photo albums clean of any saccharine couples selfies and mementos from past relationships, this drawing has been enduringly printed on the covers of thousands of books. So I've effectively cursed myself to be forever haunted by a mustachioed (and hunchbacked) incarnation of a former beau. You ask me if perhaps a subconscious connection can be drawn from my depiction of him as the poseur/thief from this classic tale of swindle and deceit. Yeah, well, maybe!

PITCHING IN A PINCH – I grew up a loyal Los Angeles Dodgers fan, but I was able to push aside my home team's rivalry with the formerly New York Giants for long enough to work on this cover about their Hall of Fame pitcher from the turn of the last century. Baseball cards from the era were a major inspiration, and I borrowed from their saturated color palettes to evoke the era. It seems to have worked: A friend of mine bought a copy of this book and assumed the cover art was from a vintage trading card until I informed him otherwise.

TEN NORTH FREDERICK – I'm not typically a proponent of using a close-up portrait on a cover. I think it imposes too much of one person's visual interpretation on the reader. But in this story of a society man destroyed, the main character's outsize ego is in such tight focus that a moody representation felt appropriate.

Adventures of Huckleberry Finn MARK TWAIN

ILLUSTRATOR: EDWARD KINSELLA III ART DIRECTOR: BRIANNA HARDEN CREATIVE DIRECTOR: PAUL BUCKLEY EDITOR: ELDA ROTOR

● **Azar Nafisi**, AUTHOR

Like all great book covers this one entices by what it reveals as well as by what it promises. The image stays in your mind independent of the story, finding its own niche in your heart, and it does so because it captures the spirit of Mark Twain's classic. While illuminating, it has its own layers and mysteries: The intimacy is theirs, the two of them—the African-American man, and the boy identified not by his face but by the wide-brimmed hat sheltering him from our gaze. They have their backs to us, the world that has turned its back to them. What are they gazing at? That golden orange river framed by trees the color of night? Not at us, but at the "unknown territory." The intimacy is theirs; the mystery is ours!

● **Edward Kinsella III**, ILLUSTRATOR

This was one of those cases where I turned in great sketches, and yet they weren't what the client was looking for. This was also one of those cases when what the client requested ended up being the best option.

I still think this is one of the best images I've ever made. ADVENTURES OF HUCKLEBERRY FINN has meant a lot to me since I was a child, and I knew that I really needed to do it justice. Twain's writing, especially in HUCK FINN, truly has the power to transport. I was on that raft with Huck and Jim. I escaped and traveled down the river with them.

It's rare that I feel completely immersed in the subject matter of what I'm illustrating, but in this case, I was. I wanted the viewer to be with Huck and Jim as well, looking down the river... looking toward freedom. I hope I got that across.

This cover image went on to win a GOLD MEDAL from the Society of Illustrators, in New York. It's an honor I never thought I'd receive, and I was absolutely thrilled that this piece in particular received the award, as I felt it was a huge leap forward for me as an illustrator.

The Adventures of Tom Sawyer MARK TWAIN

ILLUSTRATOR: EDWARD KINSELLA III ART DIRECTOR: BRIANNA HARDEN CREATIVE DIRECTOR: PAUL BUCKLEY EDITOR: ELDA ROTOR

• GOLD MEDAL, SOCIETY OF ILLUSTRATORS. PHOTO BY MATT VEE

● **Edward Kinsella III**, ILLUSTRATOR

Illustrating the cover for a classic is a daunting task, but I felt a bit of relief knowing that Hannibal, Missouri, Mark Twain's hometown, is only about an hour north from where I live. Being a Missourian, with a strong connection to the rivers, creeks, and caves of the state, I had a deeply ingrained sense of the material from the beginning.

I made the short trip to Hannibal, took a ton of reference photos, and even toured the famous cave where Twain spent time as a child. Before the trip I had thoughts of what I wanted to sketch for possible covers, but the tour solidified my hope to have the cave on the cover.

It's amazing what the right reference photos can do. I would have never thought to have those dark cuts through the rock, but I think they ended up being what makes the image so interesting.

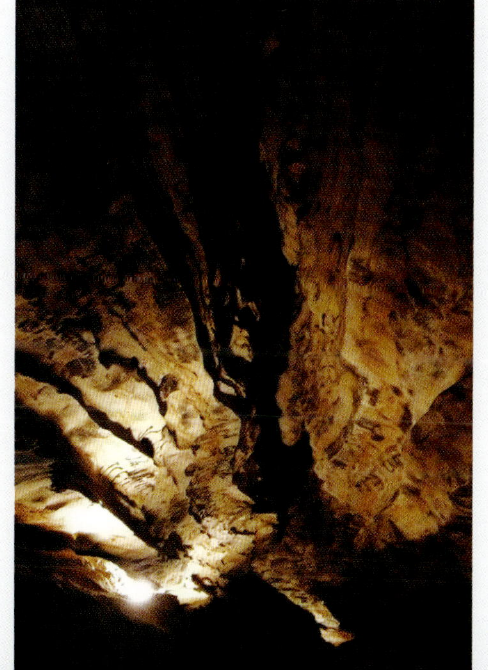

• CAVE PHOTO, EDWARD KINSELLA III

• ADVENTURES OF HUCKLEBERRY FINN DETAIL, EDWARD KINSELLA III

• THE ADVENTURES OF TOM SAWYER DETAIL, EDWARD KINSELLA III

Edward Kinsella III, ILLUSTRATOR

I figured out this technique through my own experimentation and frustration with other media. I start with a pencil drawing, rendered in only face and hand areas. I then float ink wash over that to build up the values. This essentially turns the drawing to a painting. The reason I figured this out was that I was very frustrated with losing my drawings when the painting stage happened (I used to work in acrylic). The color is gouache wash and watercolor wash. The dark areas are a waterproof ink mixture and the opaque light areas are gouache as well. It's all done on Stonehenge paper.

My biggest source of inspiration is turn-of-the-century poster art. Since I was a kid, I always loved the blend of flat and rendered in those pieces and the minimal color palettes. That juxtaposition between flat and rendered, color and neutrals, control and looseness is something I try to get in my work. I think these pieces have that balance I strive for.

Jorge Amado

SERIES ILLUSTRATED BY KRISTEN HAFF

THE DOUBLE DEATH OF QUINCAS WATER-BRAY, THE VIOLENT LAND, THE DISCOVERY OF AMERICA BY THE TURKS

CREATIVE DIRECTOR: PAUL BUCKLEY EDITOR: JOHN SICILIANO

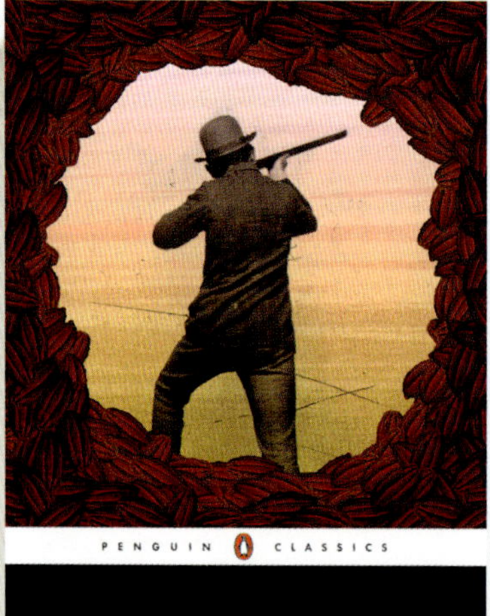

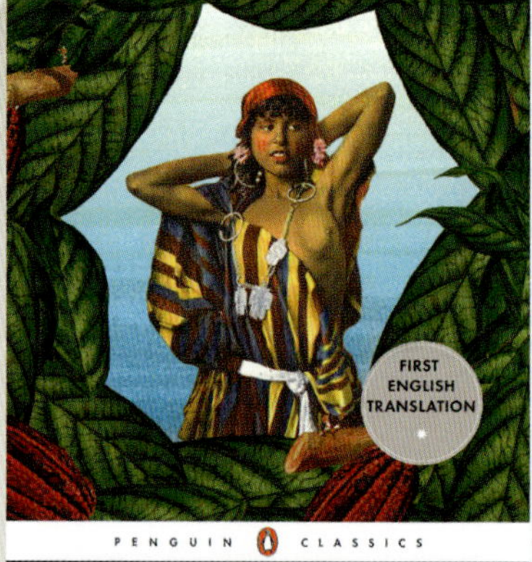

● **Kristen Haff, ILLUSTRATOR**

THE DOUBLE DEATH OF QUINCAS WATER-BRAY – I had been digging deep into collage art at this time and really wanted to come up with something unique and special. I tried to pull together a few images from the book and Paul seemed happy with them. The editor ended up choosing the two caskets on the cover. This was a good choice—it's graphic and strong—yet I still wanted the collage with the head to win. The chosen cover ultimately provided a template for the others in this series, so it was probably in my favor that it won out.

THE VIOLENT LAND – This followed the template I'd set up for this series. At the time I was struggling with a different cover that was giving me hell—and I was throwing a million different images into this template to come up with something strong. In hindsight this one feels slightly disconnected from the other ones—and I'd completely forgotten I'd created a moon version. The moon version is cool! I'll never know why it wasn't chosen. It's now just another cover to lay on the "killed" pile.

THE DISCOVERY OF AMERICA BY THE TURKS – This is the only cover I was successfully able to get boobs onto. The End.

PENGUIN  CLASSICS

JORGE AMADO

The Double Death of Quincas Water-Bray

Introduction by RIVKA GALCHEN
Translated by GREGORY RABASSA

PENGUIN CLASSICS

JORGE AMADO

The Discovery of America by the Turks

Foreword by JOSE SARAMAGO
Translated by GREGORY RABASSA

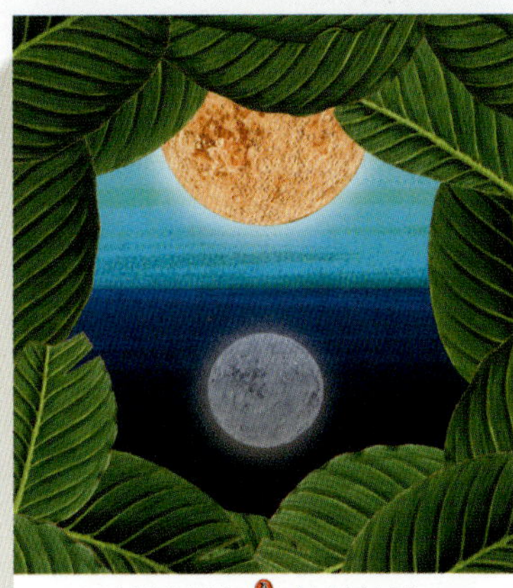

PENGUIN CLASSICS

JORGE AMADO

The Violent Land

• PUPPETEER DETAIL, CHRIS MARS

Songs of a Dead Dreamer and *Grimscribe* THOMAS LIGOTTI

ILLUSTRATOR: CHRIS MARS **ART DIRECTOR:** COLIN WEBBER **CREATIVE DIRECTOR:** PAUL BUCKLEY **EDITOR:** ELDA ROTOR

● **Chris Mars,** ILLUSTRATOR

My brother Joe has schizophrenia. The havoc this has wrought upon him has not hardened him, nor does it define him. Joe is kind, thoughtful, generous, witty.

A label is a ready tool to dismiss one's humanity, be it wielded by an individual, an organization, a party, or a nation. I was young when I learned that the hardest part of my brother's illness is not its symptoms so much as its perceptions, as well as the results of dismissal, prejudice, and pointless fear.

• HYPNAGOGIA, CHRIS MARS

I watched old horror movies cheering for monsters, or if not cheering for them, hoping for them...hoping for understanding, for peace.

Thomas Ligotti understands that the absence of hope is the most terrifying thing of all. It is my great honor to have my work associated with his, a man whose world is as fantastic to enter as it is to escape from.

The Portable
Malcolm X Reader

APPROVED COVER (LEFT), UNUSED COMPS (CENTER, RIGHT)

CREATIVE DIRECTOR: PAUL BUCKLEY **EDITOR:** BRITTNEY ROSS

• APPROVED COVER

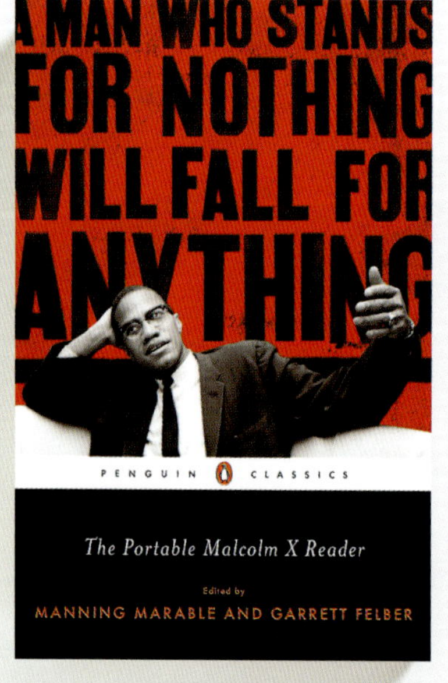

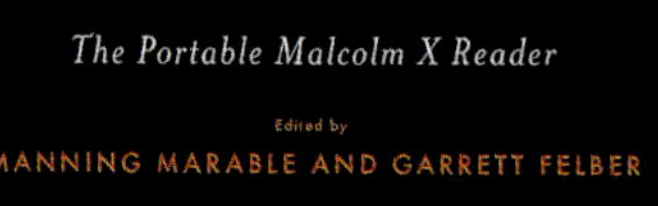

● **Kristen Haff,** ILLUSTRATOR

To the average person, the name Malcolm X conjures images of courage and human rights advocacy. When the name was spoken to me, my mind went blank. Such a magnitude of bravery and wisdom—how is someone supposed to distill that down into a fitting cover? "Malcolm . . . X . . . Malcolm . . . X . . . I know! I'll put a large *X* over his face. . . . No . . . no that's stupid. . . . I know! I'll put his face *in* an X! . . . No . . . NO!" Overcome with self-contempt, I scoured the Internet, searching for inspiration. I stumbled across a few great images, inspiring quotes, a Jaya Miceli cover that I vaguely ripped off, and voilà—a cover was born.

Twelve Years a Slave

SOLOMON NORTHUP

APPROVED COVER (LEFT), UNUSED COMPS (CENTER, RIGHT)

CREATIVE DIRECTOR: PAUL BUCKLEY **EDITOR:** JOHN SICILIANO

• APPROVED COVER

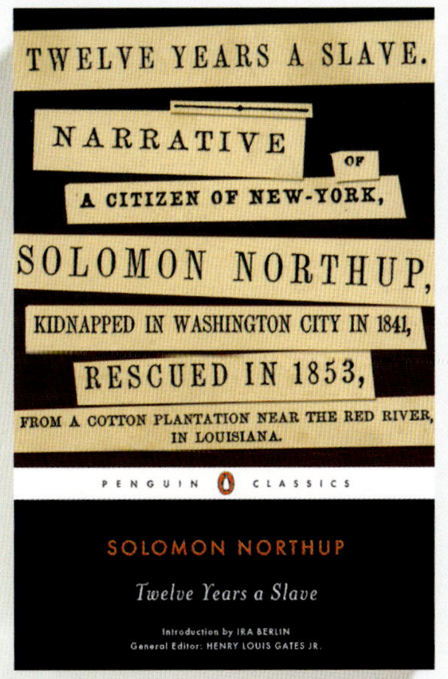

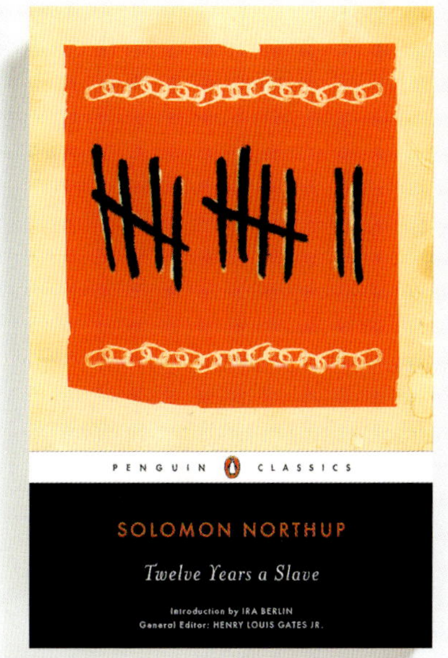

● **Kristen Haff**, ILLUSTRATOR

I don't know why this particular cover was easy, but it was. I had been researching graphic woodblock cuts when this was assigned, and I created a few different designs with chains and various scratches with a cut-up eraser and an ink pad. I imagined Solomon Northup in confinement, creating crude tools to count the passing days. Further Internet digging surfaced an archived first edition of Northup's narrative. The type was set so beautifully on its cover page, I couldn't resist pulling it into its own design, which ended up becoming the cover. Then, they took this cover and replaced it with the movie poster of **TWELVE YEARS A SLAVE**, costarring Brad Pitt. And now, because of all this, I consider myself closer to Brad Pitt than the average person.

Jason and the Argonauts APOLLONIUS OF RHODES

ILLUSTRATOR: ANGIE WANG **ART DIRECTOR:** JOHN-PATRICK THOMAS **CREATIVE DIRECTOR:** PAUL BUCKLEY **EDITOR:** ELDA ROTOR

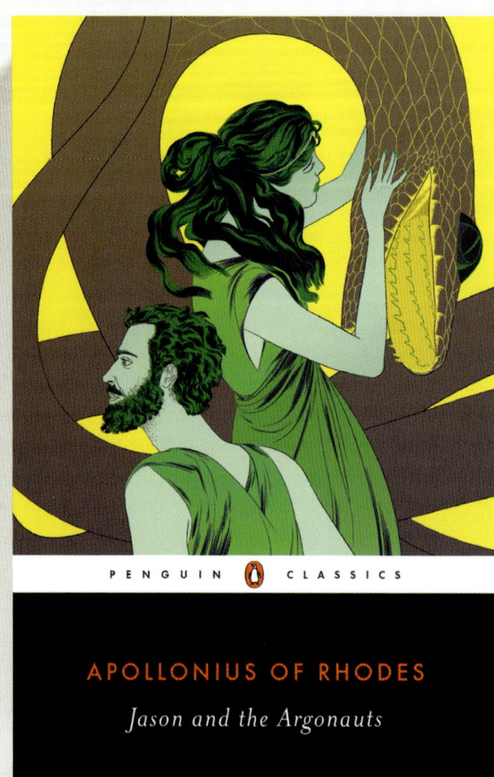

PENGUIN CLASSICS
APOLLONIUS OF RHODES
Jason and the Argonauts

• SKETCHES, ANGIE WANG

● **Angie Wang,** ILLUSTRATOR

Since I took four years of ancient Greek in college, I wound up doing a lot of my own translation from ancient Greek to English on the Perseus Digital Library to figure out what exactly was happening with the monstrous serpent and the fleece in the scene I intended to illustrate. Was it actually a serpent or was it some kind of dragon? Did it have legs? Where were they standing? My background in a long-dead language finally came in handy. I had access to notes and scholarly commentary on the scene that most illustrators might not have been able to look up.

I was a little reluctant to work in the inky, high-gloss style that had been requested of me, to be honest. It's a style I'd given up due to its many limitations, but it is tremendously satisfying to execute and the results are easy to like. Using an acidic color scheme made the cover pop; I'd been asked for more of a modern, dynamic take on the book, so it seemed appropriately opposed to the red-figure scenes that evoke antiquity.

Shirley Jackson

SERIES ILLUSTRATED BY BRIANNA HARDEN

COME ALONG WITH ME, THE ROAD THROUGH THE WALL, HANGSAMAN

CREATIVE DIRECTOR: PAUL BUCKLEY EDITOR: ELDA ROTOR

Brianna Harden, ILLUSTRATOR

I had an early breakthrough as a cover designer thanks to a lesson from a senior colleague, after he saw me toiling away to digitally create a Xerox-textured effect. He patiently walked me to our busted old black-and-white copy machine, and asked why I was working so hard to re-create what a machine could authentically do for me in seconds. By printing out art or typography and then repeatedly feeding the results back through the copier, I could instantly achieve a gritty, distressed look that saved me hours of needlessly faux-distressing my work in Photoshop.

I giddily began applying this newly discovered technique whenever I could, and for the eerie domestic horror of the Shirley Jackson novels, the style was an obvious fit. The elements on the covers were constructed by collage: Photographs of wood grain were photocopied and then cut and rearranged to look like a chest or a desk, and pictures of brick walls were trimmed with an X-acto knife and re-constructed piece by piece. The process was a puzzle, and it felt like sculpture in two dimensions.

Across the course of creating art for the series, I gathered dozens of images of wood boards, fabric, twigs, brick walls, and people parts. Sourcing the photographic bits and pieces was almost as much fun as pasting them together—for example, the neckline on the young woman on HANGSAMAN may or may not be lifted from a photo of Elizabeth Taylor.

Black SPINES

ILLUSTRATED BY NICK MISANI

THE POETICS OF SPACE, THE PORTABLE EMERSON, THE ANALECTS

CREATIVE DIRECTOR: PAUL BUCKLEY   EDITORS: ELDA ROTOR, JOHN SICILIANO

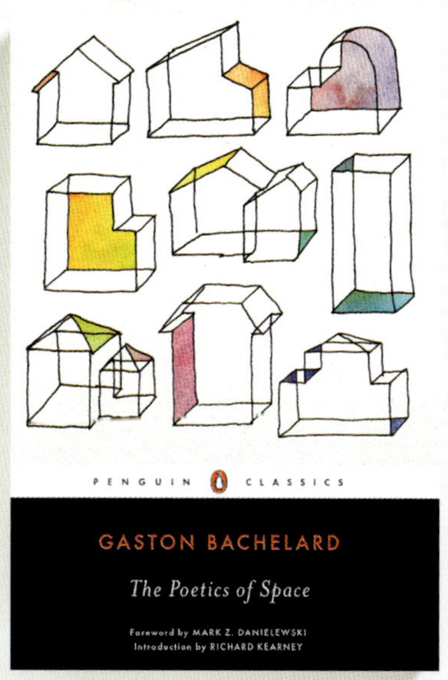

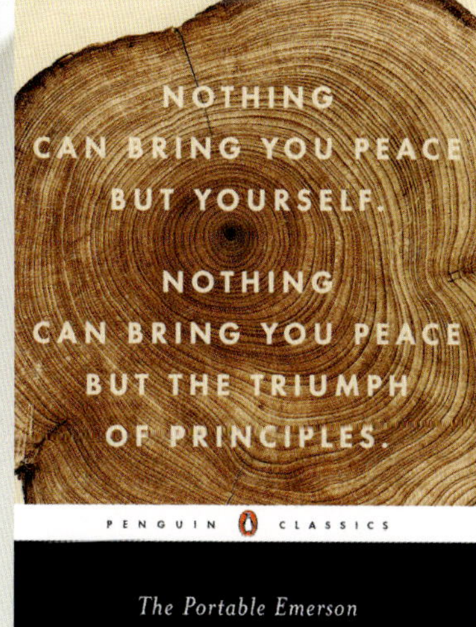

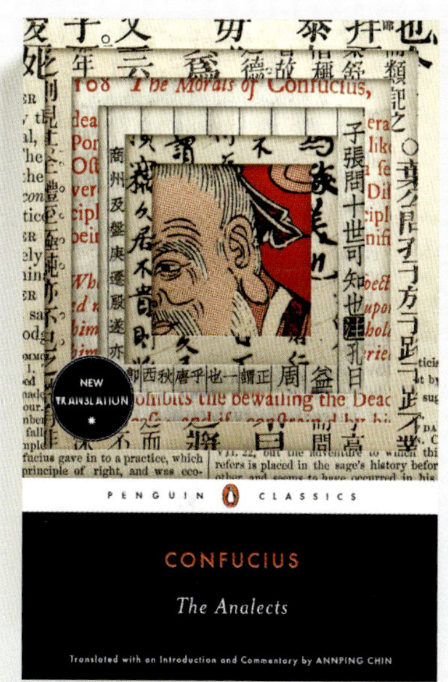

● **Nick Misani, DESIGNER**

THE POETICS OF SPACE – For such an esoteric, lofty text whose themes are as abstract as its language is poetic, I opted for simplicity and metaphor. Color washes pool into impossible, intimate spaces within hand-drawn homes. These imagined alcoves transcend tangible architecture, each containing an amalgam of different associations, emotions, recollections, and colors. It's these physical and mental spaces that transform homes from geometric arrangements of material to lived-in, breathed-in environments.

THE PORTABLE EMERSON – The striking photograph of a sawn tree overlaid with a resolute quote, plainly typeset, strives to convey the communion with nature, vigorous self-reliance, and newfound American independence that embody Emerson's work. As it is, this book was very much overdue and at the last minute we weren't able to secure rights for an image we all loved. I found this alternative photograph and rushed it upstairs to show the editorial team. With Elda on board, I made my way to the corner office of Kathryn Court, our president and publisher, who I knew hates beige. Always gracious, though no less intimidating, she approved the cover after only a moment's hesitation, mentioning its being "so beige."

THE ANALECTS – The original text can go from being somewhat vaporous to downright incomprehensible, but the extensive commentary enlightens and contextualizes each quote, allowing us to get closer to grasping Confucius's original meaning. Initially, the collage on the cover was simply meant to frame Confucius with a variety of different translations and rewritings of the text. However, upon further discussion of the concept with the scholar and translator, Annping, we decided to add intentionality to the layers by selecting significant editions of the text from the Yale archives and arranging them chronologically.

On Being Different

MERLE MILLER

UNUSED COVERS (LEFT), APPROVED COVER (RIGHT)

ILLUSTRATOR: KRISTEN HAFF CREATIVE DIRECTOR: PAUL BUCKLEY EDITOR: ELDA ROTOR

● **Kristen Haff**, ILLUSTRATOR

One of the hardest parts of the classic series is that all of these books are enormous human achievements. Most of them contain politically charged or groundbreaking ideas that caused a rift during their time. The impact of these books would hover over me like a giant anvil waiting to drop. "Design something beautiful; the book deserves it!" would be whirling around in my mind. So this one got kicked off to me; Paul Buckley slapped the manuscript on my desk with some line like "Don't fuck it up, Haff." A combination of panic and annoyance killed any creative inclination I'd initially had. I came up with a few "unique" ideas, one being a simple, solid wash of pink. Paul looked it over. "I like it," he said. "It just needs something. ...What about...a little ti-i-i-ny rainbow sticker, right in the middle?"

I tried it. For some reason the editor didn't go for it. She killed the rest of my precocious designs—an image of the author laid over a pile of gold glitter...a pink triangle pinned to a jean vest...rows of white laundry interrupted by a single pink shirt ...and perhaps the most horrific: soldiers raising a rainbow flag over a battlefield à la Iwo Jima. After days of agonizing over how to communicate the author's triumphant and pioneering work, I landed on this groundbreaking solution: a simple rainbow pattern. The estate loved it.

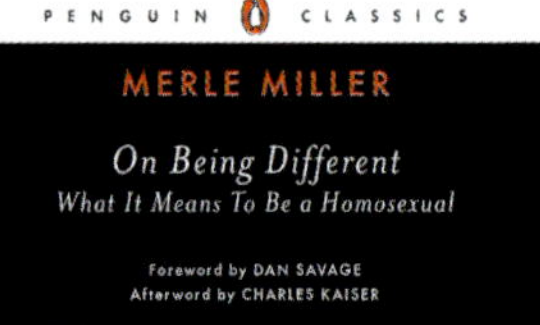

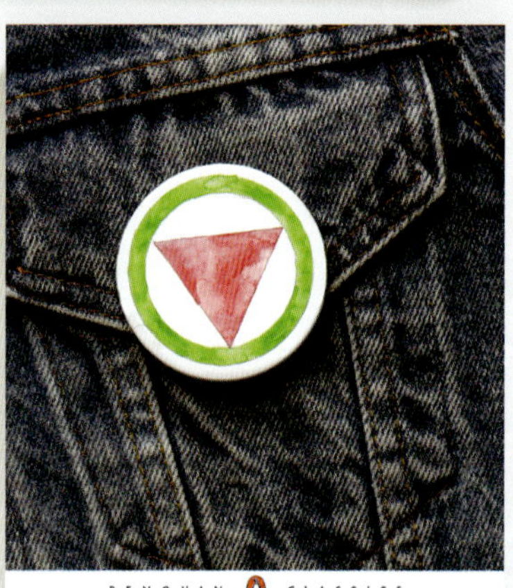

PENGUIN CLASSICS
MERLE MILLER
On Being Different
What It Means To Be a Homosexual
Foreword by DAN SAVAGE
Afterword by CHARLES KAISER

Around the World in Seventy-Two Days and Other Writings NELLIE BLY

ILLUSTRATOR: JOHN-PATRICK THOMAS **CREATIVE DIRECTOR:** PAUL BUCKLEY **EDITOR:** HENRY FREEDLAND

● **Maureen Corrigan,** JOURNALIST / AUTHOR

She's dressed for departure in an age when women most often stayed put—seated in drawing rooms, beside sickbeds, or behind sweatshop sewing machines. The wide world at her back, Nelly Bly looks confidently out of the frame. Maybe she's looking into the future, where the generations of girls she's inspired are themselves imagining careers as crusading journalists—ones whose adventures also make headlines and right injustices.

● **John-Patrick Thomas,** ILLUSTRATOR

After your hundredth comp lands in the recycle bin, your mechanical comes back from the editors for the tenth pass, and you sense the familiar feeling of your eyes bleeding from too much screen time, being assigned a Classics cover brings you back to life in spades. Once I'd read the manuscript and done some research on Nellie Bly, I realized she was one badass lady and I'd better not screw it up. Starting her career in the late nineteenth century, she single-handedly exposed the heinous treatment of the "insane" (many were not and were nonetheless forced into institutions), dined with Jules Verne in France, visited a leper colony in China, and bought a pet monkey in Singapore during her record-breaking solo circumnavigation of the world—in which she clocked just shy of twenty-five thousand miles in seventy-two days. Afraid of being haunted by this fearless journalist, inventor, and suffragette, I set to working on this portrait of her nestled in turn-of-the-century reportage and world travel. This cover came together quite painlessly, too. Everyone seemed to be on board with the first few sketches and barely any revisions were requested.

The Story of Hong Gildong

ILLUSTRATOR: SACHIN TENG **ART DIRECTOR:** MATT VEE **CREATIVE DIRECTOR:** PAUL BUCKLEY **EDITOR:** SAM RAIM

● **Minsoo Kang,** EDITOR

The brilliance of Sachin Teng's cover illustration of **THE STORY OF HONG GILDONG** lies in that rather than introducing the work as a venerable classic of Korean literature, it perfectly captures the essence of the narrative as an exciting and action-packed adventure of an extraordinary hero. While all modern Koreans are familiar with its basic plot, few have actually read the original work in its entirety, being more familiar with cartoon and storybook versions that were part of their childhood. In his artwork, Teng points to elements of the iconic image of the hero that would be immediately recognizable to Koreans, including his blue shirt and straw hat, but makes it a wholly original interpretation that is unique to his style.

● **Sachin Teng,** ILLUSTRATOR

Originally the straw hat was off to the side because I wanted it to fly around a bit. I was already finished with the full-color illustration when I was asked to put the hat on top of his head instead because he wasn't immediately recognizable as Hong Gildong. Don't get me wrong—they were right. But I was still stuck with an illustration I had already finished, panicking over how I was going to move the hat without it looking as though it was an afterthought, with a suspicious hat-shaped hole in the illustration like in a Looney Tunes cartoon.

• SKETCHES, SACHIN TENG

Black SPINES

ILLUSTRATED BY MATT VEE

COMMON SENSE, THE SCARLET LETTER

CREATIVE DIRECTOR: PAUL BUCKLEY **EDITOR:** ELDA ROTOR

● **Matt Vee, ILLUSTRATOR**

COMMON SENSE – The final cover you see here had always been in my periphery, but it was buried beneath the more obvious attempts I'd made in the process: bloody stars, "Join, or Die," a chess metaphor, oof. But when the chosen cover was finally agreed upon, I felt I'd struck a nerve with our publisher, who said she didn't see what we all saw in it. The room smiled, finding it hard to overlook her British accent. The irony wasn't lost on us, and she eventually caved to the consensus of the group. God save Queen Penguin—thanks, Kathryn!

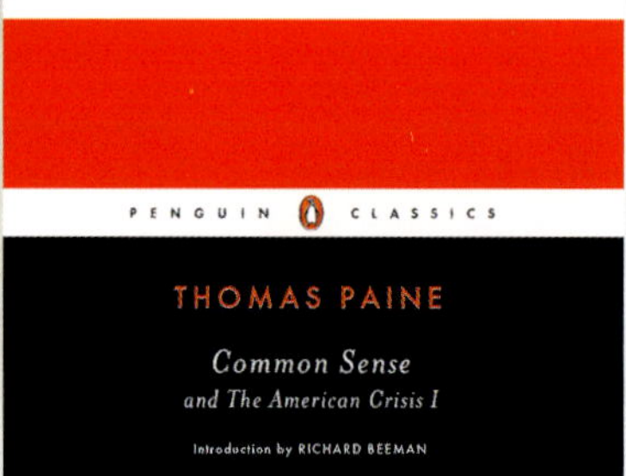

APPROVED COVER •

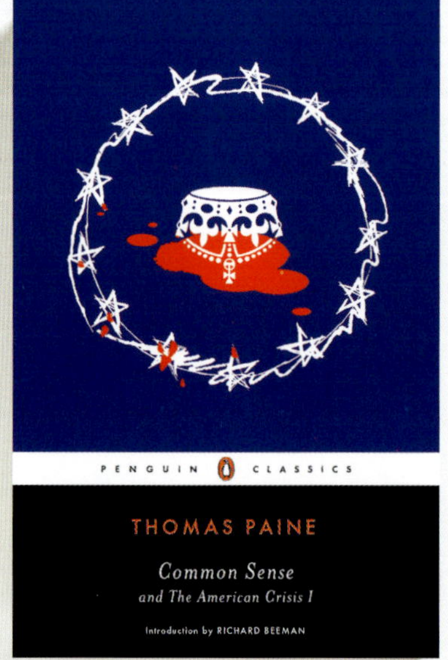

THE SCARLET LETTER – Black spines are often a much-appreciated respite from the chaos of seeking approval on a season's worth of book covers. Just reimagine the classic in a modern way—no house style, no type is necessary, no hard rules in general... unless it's called **THE SCARLET LETTER**. It demands a *certain* vowel of a *certain* color.

At first glance, the final cover is quite quaint. But Elda and Co. were quite taken with it once they found Hester and Pearl hiding inside the titular red *Aa*. A far cry from the week before, when we were down to the wire. We're still tweaking details, minutes before the meeting. I fix the eyes for Paul, and he (cheekily) mentions he should win art direction of the year for this one. The covers were killed moments later. *Classic Penguin.*

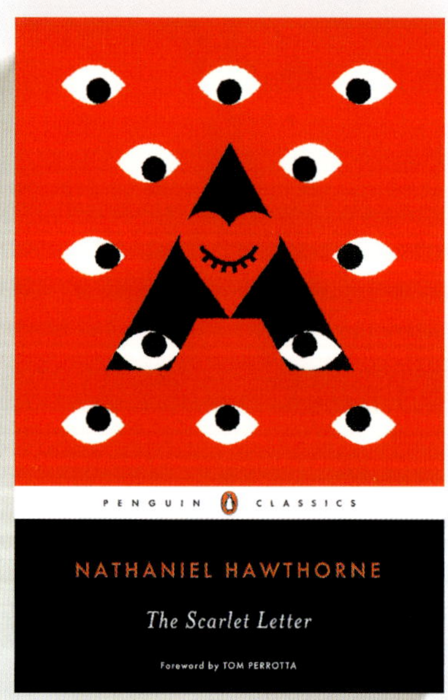

PENGUIN CLASSICS

BLACK SPINES

NATHANIEL HAWTHORNE

SIEGFRIED SASSOON

Memoirs of a Fox-Hunting Man

The Memoirs of George Sherston

ART DIRECTOR: BRIANNA HARDEN

SIEGFRI

Memoirs of

The Memoir

CREATIVE D

● **Matt Wood, ILLUSTRATOR**

Depicting Siegfried Sassoon's thinly fictionalized trilogy recounting his experiences in WWI was challenging. The art directors and I dug deep to find the best solutions for his portrayal of trench warfare. Sassoon's angry and compassionate words give a dynamic quality to his descriptions of the war, which the art directors and I wanted to convey in each of the three book covers. Throughout the trilogy, the protagonist seems to be in a constant state of overlapping confusion and clarity. There is a calmness to

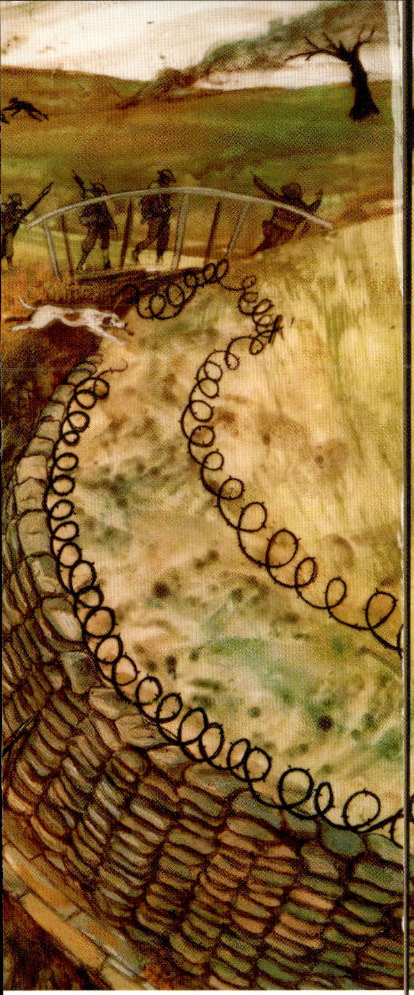

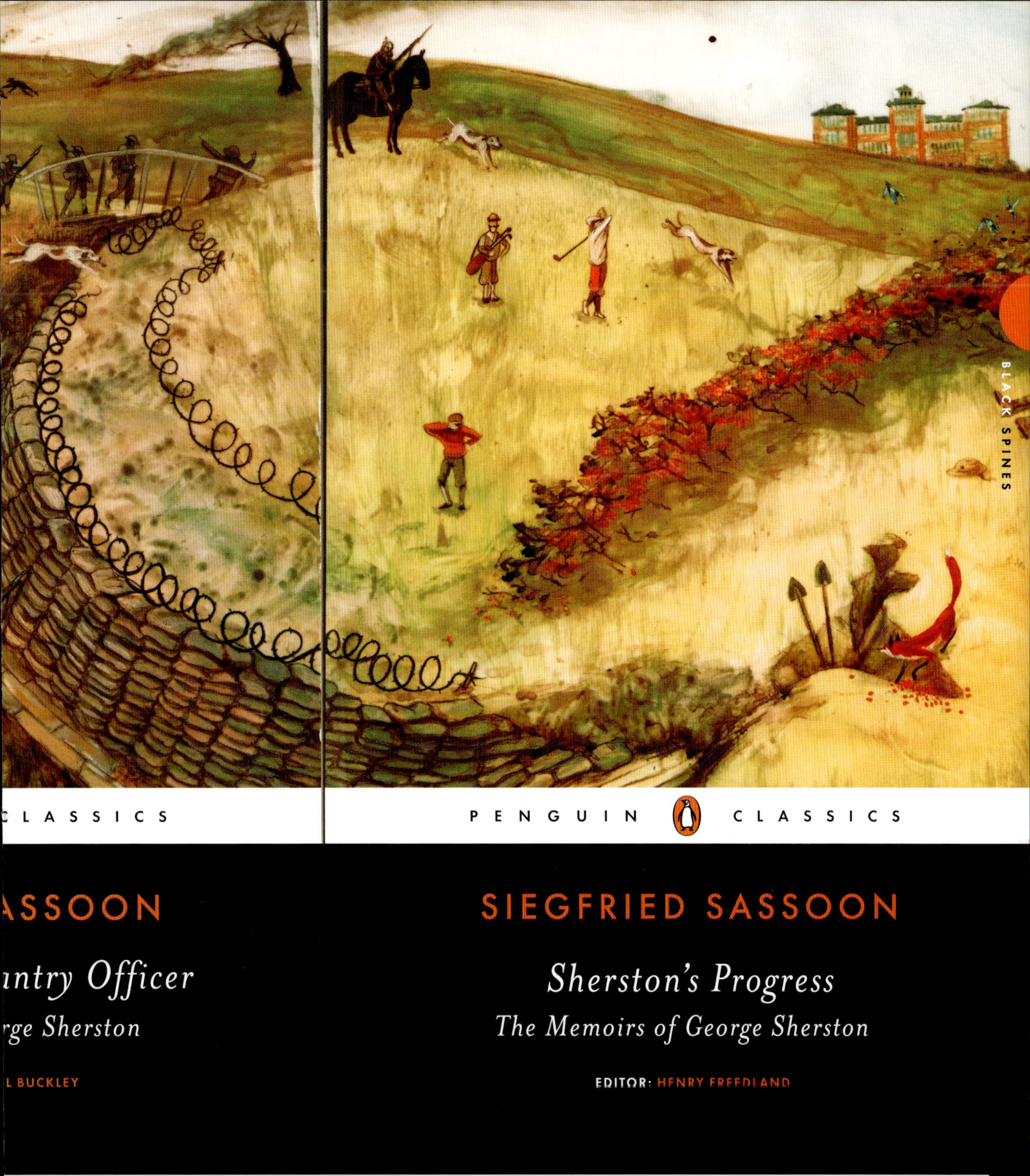

BLACK SPINES

CLASSICS

PENGUIN CLASSICS

ASSOON

ntry Officer

rge Sherston

L BUCKLEY

SIEGFRIED SASSOON

Sherston's Progress

The Memoirs of George Sherston

EDITOR: HENRY FREEDLAND

the chaos as Sassoon's story progresses. By electing to employ a single image for the covers, split into a triptych, we hoped to convey this calm chaos. From his nostalgic memories of country life as a fox hunter before the war, through his shockingly realistic depictions during the war, and into the growth of his pacifist feelings after the war, we wanted it all to be seen and understood seamlessly and simultaneously.

The Power and the Glory GRAHAM GREENE

DESIGNER: PAUL BUCKLEY **EDITOR:** JOHN SICILIANO

Paul Buckley, DESIGNER

This is the second book in a thus far rarely appearing Penguin Classics series the folks upstairs call our "Black Tie series." I'm not sure why that moniker—maybe because they're a bit fancy. These books are born of an interesting idea from Patrick Nolan and Elda Rotor as a route they might want to take during a special occasion for a classic title—in this instance it was in celebration of the seventy-fifth anniversary of this novel. The series consists of a jacket over a "regular" black spine Penguin Classic. We have incorporated the die cut so that one realizes there is another cover under there.

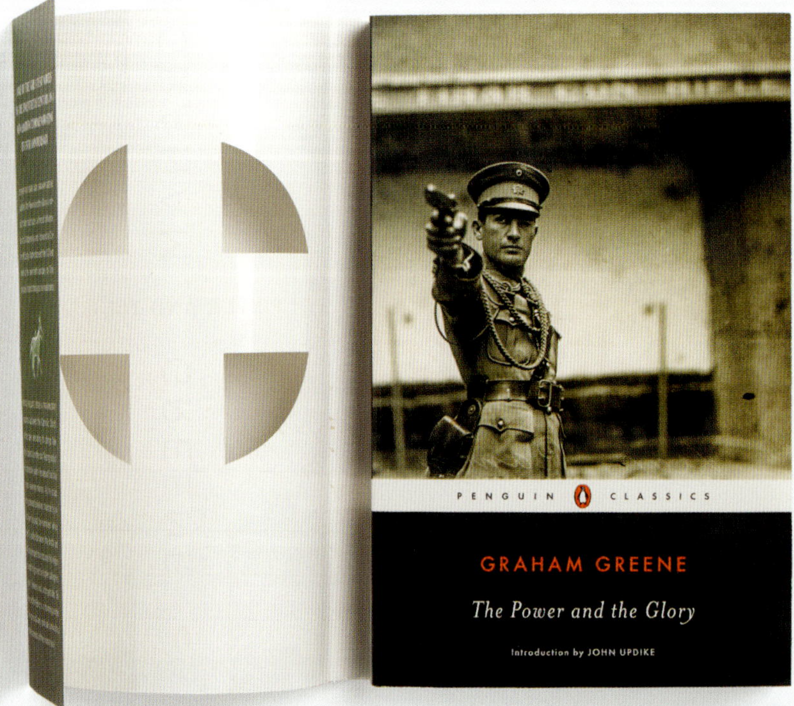

I really love this book, and the actual historical backdrop in which it takes place is quite amazing. During the period in Mexico's history known as the Cristero War, Catholicism was outlawed and priests were given the choice to renounce their faith or face a firing squad. Some priests rebelled and roamed the country, furtively practicing their faith as they walked from small town to small town, hoping to avoid betrayal and prosecution. The protagonist in Graham Greene's book is never named; he is just called "The Priest"—or "The Whisky Priest," due to his constant desire for alcohol. His adversary is "The Lieutenant," who hunts him mercilessly through the pages of the book.

The top cover is from a sketch I came up with during the packaging meeting when this book was being briefed to me, an ornamental Mexican cross based on iron crosses of the region, which allowed me to create four die-cut windows from the leftover negative space in which to show the image underneath. For that, I wanted the viewer to see the last thing a reluctant priest would see: a man with a gun.

• "THE PRIEST" WAS LOOSELY BASED ON A PRIEST OF THE TIME NAMED MIGUEL PRO, WHO IS SHOWN HERE FACING HIS FIRING SQUAD. HE REFUSED A BLINDFOLD AND BLESSED THE SOLDIERS. PHOTO, KEYSTONE-FRANCE / GETTY IMAGES

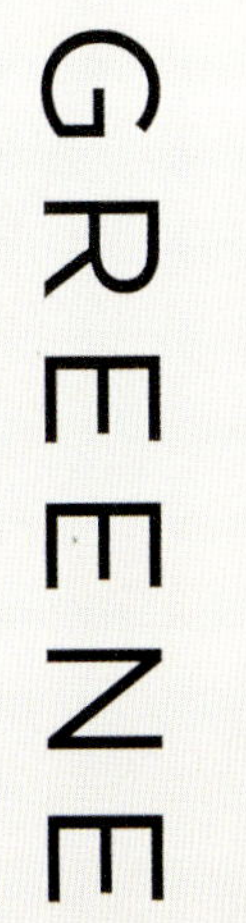

GRAHAM
SEVENTY-FIFTH ANNIVERSARY
THE POWER AND THE GLORY
GREENE
Introduction by JOHN UPDIKE
PENGUIN CLASSICS

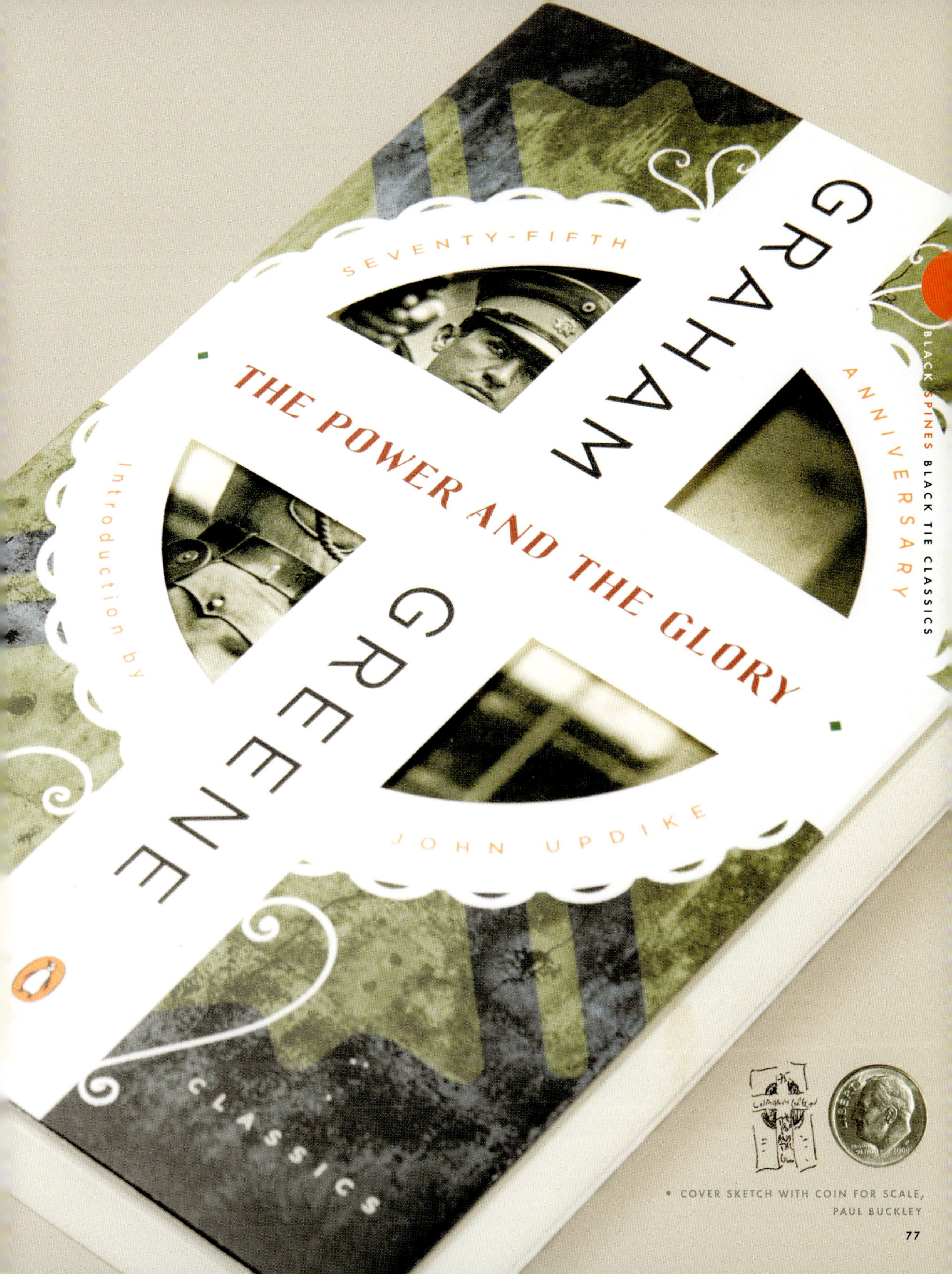

• COVER SKETCH WITH COIN FOR SCALE, PAUL BUCKLEY

Deluxe

CLASSICS

РУКОПИСИ
НЕ·ГОРЯТ
ЗА·МНОЙ,
ЧИТАТЕЛЬ!
WWW.PENGUINCLASSICS.COM
ART DIRECTION:
PAUL BUCKLEY
COVER ART: C.C. ASKEW

Mikhail Bulgakov · The Master & Margarita
DELUXE CLASSICS
50
ANNIVERSARY
A Penguin Book
Literature
U.S. $17.00
CAN. $23.00
ISBN 978-0-14-310827-6
51700
EAN 9 780143 108276
PENGUIN
CLASSICS
DELUXE
EDITION

A NEWLY REVISED TRANSLATION BY
RICHARD PEVEAR AND
LARISSA VOLOKHONSKY
FOREWORD BY
BORIS FISHMAN
THE MASTER & MARGARITA
MIKHAIL · BULGAKOV
50
ANNIVERSARY
PENGUIN CLASSICS DELUXE EDITION
MIKHAIL BULGAKOV · THE MASTER & MARGARITA
50
ANNIVERSARY
PENGUIN CLASSICS DELUXE EDITION

The Master & Margarita MIKHAIL BULGAKOV

ILLUSTRATOR: C.C. ASKEW CREATIVE DIRECTOR: PAUL BUCKLEY EDITOR: JOHN SICILIANO

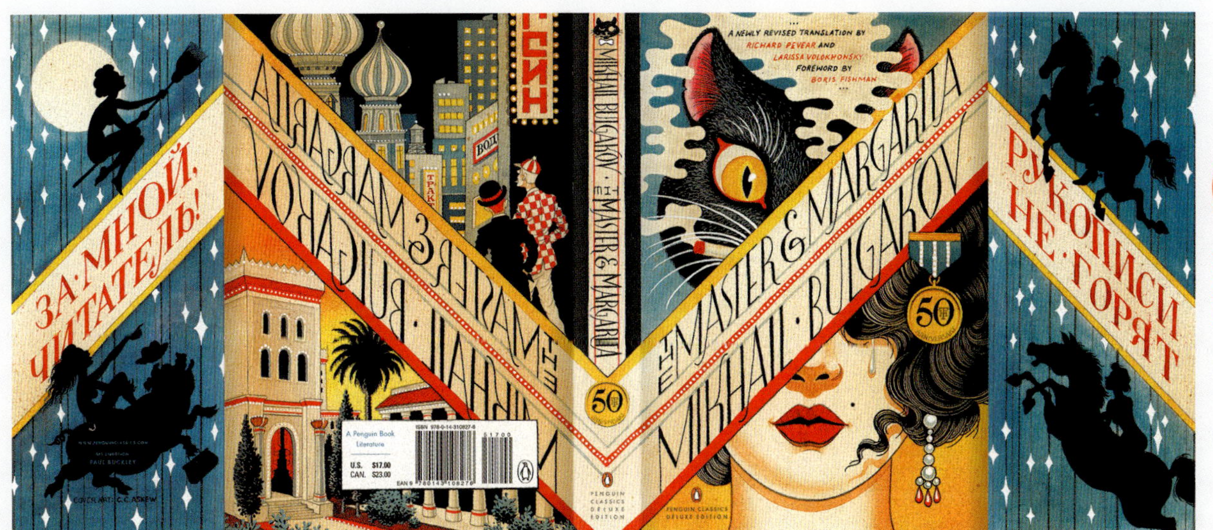

Paul Buckley, CREATIVE DIRECTOR

I met Chris when I was putting together the Penguin Ink series; he illustrated *Waiting for the Barbarians* for me. I loved that piece so much that I purchased it from him, and I've had a C. C. A. art crush ever since. Like many tattoo artists, Chris can effortlessly draw circles around many others, and his craft of type and design is no mere secondary thing. All this was done by hand and was mailed to me in separate pieces—each flap, the spine, the front, and the back—which were then scanned and color corrected and pieced together. It had been many, many years since anyone had sent me physical art. It was like it was 1990 all over again, perestroika and all.

C.C. Askew, ILLUSTRATOR

THE MASTER & MARGARITA is a book I've loved and reread many times over since the age of fifteen, and I had already done several illustrations for it before, so right off the bat I had one big problem: competing not only with the work of previous illustrators but with myself as well. To do this piece in a new way that still reflects my style forced me into a lot of visual self-analysis, and to work just a bit beyond my usual comfort zone. I expanded my wonted color palette and challenged myself to balance iconic elements, such as Behemoth, with less-often-addressed imagery, including the city of Jerusalem.

I wanted this piece to have a unifying element that is only visible when the book is viewed as a whole, and not as separate panels. I used the diagonal lettering strips on each panel to form a sort of great big M within an M, which becomes apparent only when the book is laid facedown with the flaps open. Of course, that's not the best way to treat a book, but I hope that in some way, perhaps a bit subliminally, the effect might be achieved without having to undermine the structural integrity of the binding.

Fear of Flying

ERICA JONG

ILLUSTRATOR: NOMA BAR **DESIGNER / CREATIVE DIRECTOR:** PAUL BUCKLEY **EDITOR:** ELDA ROTOR

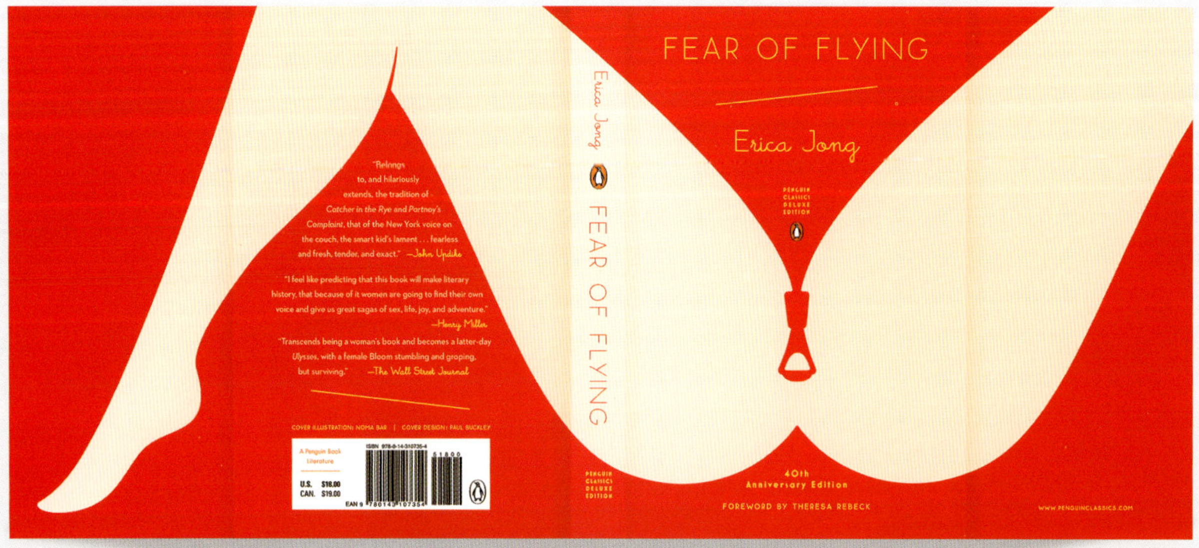

● **Erica Jong**, AUTHOR

When I saw the new cover for the Penguin Classics Deluxe Edition of **FEAR OF FLYING**, I was absolutely delighted. I love the combination of red and cream, which has a great graphic quality. It is sexy without being vulgar. I was thrilled it was celebrated as one of the best covers of 2013.

FEAR OF FLYING has had many covers in the forty-four years since it was originally published. There was the famous cover of a naked navel revealed by the V-shaped opening of a zipper. There was a flying banana (which, thankfully, didn't last long). There were many varieties of hot pink airplanes. There was a Statue of Liberty cover invented by my Danish publishers.

As the book established itself as a classic, the covers became more discreet. Although there are occasional mass-market reprints in which we see navels and bananas, we are starting to get more artistic covers as years go by.

When I was writing **FEAR OF FLYING**, I thought of it as the "Portrait of the Artist as a Young Woman." I never thought it would be seen as a sexy book. I described Isadora Wing's sexual feelings because it was important to show that intellectual women also have sexual fantasies. We are both minds and bodies. Why does this shock people?

The most important thing about my heroines, from Isadora Wing to Fanny Hackabout-Jones to Leila to Sappho to Vanessa Wonderman, is that they are full human beings. They are mothers, lovers, actors, poets, and painters. They succeed in many areas—balancing children, books, artworks, movies, stage plays, works of all sorts. It is important to show the full range of women's lives.

The Penguin Classics cover of **FEAR OF FLYING** suggests an exuberant and sexual woman. Behind that exuberance is a full mind and imaginative talents that need to be expressed. My job as an author is to encourage all my readers to reach for satisfying lives. A woman's life is always in flux. We go from being little girls to adolescents longing for sexuality to mothers, grandmothers, and mentors. Change gives us flexibility and enlightenment, and as older women we finally become wise.

FEAR OF FLYING

Erica Jong

PENGUIN CLASSICS DELUXE EDITION

40th Anniversary Edition

FOREWORD BY THERESA REBECK

Kama Sutra

VATSYAYANA

ILLUSTRATOR: MALIKA FAVRE **CREATIVE DIRECTOR:** PAUL BUCKLEY **EDITOR:** ELDA ROTOR

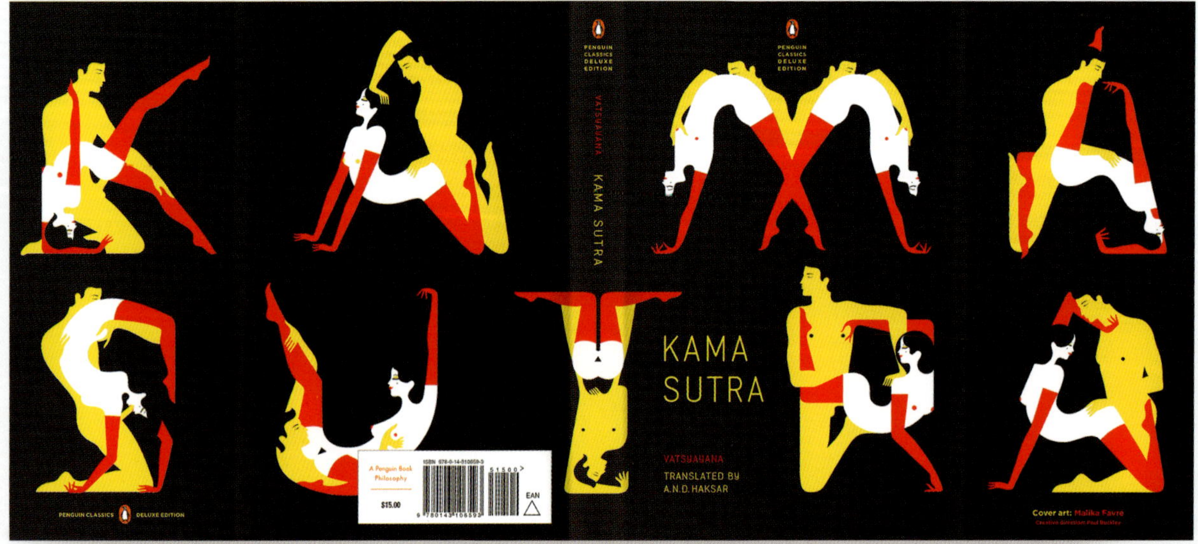

Paul Buckley, CREATIVE DIRECTOR

The **KAMA SUTRA** is over two thousand years old, and as long as we continue to have only two arms, two legs, a thing-amajig, and a whosiewhatsit, there are only so many positions we can wrangle our bodies into. So this ancient guide on what you might try to do is still very relevant, and in illustrating that, the challenge with which artists historically have struggled is just how one renders that sort of thing with taste, dignity, and a flair for the erotic-dramatic. Americans are, by and large, a prudish bunch—I'm just waiting for the Pilgrims to make a comeback. So I went overseas to the land of Malika, and a new classic born of an old classic was beautifully, perfectly, brought to life.

Malika Favre, ILLUSTRATOR

The **KAMA SUTRA** cover was my dream project and, on paper, an obvious one for me. I really thought it would be a breeze, but I still remember the struggle I went through in nailing that concept. I kept sending sketches over and over again to Paul, and his feedback was the same, short and to the point: It was too prudish and, apparently, so was I. I reached a point where it became a matter of French pride, and I somehow landed on the idea of explicit typographic positions wrapping around the book. It was a hit and a smooth road until final approval. In retrospect, it was all worth it, and I couldn't imagine another cover than the one we produced together.

• PHOTO, MALIKA FAVRE

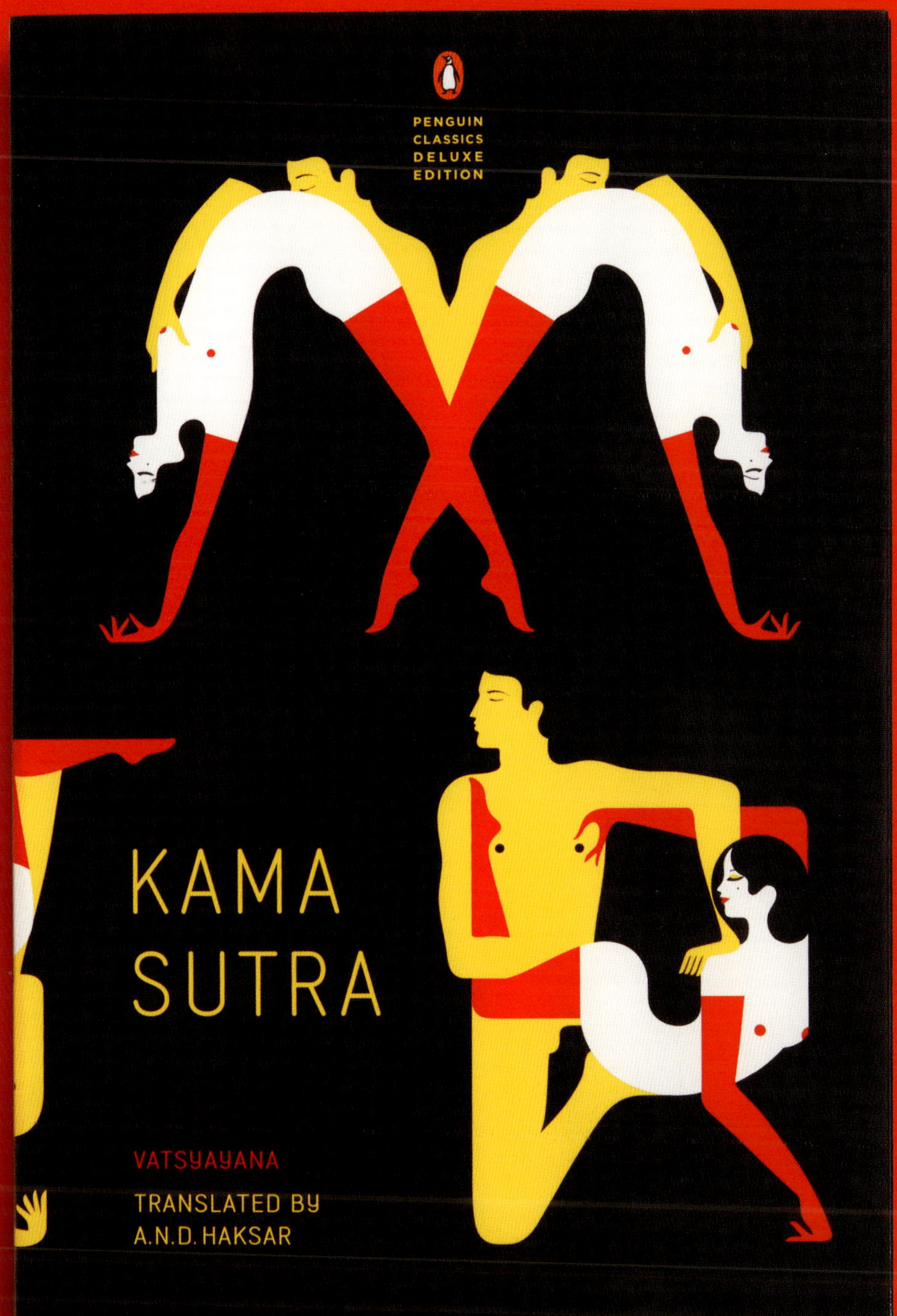
PENGUIN
CLASSICS
DELUXE
EDITION
KAMA
SUTRA
VATSYAYANA
TRANSLATED BY
A.N.D. HAKSAR

• KAMA SUTRA ALPHABET, MALIKA FAVRE

The Liars' Club

MARY KARR

ILLUSTRATOR: BRIAN REA DESIGNER / CREATIVE DIRECTOR: PAUL BUCKLEY EDITOR: JOHN SICILIANO

● **Paul Buckley,** DESIGNER / DIRECTOR

Brian Rea is one of the most successful illustrators working today. His deceptively simple drawings brilliantly conceal a flawless sense of design and composition and an innocent invitation to look upon the work no matter how rough the subject. There's a complete and uncluttered honesty inherent in the work, not unlike the kid in the restaurant who says far too loudly, "Mommy, why is that man in that booth crying?" This memoir of childhood told from the perspective of a very young Mary Karr perfectly matches Brian's voice and is chockablock with one amazing visual after another. He dove in deep and did what seemed like one hundred drawings, which we then narrowed down and arranged into what you see here.

● **Brian Rea,** ILLUSTRATOR

THE LIARS' CLUB was one of the toughest projects I've worked on. After reading the book, taking notes on it, researching the hell out of the details, and sketching pages and pages and pages of ideas (seriously, pages of ideas), I was desperate to visually match the depth of storytelling that exists in the book. It's so damn good, it's such a classic, plus Lena Dunham wrote the foreword—hell, I hope I got close.

• SKETCHES, BRIAN REA

THE LIARS' CLUB

MARY KARR

Crime & Punishment

FYODOR DOSTOYEVSKY

ILLUSTRATOR: ZOHAR LAZAR **CREATIVE DIRECTOR:** PAUL BUCKLEY **EDITOR:** JOHN SICILIANO

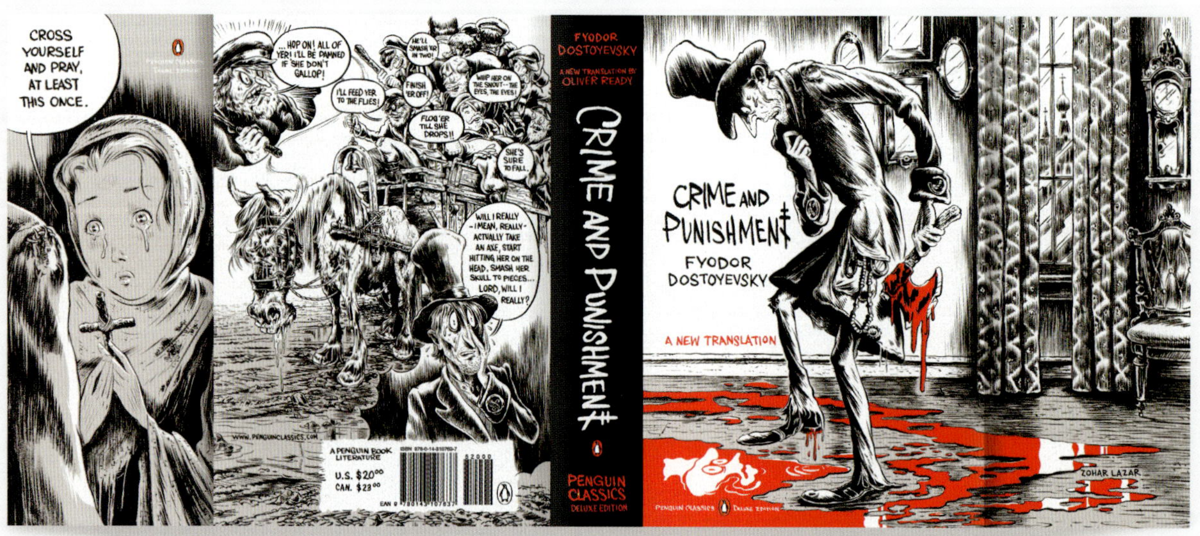

● **Zohar Lazar,** ILLUSTRATOR

I imagined the Rodya of my cover as an innocent boob perpetually waking into a hilariously terrifying nightmare of his own making, a pompous doofus who takes the long, bumbling road to his own salvation. The drawings came to me almost immediately. The poor guy stands comically, on one leg, utterly grossed out by the sight of blood. Gazing into the puddle, he is startled by his own ghostly reflection. . . . This guy isn't a murderer; he's a pussycat. On the back, I depicted him waking from a dream of his childhood, in which a drunken mob of sadistic idiots torture a tired old nag. Rodya is appalled that he would have anything in common with these guys, even as he contemplates cold-blooded murder. I modeled his expression (hand to his face) after my own when I realized that I had been assigned the cover of CRIME AND FUCKING PUNISHMENT. "Holy shit!" I thought. This is a book that countless high school students carry about (cover out) to show their depth and refined tastes in literature. I hope I lived up to the task.

• SKETCH, ZOHAR LAZAR

DELUXE CLASSICS

PENGUIN CLASSICS

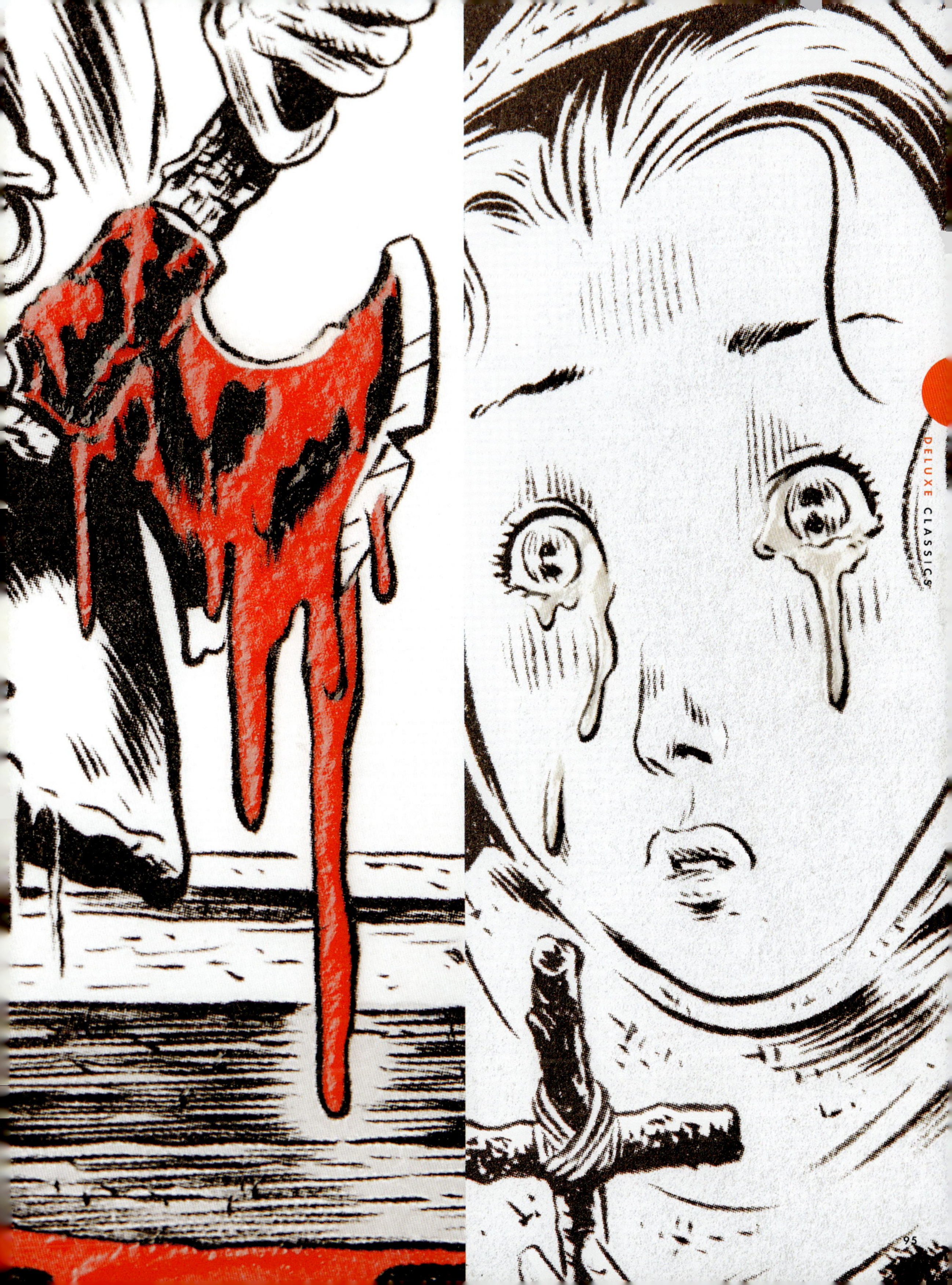

ESSAYS BY JENNIFER BUEHLER,
E. M. FORSTER AND E. L. EPSTEIN
COVER ART BY ADAMS CARVALHO
PENGUIN CLASSICS
DELUXE EDITION
www.penguinclassics.com

William Golding
Deluxe Classics
Lord of the Flies
Penguin Classics Deluxe Edition

WILLIAM GOLDING

LORD of the FLIES

PENGUIN CLASSICS DELUXE EDITION

LORD of the FLIES

FOREWORD BY LOIS LOWRY

INTRODUCTION BY STEPHEN KING

WILLIAM GOLDING

Lord of the Flies

Deluxe Edition WILLIAM GOLDING

ILLUSTRATOR: ADAMS CARVALHO **CREATIVE DIRECTOR:** PAUL BUCKLEY **EDITOR:** ELDA ROTOR

• SKETCHES, ADAMS CARVALHO

Adams Carvalho, ILLUSTRATOR

Fortunately we all agreed on which image created the best cover. The boy on the cover is almost literally a portrait of a young British punk. I think this cover says everything using very little information—just a young face in profile shouting through a mouthful of blood to portray a return to savagery within a group of young children. The cover image is almost a mirror of the back cover image: The boy becomes just like a wild boar.

Paul Buckley, CREATIVE DIRECTOR

I was asked to commission **LORD OF THE FLIES** twice in one season, hence these two cover solutions back-to-back. Elda Rotor and Kathryn Court wanted both versions, as this book has wide crossover appeal between young adults and adults, and they wanted a separate cover for each market. The book has some pretty rough scenes and themes, so how to differentiate the art? Does the younger crowd need something softer? Or maybe it should be even gorier than the adult version.

After pondering the situation I decided to hire two artists whose work I admire greatly but who come at things very differently. Kikuo is more refined and controlled, while Adams's work has a raw, drippy, xeroxy quality. I never told the other there were two versions being done or which market I was hiring them for, as I was worried that if I said something along the lines of "I really need you to think about the young-adult audience while you're solving this," or the adult market, that might begin to skew the work in some forced way or make the solutions too predictable. So I just sat back and waited to see what each artist brought to the table,

(CONTINUED ON NEXT PAGE)

Lord of the Flies

Young Adult WILLIAM GOLDING

ILLUSTRATOR: R. KIKUO JOHNSON **CREATIVE DIRECTOR:** PAUL BUCKLEY **EDITOR:** ELDA ROTOR

● **R. Kikuo Johnson,** ILLUSTRATOR

LORD OF THE FLIES is the story of a slow descent into chaos. When I was assigned the cover, my instinct was that a very dramatic or violent image would be a spoiler for the novel's savage final chapters. I figured it was better to aim for a colder, cerebral reaction rather than a visceral one.

I came up with an image of a shirtless boy wiping the sweat from his brow while flames rise from the palm trees overhead. He casually removes his cap, the lone symbol of modern civilization in the image, as the world burns down around him. His delayed reaction to the slow blaze seemed like the perfect metaphor for the book's gradually ratcheting mayhem. I was so sure that this image should be the cover, I made the illustrator's fatal mistake of investing hours in completing the final artwork before a sketch was ever approved.

To my disappointment, my most dramatic and sensational sketch was the one that was ultimately chosen. It features a feral boy in chiaroscuro, mid-breath, engulfed in flames. It turned out to be the far better cover, and I'm grateful it is the one readers will see.

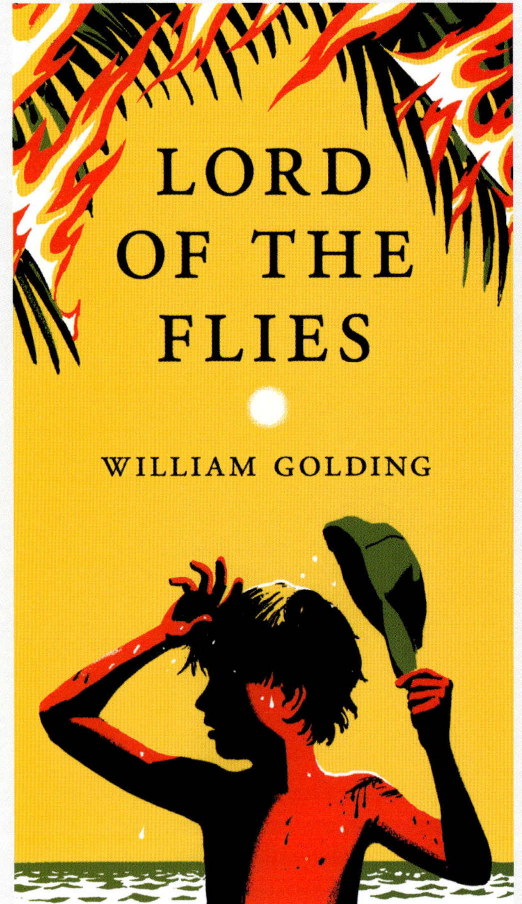

• SKETCH, R. KIKUO JOHNSON

(CONTINUED FROM PREVIOUS PAGE)

relying on my instinct that each would feel right stylistically according to the way I had perceived how they'd solved other works I'd seen by them—fingers crossed! And I'd never seen typography by either, so the design was a bit of a second gamble.

I think it all worked out nicely, but I'm not convinced, at least for this book, that you need two different covers for the two markets. But I could easily be wrong about that, as that is neither my call nor my skill set. I just do the covers I'm told to do and hope everything works out for the best.

WILLIAM GOLDING
LORD of the FLIES
Afterword by
Lois Lowry

The Haunting of Hill House SHIRLEY JACKSON

ILLUSTRATOR: ARON WIESENFELD DESIGNER / CREATIVE DIRECTOR: PAUL BUCKLEY EDITOR: ELDA ROTOR

● **Aron Wiesenfeld**, ILLUSTRATOR

The first sketch I sent in was pretty detailed, and had all the characters from the book doing things that hinted at their role in the story. Paul's reply was that because the book is so widely known, I didn't need to "illustrate" the story, and could be more subtle. That was enormously relieving. It meant I could make the kind of image I love to make. So I did a lot of really quick charcoal sketches intended more to capture a mood than anything else. The one they chose was just a very simple image of the main character standing in a dark forest. It doesn't really tell anything about the story, but I think it's a lot more provocative than the first idea would have been.

• PROCESS PHOTO, MONICA WIESENFELD & SKETCH, ARON WIESENFELD

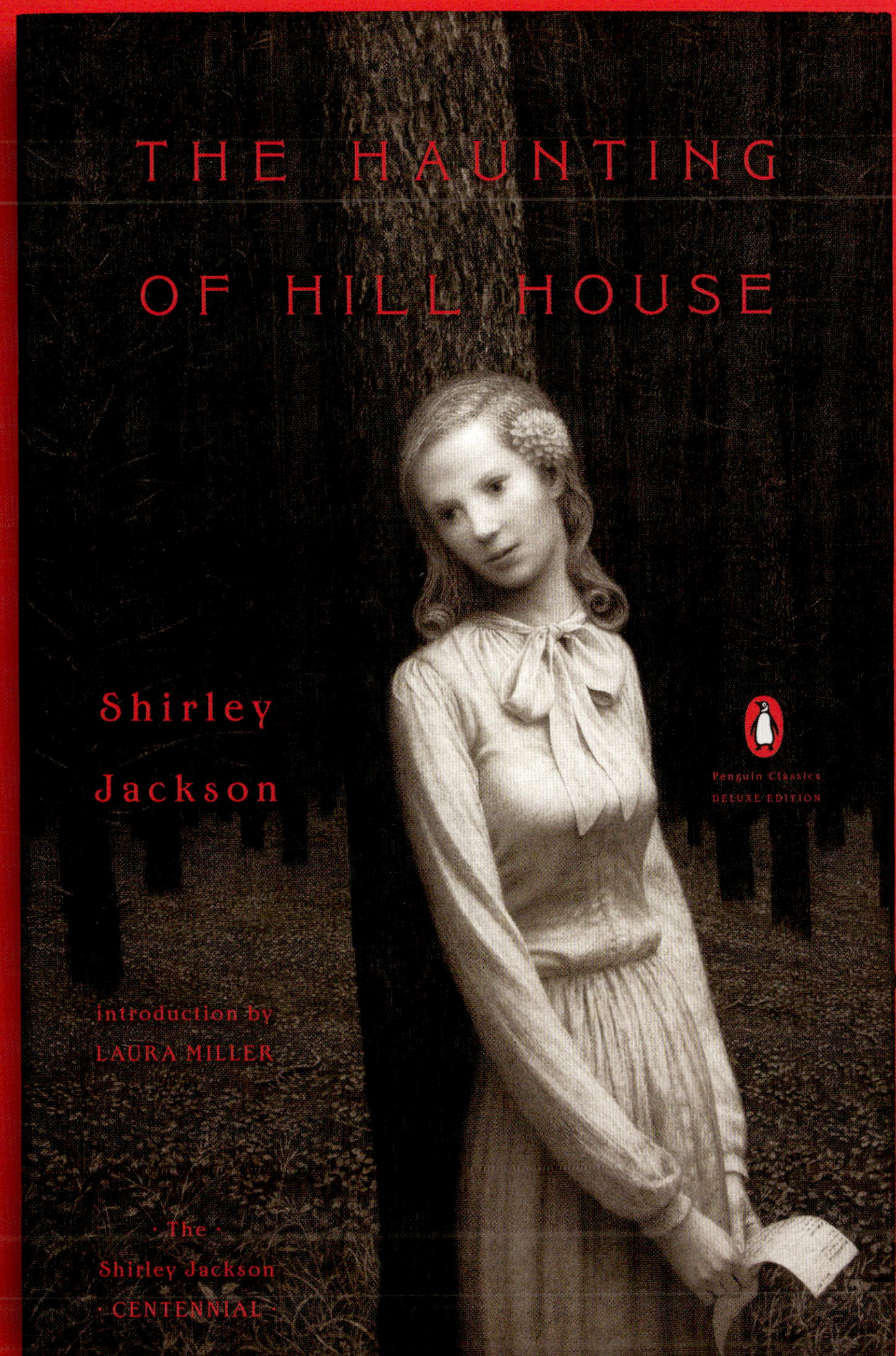
THE HAUNTING
OF HILL HOUSE
Shirley
Jackson
Penguin Classics
DELUXE EDITION
introduction by
LAURA MILLER
· The ·
Shirley Jackson
· CENTENNIAL ·

• THE HAUNTING OF HILL HOUSE SKETCHES, ARON WIESENFELD

COVER ART: *BAKEA*

COVER DESIGN & ART DIRECTION:

PAUL BUCKLEY

PENGUIN CLASSICS  DELUXE EDITION

PENGUIN CLASSICS READERS GUIDE AVAILABLE ONLINE AT WWW.PENGUINCLASSICS.COM

Alice's Adventures in Wonderland
and Through the Looking-Glass
DELUXE CLASSICS
PENGUIN
CLASSICS
DELUXE
EDITION
LEWIS
CARROLL
A Penguin Book
Literature
U.S. $16.00
CAN. $18.00
U.K. £10.99
ISBN 978-0-14-310762-0
51600
EAN 9 780143 107620

150th-Anniversary Edition

Alice's Adventures in Wonderland

and

Through the Looking-Glass

Penguin Classics Deluxe Edition

Lewis Carroll

Introduction by Charlie Lovett

Alice's Adventures in Wonderland and Through the Looking-Glass

Penguin Classics Deluxe Edition

Lewis Carroll

Alice's Adventures in Wonderland & Through the Looking-Glass LEWIS CARROLL

ILLUSTRATOR: JUAN GÓMEZ AKA BAKEA **DESIGNER / CREATIVE DIRECTOR:** PAUL BUCKLEY **EDITOR:** ELDA ROTOR

DELUXE CLASSICS

Paul Buckley, DESIGNER / CREATIVE DIRECTOR

It was a very long road getting here. Literally. Thousands of miles, in fact. And a few bumpy stretches along the way.

When I was thinking of who to hire for this, I received a lovely e-mail from Ivan Canu, who is the director of Mimaster, a highly influential illustration college in Milan, inviting me there to do three things: give a lecture, review student portfolios, and last and definitely not least, assign the students a book cover and then fly over there and hopefully choose one that we would print—for reals. Generally, I decline 90 percent of the things I get invited to, for one reason or another—most often because I don't want to teach during my vacations (and my wife, Ingsu, deserves vacations where I'm actually present), and putting a speech and work together for a presentation is really hard to do; it's a tremendous amount of work. So I generally decline and will never become the big shot my ego wants me to be—bigshotdom is just way too much goddamn work.

But this was Italy, and Ingsu's eyes lit up, and away we flew—and I assigned the students this book, never giving thought to the fact that they only had four weeks to become familiar with it, do covers for it, and "it" was two books.

(CONTINUED ON NEXT PAGE)

(CONTINUED FROM PREVIOUS PAGE)

Milan was lovely and the people were fantastic, but of the thirty or so options I saw for Lewis Carroll, nothing was solid enough. This was entirely my fault. There were some great ideas presented, but it was just too big a commission for students. So I flew back to NYC and reported to the powers that be in-house, who'd trusted my instincts that this would work ("We'll have so many things to choose from!"), that I had come back empty-handed.

Since then, I have twice worked with Ivan and Mimaster and have commissioned the students to do the art for one of our black spine classics, and that seems to be working out fine for everybody. It's far less complicated, no type or design, no deluxe packaging—just read the material and illustrate what you see to fit in a square space. And great folks like Riccardo Vecchio and Emiliano Ponzi are teaching these students along the way.

So for phase two of solving this cover, I reached out to Juan, whose work I'd been admiring a long time. He works in a manner in which he puts these absolutely crazy characters in real photographic environments, and I knew he'd be perfect. As we got further along with solving the illustration, it became apparent that Juan wanted to do the type as well. On my end, I was hesitant. Within the Deluxe series, and in general, I do enjoy commissioning artists who are also very proficient with type, and that is clearly apparent within these pages . . . but though I truly love Juan's art, I was not sure about the few type samples I'd found online being right for this, and it was taking us a long time to get the art where we needed it to be.

But eventually we got the illustration done—and what an amazing job Juan did. But we just did not like the type he was submitting. And then we ran out of time. So I was forced to do the typography overnight and it caused a bit of a rift between us. A number of e-mails were sent, Juan reiterating his displeasure, while I reiterated that it's a really nice collaboration and we should both be proud of this cover. I really do appreciate that these things are subjective—maybe 100 percent of the people looking at both type solutions find mine inferior—but I also appreciate that I was the one doing the commissioning (for illustration, not design) and the type just didn't work for us here. Finally, when I thought we had moved past this, I received an e-mail stating that due to a language barrier (he lives in Spain), Juan believed he was not able to properly convey to me the extent of his displeasure and asking if Penguin could offer a translator so that he could respond to me in Spanish . . . [art director puts gun in mouth . . .].

From Milan to Spain to NYC, it took what it took, I'm glad it's over, and I love this cover, warts and all.

—PB

Juan Gómez aka Bakea, ILLUSTRATOR

When I got the e-mail in which Paul asked me if I wanted to do the cover it was like a dream come true. I was being asked to do the cover of one of my all-time favorite books! Later on, as it also happens in the book, things didn't go so well....

I'm happy with the final result, but I'm sure that we could've done better. The typography aspect of the design was a bump in the road that I still doubt if we avoided successfully.

Finally, just a couple things: (1) Thanks; and (2) Paul, I still believe "that simple Bodoni" looked better.

James and the Giant Peach ROALD DAHL

ILLUSTRATOR: JORDAN CRANE **CREATIVE DIRECTOR:** PAUL BUCKLEY **EDITOR:** JOHN SICILIANO

● **Jordan Crane, ILLUSTRATOR**

Every single cover that has ever been done for this book has one thing in common: a giant peach. So I went the other way. I swore off peaches. No peaches. Anyhow, it's in the title; no need to be redundant with my images. Start at the bottom. Before the peach. That awful moment of hopelessness when James trips and loses the magic worms is the first seed of the adventure. The magic starts with the little green worms. That's when the book changes, when it gets its power. Everything grows from there.

DELUXE CLASSICS

The Divine Comedy

DANTE

ILLUSTRATOR: ERIC DROOKER **CREATIVE DIRECTOR:** PAUL BUCKLEY **EDITOR:** JOHN SICILIANO

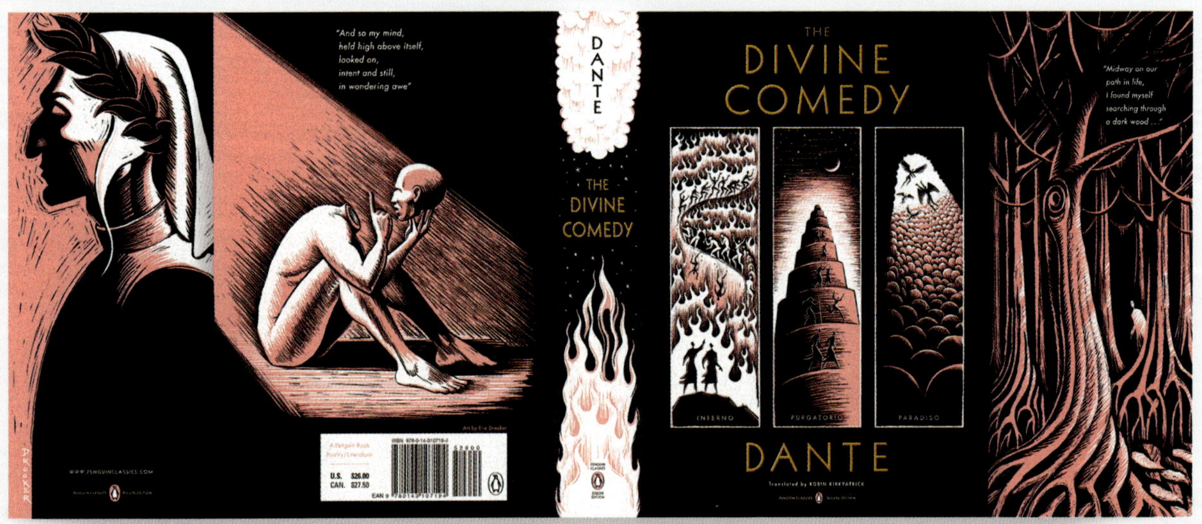

● **Eric Drooker, ILLUSTRATOR**

When illustrating someone else's words, I try to climb inside the head of the author. As I read the opening lines of **THE DIVINE COMEDY**, it occurred to me that the author was in the midst of a harrowing midlife crisis. Wracked with guilt and regret, Dante has evidently lost his path, and now finds himself all alone in the middle of the deep, dark forest.

"Wonderful," I said to myself, "such familiar territory! Who can't relate to being lost in the woods? At any age . . . in any century?"

My first cover sketch was of the author holding his own severed head in his hand in a vain attempt at being more mindful. "And so my mind, held high above itself, looked on . . ." The editor liked the idea—at first—but soon demanded something more encompassing on the book's front cover.

In my triptych, *Inferno* is the most vivid, as it is the most memorable chapter in the book. Fortunately, Penguin soon published a stand-alone edition of Dante's *Inferno*, with this powerful drawing on the cover.

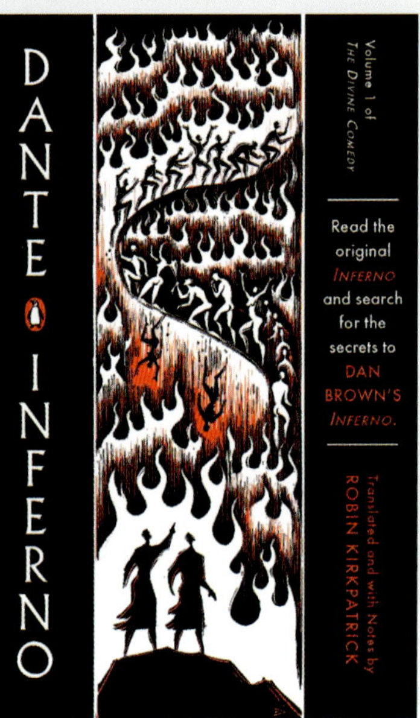

• INFERNO COVER, ERIC DROOKER

THE

DIVINE COMEDY

Translated by ROBIN KIRKPATRICK

PENGUIN CLASSICS  DELUXE EDITION

DELUXE CLASSICS

Middlemarch

GEORGE ELIOT

DESIGNER / ILLUSTRATOR: KELLY BLAIR **ART DIRECTORS:** ROSEANNE SERRA & PAUL BUCKLEY **EDITOR:** ELDA ROTOR

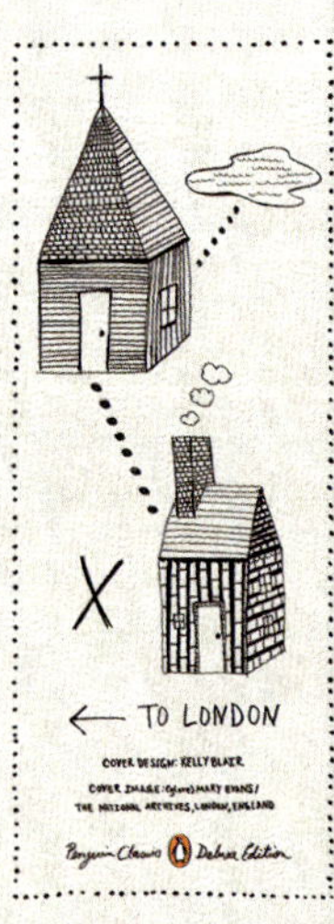

● Rebecca Mead, FOREWORD

In one climactic encounter toward the end of **MIDDLEMARCH**, Dorothea Brooke, the heroine of George Eliot's novel, takes off her gloves "from an impulse she could never resist when she wanted a sense of freedom"—a telling reminder of that era's constraints upon women, sartorial and otherwise. The inspiration for this cover came from a real glove that is preserved in the British National Archives. Cunningly designed by George Shove, and coinciding with the Great Exhibition in Hyde Park in 1851, the glove offers its wearer something like the freedom of the novelist: the precious liberty to plot her own course.

● Kelly Blair, DESIGNER / ILLUSTRATOR

The Green Dragon, Freshitt Hall, the Garths' house, St. Peter's Place, the White Hart, the Tankard, Tipton, Lowick Gate, Vincey's warehouse. These are all places one finds when meandering through the pages of **MIDDLEMARCH**.

This cover takes direct inspiration from a beautiful vintage map of the Great Exhibition of London on a white leather glove. Re-creating this image with a map of Middlemarch was a real pleasure. It was easy to imagine wandering the landscape, finding my way through this dense, fascinating world. I'd have this left glove in hand, making an occasional stop for a strong cup of tea. Perhaps along the way I'd make a map on the right glove of all the characters I met.

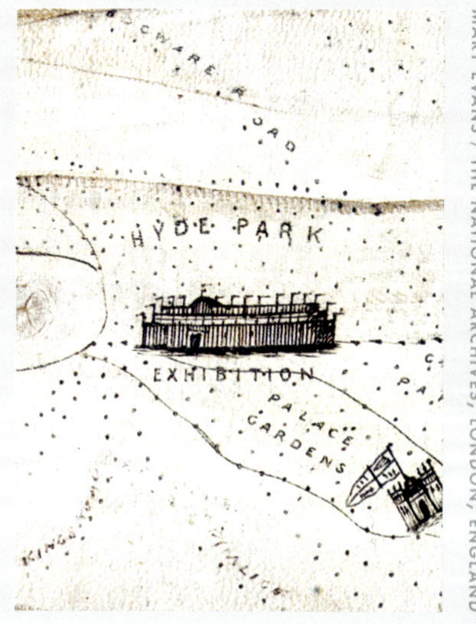

MARY EVANS / THE NATIONAL ARCHIVES, LONDON, ENGLAND

• GREAT EXHIBITION GLOVE OF LONDON

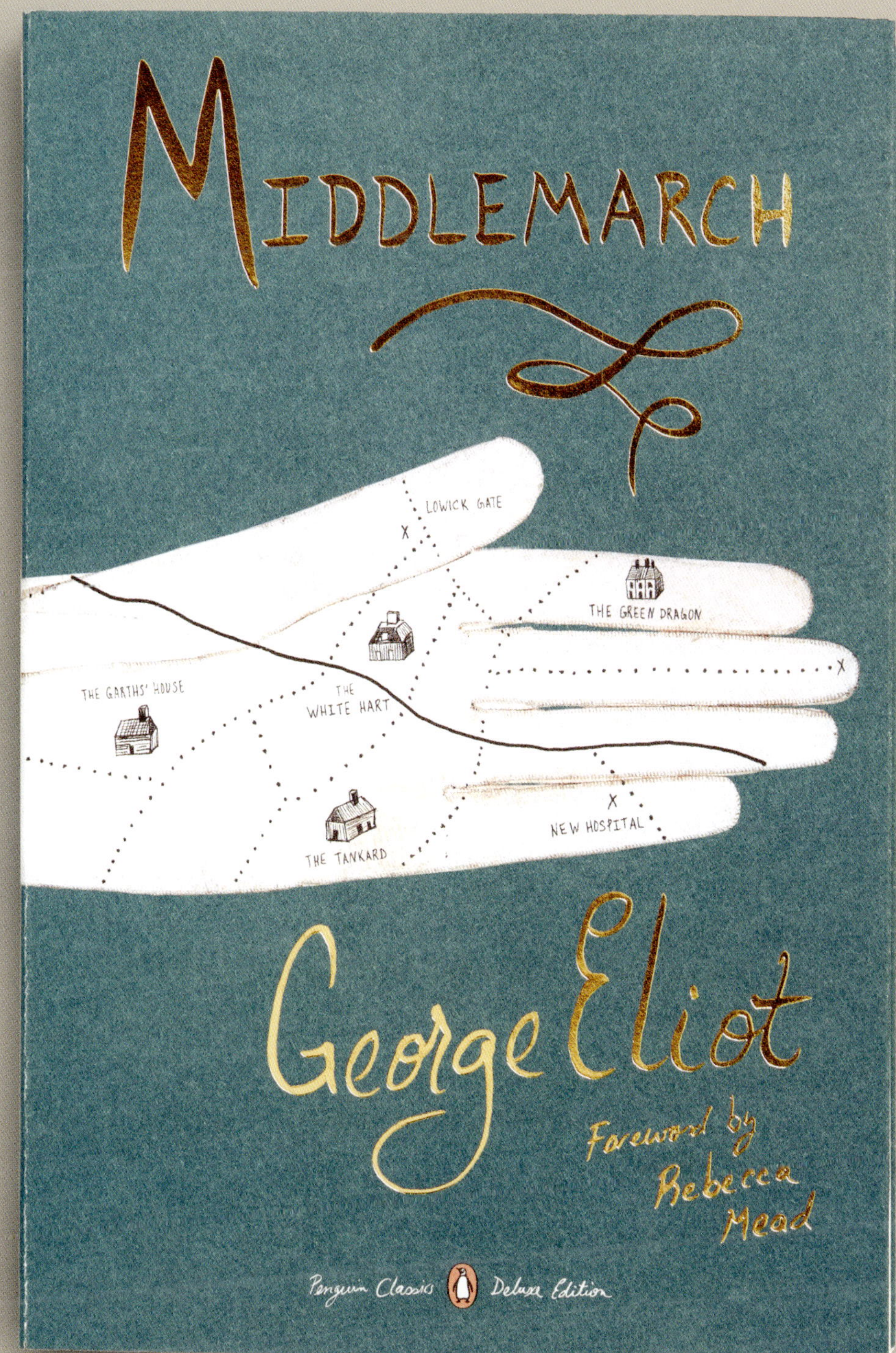

DELUXE CLASSICS

Titanic:
First Accounts

ILLUSTRATOR: MAX ELLIS **ART DIRECTOR:** ROSEANNE SERRA **EDITOR:** ELDA ROTOR

● Tim Maltin, EDITOR

Titanic was a floating palace and this beautiful cover shows a cross-section of the ship, which was a microcosm of the highly stratified society of the Gilded Age, before the horrors of the First World War brought greater equality. *Titanic*'s thirteen hundred passengers had nine hundred crew members to look after them. Max Ellis's remarkable cover for TITANIC: FIRST ACCOUNTS clearly shows these levels of society, with the "black gang" of stokers in the bowels of the great ship and the luxuries of the first class gymnasium on the boat deck, one hundred feet above.

● Roseanne Serra, ART DIRECTOR

Working with Max Ellis on TITANIC was a real trip. I needed someone extremely technical. I learned a lot about the interior and building of the ship through him. Did you know that the ship was built not only as a structural beast but to be aesthetically pleasing on the outside also? Originally it had three smokestacks but that looked off to the designers, so they added another. The three front stacks are above the main fuel furnaces. The fourth stack, in the back, is added just for balance. It is not a working smokestack. The tiny bit of smoke that does come out of the side of the stack is exhaust from the kitchen below.

PENGUIN CLASSICS 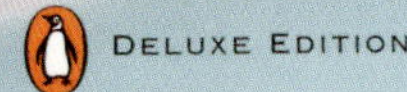 DELUXE EDITION

TITANIC

FIRST ACCOUNTS

EDITED WITH AN INTRODUCTION BY TIM MALTIN

AFTERWORD BY NICHOLAS WADE

FIRSTHAND ACCOUNTS BY LAWRENCE BEESLEY, MARGARET BROWN, ARCHIBALD GRACIE, AND MORE

• TITANIC DETAIL, MAX ELLIS

● **Max Ellis,** ILLUSTRATOR

I was on holiday on Bali and had had a few cocktails when I received the commissioning e-mail and immediately accepted the job, wrongly assuming it was to be a wreck illustration. (I've produced hundreds of schematics of sunken vessels for a dive magazine.) I arrived home two weeks later to find out I'd agreed to produce a cover of a cross-section of the fully laden *Titanic* on its maiden voyage!

There was no single source of reference, so what followed was a month of intensive, hysterical research, plowing through engineering drawings and stalking online forums trying to fill in the many gaps in the basic information needed to start the artwork. Many details simply weren't available (for instance, a liner pitches up at the bow and stern to add stability). The squash court was placed in the forward section. I needed to know if the floor sloped or was built up level, but even watching archive film footage from the sister ship, the *Olympic*, couldn't shed any light, so I just had to guess. I look back at the image now and can't believe I created it and am fortunate enough to be part of this amazing history.

The Communist Manifesto KARL MARX, FRIEDRICH ENGELS

ILLUSTRATOR: PATRICE KILLOFFER **CREATIVE DIRECTOR:** PAUL BUCKLEY **EDITOR:** ELDA ROTOR

● **Patrice Killoffer,** ILLUSTRATOR (TRANSLATED FROM FRENCH BY SAM RAIM)

When Penguin asked me to do the cover for **THE COMMUNIST MANIFESTO**, by Karl Marx and Friedrich Engels, I was very happy, first of all because it was for Penguin and for a very beautiful collection illustrated by prestigious artists. But most of all because it was *this* book. It's a classic, of course, but above all it's a book of which we can certainly say: It changed the world. That makes this book something more than a classic. And it's also more than just a political book. In it there is philosophy, humor, literature, history, anger, irony—everything!

How do we take all these things into account?

It was intimidating enough. And coinciding with all this, there was my life at that time: a recent breakup, a new relationship with a completely crazy Spanish woman, and a son who had tried to kill himself (not too seriously, but nevertheless . . .).

With all of this, I wasn't behaving very professionally. I wasn't responding to e-mails and I finally turned in my drawing very late, once they started to threaten me. I think I've been on Penguin's blacklist ever since.

Anyhow, all the same I'm very happy to have had this ultimate challenge to surmount. Encountering this kind of thing is exactly why I chose this job. Illustrating **THE COMMUNIST MANIFESTO** . . . I think I'm a bit of a masochist.

One small regret, nevertheless: I had an idea, in the first place, to represent capitalists not as pigs in top hats with fat cigars, as is the tradition, but as penguins. It seemed a perfect opportunity: penguins in tuxedos, hats, and cigars . . . but the idea didn't please them. I'm still wondering why.

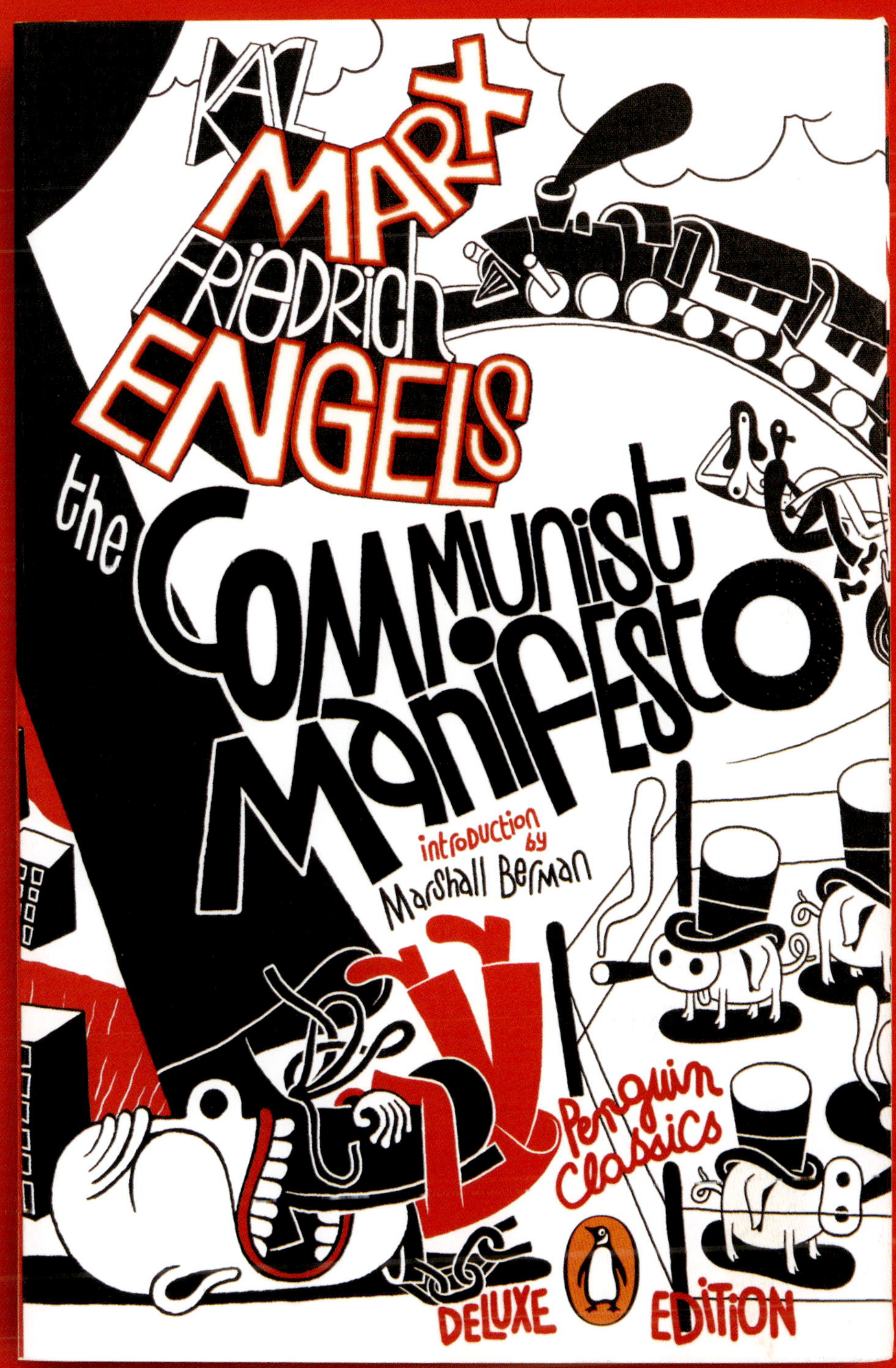
Karl
Marx
Friedrich
Engels
the
Communist
Manifesto
introduction by
Marshall Berman
Penguin
Classics
DELUXE
EDITION

Emma

JANE AUSTEN

ILLUSTRATOR: DADU SHIN **ART DIRECTOR:** BRIANNA HARDEN **CREATIVE DIRECTOR:** PAUL BUCKLEY **EDITOR:** ELDA ROTOR

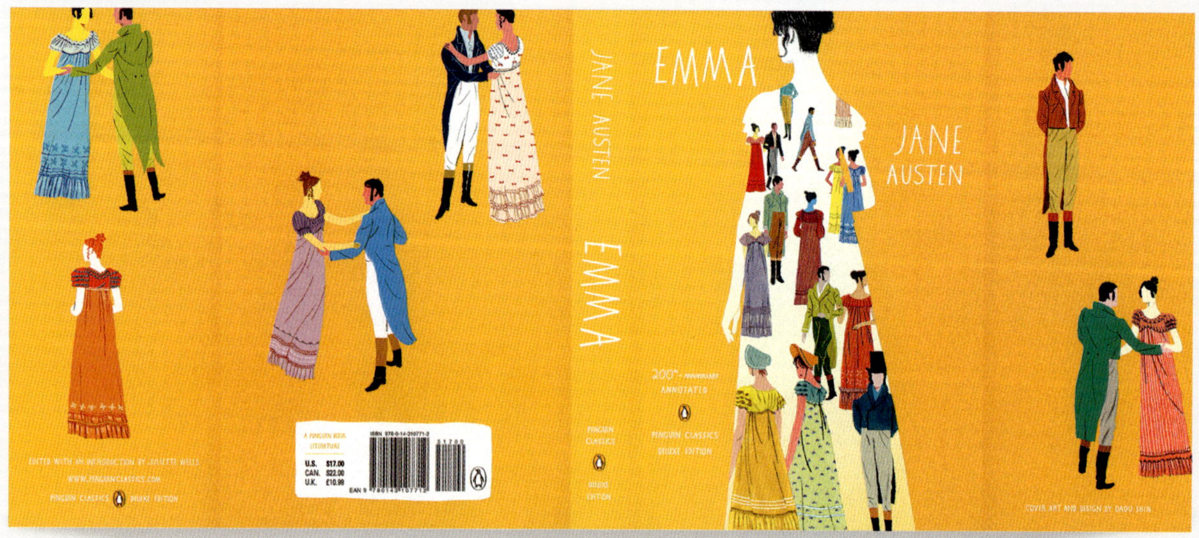

● Dadu Shin, ILLUSTRATOR

There have been many covers created for Jane Austen's **EMMA**. A quick google search will show that many of them are the same type of image: a straightforward portrait of the book's protagonist, Emma. For the two hundredth anniversary edition, our goal was to do something different. We ended up going with an image that I think clearly illustrates the book's focus on relationships and how Emma is the window to those relationships. I did wonder if I should have done something more representative of social status and how it pertains to gender roles, but I'm at peace with the final cover.

• SKETCH, DADU SHIN

EMMA
JANE
AUSTEN
200th - ANNIVERSARY
ANNOTATED
PENGUIN CLASSICS
DELUXE EDITION

The Call of Cthulhu and Other Weird Stories **H.P. LOVECRAFT**

ILLUSTRATOR: TRAVIS LOUIE **DESIGNER / CREATIVE DIRECTOR:** PAUL BUCKLEY **EDITOR:** ELDA ROTOR

● **Travis Louie,** ILLUSTRATOR

There is something about slowly losing it while being really afraid that characterizes H. P. Lovecraft's writings for me. When asked to do the cover of **THE CALL OF CTHULHU AND OTHER WEIRD STORIES**, I was excited to read his work again, even though it reminded me that I might be getting a little more insane every year and that my impending doom will revolve around extraterrestrials and ancient sea gods dancing in my backyard like they're in a holiday ballet with people in rodent suits and fancy hats. It's only a matter of time, really. The signs are everywhere and Lovecraft knew even back in the 1920s. When my postman says things like, "We're all doomed! Have a nice day!" I'm reminded that the doomsday clock is always ticking. Even if you haven't nearly run over someone who planted himself face-first on your car windshield screaming, "They're already here!" you feel it...don't you? I'm not running around my house pulling at my hair or staring into the abyss of my bathroom mirror with a look of despair just yet, but I am definitely prepared to, thanks to Lovecraft.

● **S. T. Joshi,** CRITIC / HISTORIAN

The covers of these two* books convey in a singularly effective fashion the utterly alien nature of H. P. Lovecraft's monsters. His signature contribution to literature was the creation of extraterrestrial entities who constituted a radical departure from the conventional ghosts, witches, vampires, and werewolves of Gothic tradition, and the artists of both these covers have fittingly portrayed the outré nature of Lovecraft's imaginative landscape. Beyond mere grisliness, these covers provide intriguing hints of the wonder and awe that Lovecraft's characters feel in their contemplation of a boundless universe where anything is possible.

*see pg. 214 for THE THING ON THE DOORSTEP

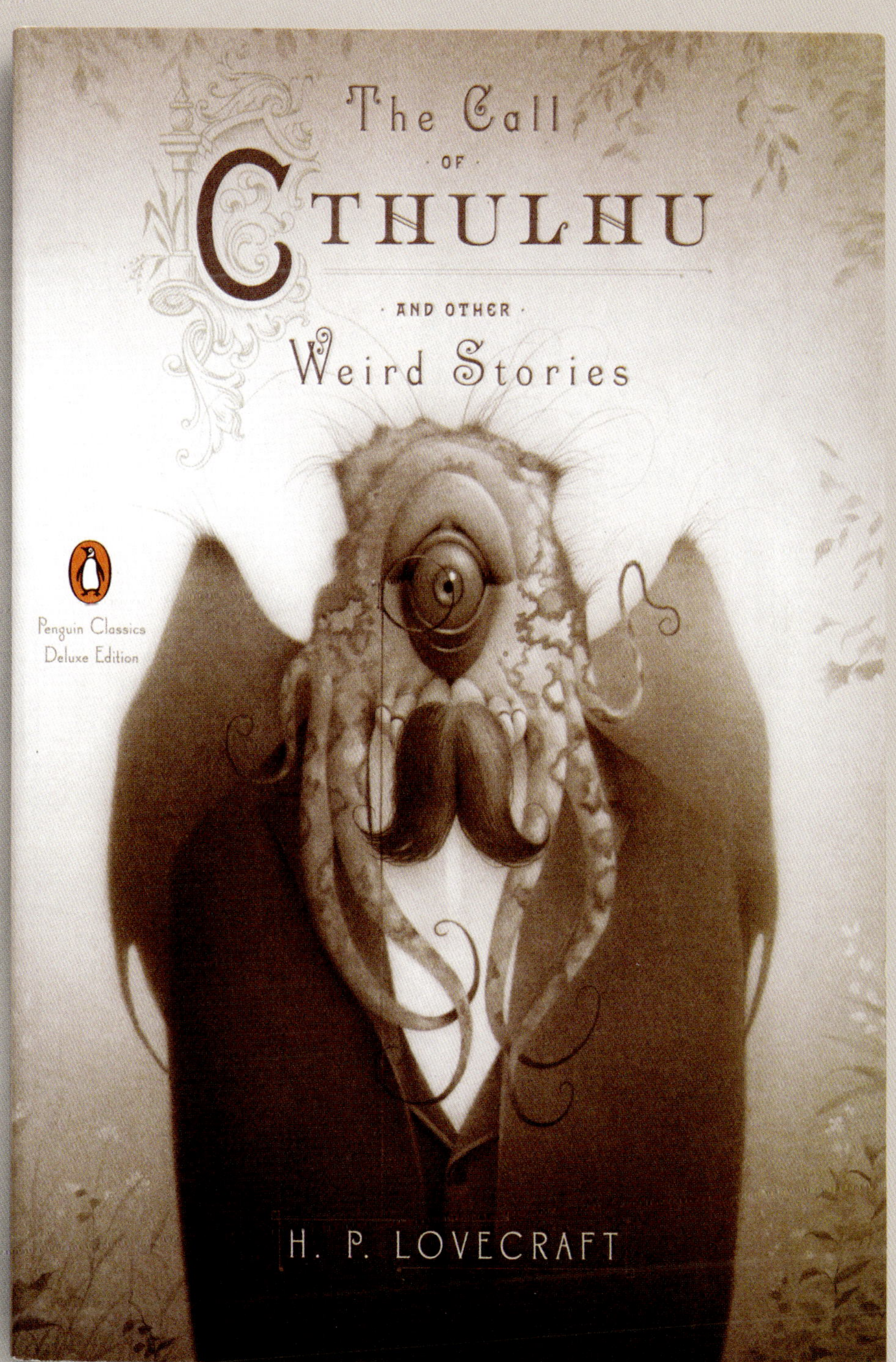

The Call
of
Cthulhu
and other
Weird Stories
Penguin Classics
Deluxe Edition
H. P. LOVECRAFT

When Victor Hugo began
work on Les Misérables in
the 1840s, he was already a
established author who ha
found success with
The Hunchback of Notre-Dame

When the novel was finally
published in 1862,
it was greeted with much
fanfare and publicity—

mixed reviews
from critics.

Nevertheless, the novel became an instant bestseller. So great was the impact that some of the social issues addressed in the book were taken up by the French National Assembly.

Les Misérables remains
Hugo's most enduring work
and is regarded as one of
the most important novels
of the 19th century.

Art and Design by
Jillian Tamaki

Marius
Cosette
Introduction by
Robert
Tombs
Jean
Valjean
Fantine
Eponine
Gavroche
Javert
A Penguin Book
Literature
U.S. $25.00
CAN. $28.00
ISBN 978-0-14-310756-9
52500
EAN 9 780143 107569

PENGUIN
CLASSICS
DELUXE
EDITION
"As long as there are ignorance and poverty on earth, books of this kind may serve some purpose."
Les Misérables
Victor Hugo
New Translation by
Christine Donougher

Les Misérables

VICTOR HUGO

ILLUSTRATOR: JILLIAN TAMAKI **CREATIVE DIRECTOR:** PAUL BUCKLEY **EDITOR:** ELDA ROTOR

● **Jillian Tamaki,** ILLUSTRATOR

I hadn't read **LES MISÉRABLES** before taking this job. I hadn't even seen the musical. There's something nice about going in totally fresh like that—you read the work very attentively and aren't swayed by your nostalgia or existing relationship to the piece. I was surprised how much I enjoyed the story too. I've always appreciated a large cast, melodrama, and rambling, chapter-long asides. (Confession: I ended up listening to the audiobook. I'm not a very fast reader.)

While preparing for this blurb, I looked at my sketches to revisit my thought process. Usually I like to present several unique ideas to clients, but in this case the design came to me very easily: a dense, lush, iconic treatment which mirrored the scope of the book. That said, I was most struck by images that reflected human cost—specifically Fantine, destitute, selling her hair and teeth; hence their appearance on the spine of the book.

• SKETCH, JILLIAN TAMAKI

Fairy Tales from the Brothers Grimm PHILIP PULLMAN

DESIGNER: ALISON FORNER **CREATIVE DIRECTOR:** PAUL BUCKLEY **EDITOR:** JOHN SICILIANO

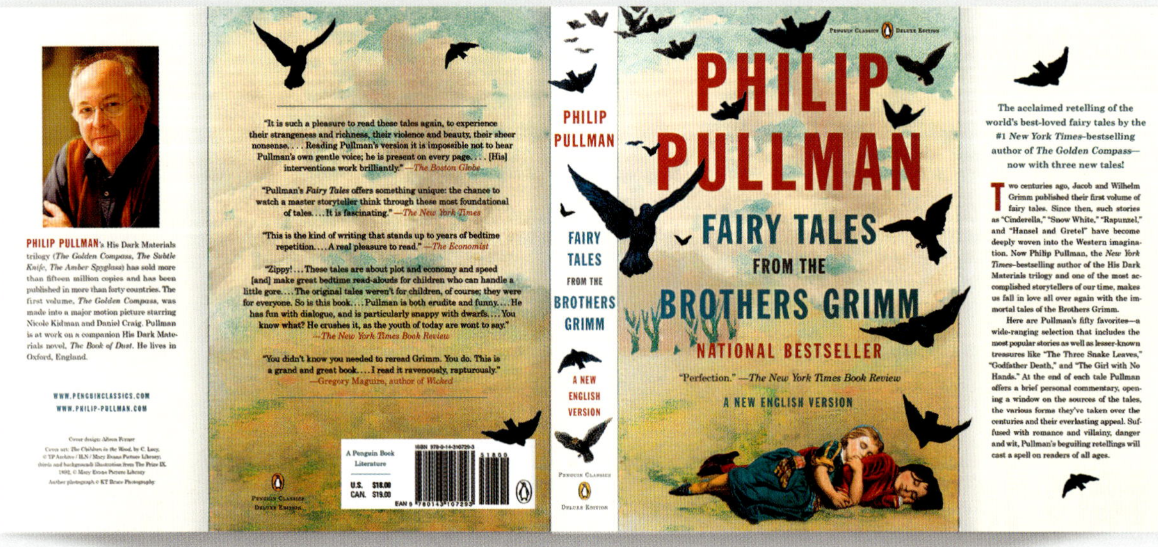

• APPROVED COVER

● Alison Forner, DESIGNER

Barbara de Wilde once said she wished someone would hire her to "throw blood on something . . . anything." This was in response to a question about the lack of interesting design work offered to women. When Paul contacted me to work on Philip Pullman's **BROTHERS GRIMM** retelling, I was at a point in my career where I could relate to Barbara's frustration—even though the work I was doing at Ecco skewed more literary, my freelance work was a steady stream of child-rearing books, self-help, and the occasional chick lit novel.

In his e-mail, Paul said, "These are dark stories . . . everyone always makes them look too nice . . . go dark, really dark." I'm pretty sure I accepted the job within seconds.

The fact that he thought of me—a woman—for something that needed to "go dark" meant so much. Although a different cover was ultimately chosen—both covers definitely have their merits—I do feel that throwing a little blood on the **BROTHERS GRIMM** would have been a bold, irreverent choice and completely unexpected.

The Brothers Grimm's Fairytales

SELECTED AND RETOLD BY

PHILIP PULLMAN

DELUXE CLASSICS

• UNUSED COVER, ALISON

Herzog

SAUL BELLOW

DESIGNER: LYNN BUCKLEY **CREATIVE DIRECTOR:** PAUL BUCKLEY **EDITOR:** BEENA KAMLANI

● **Lynn Buckley,** DESIGNER

Roseanne Serra first sent this assignment to Jen Wang, who did some brilliant work. But the author's estate proved to be a bit difficult to please. So, it was rather late in the season, and we were without an approved comp. Luckily, our publisher, Kathryn Court, remembered a killed comp for another book, *Music for Wartime.* Finally, a publisher really meant it when she said, "But save it; we can use it on another cover." That ubiquitous phrase, striking pain in the hearts of designers everywhere, usually means it will never see the light of day. Looking back on it, the original *Music for Wartime* comp was not great. But I see the inkling of the final HERZOG cover, as well as the final jacket for *Music for Wartime.*

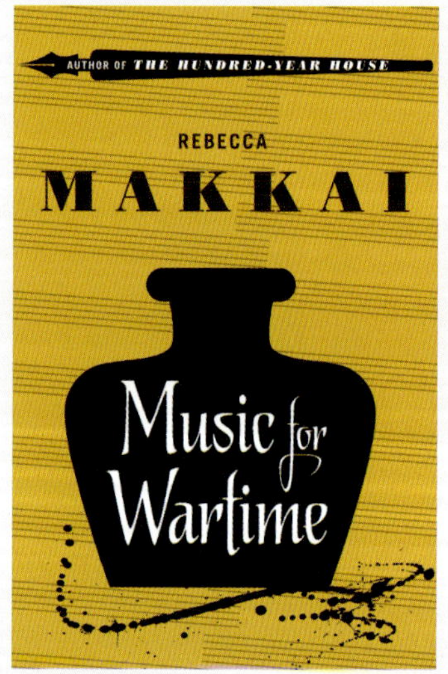

• MUSIC FOR WARTIME SKETCH, LYNN BUCKLEY

• HERZOG UNUSED COVERS, JEN WANG (ART DIRECTOR: ROSEANNE SERRA)

PENGUIN CLASSICS DELUXE EDITION
HER-
SAUL BELLOW
ZOG
INTRODUCTION BY PHILIP ROTH

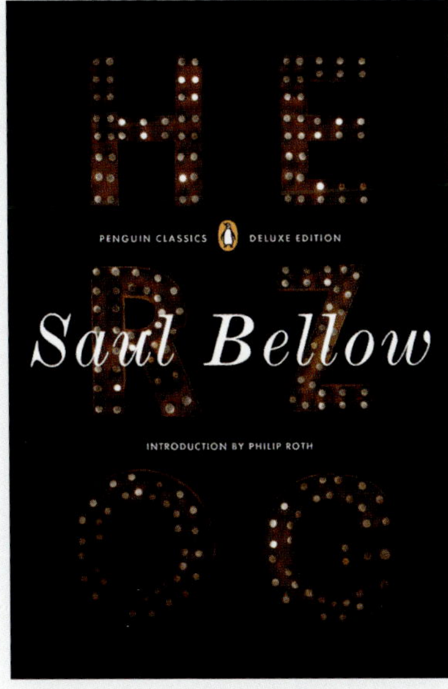

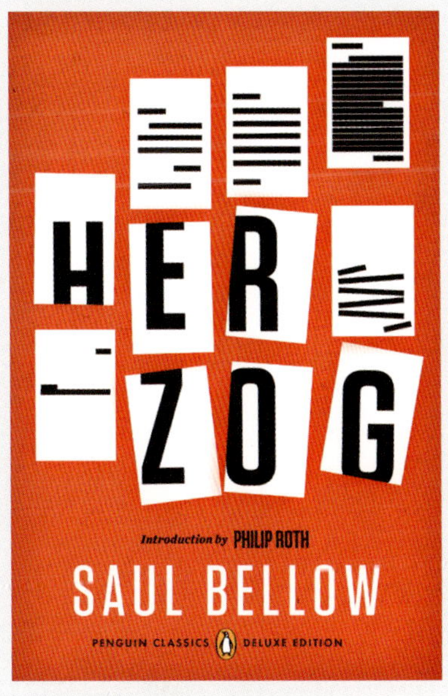

● **Lynn Buckley**, DESIGNER

Back to the design process for **HERZOG**. So, I began reworking the cover. The protagonist's character was said to be based on Saul Bellow himself. So I tried Bellow's signature, with a wood-grain texture echoing a desktop and '60s design. Unfortunately, I was told the publisher "doesn't like wood grain" and the signature wasn't quite working. But, again, the cover got better. I was pleased with the final type choice, and though I showed many color options for the background, they went for green. It's my favorite color, but I've often been told green covers don't sell, so this was another personal coup. To top it off, you gotta love the opportunity to do a lot of ink splattering.

• MUSIC FOR WARTIME
FINAL COVER, LYNN BUCKLEY

• HERZOG SKETCH, LYNN BUCKLEY

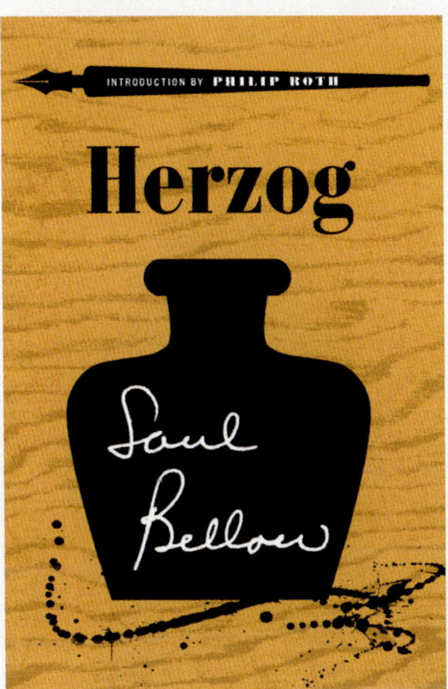

COVER ART AND DESIGN
BY ADAM SIMPSON
PENGUIN CLASSICS DELUXE EDITION

RACHE
INN
DELUXE CLASSICS
A PENGUIN BOOK
LITERATURE
U.S. $25.00
CAN. $33.00
U.K. £14.99
ISBN 978-0-14-310713-2
52500
EAN 9 780143 107132

SHERLOCK HOLMES

THE NOVELS

THE VALLEY OF FEAR

PENGUIN CLASSICS DELUXE EDITION

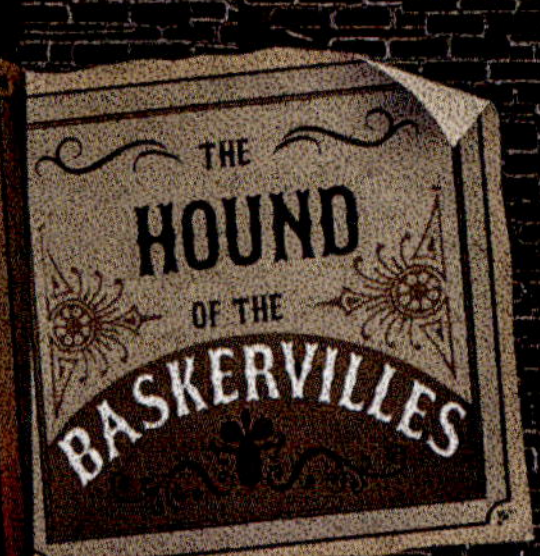

SIR ARTHUR CONAN DOYLE

INTRODUCTION BY MICHAEL DIRDA

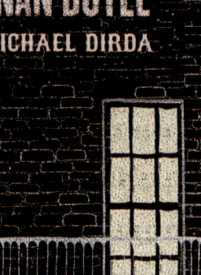

SHERLOCK HOLMES THE NOVELS SIR ARTHUR CONAN DOYLE

PENGUIN CLASSICS DELUXE EDITION

Sherlock Holmes

The Novels SIR ARTHUR CONAN DOYLE

ILLUSTRATOR: ADAM SIMPSON   CREATIVE DIRECTOR: PAUL BUCKLEY   EDITOR: ELDA ROTOR

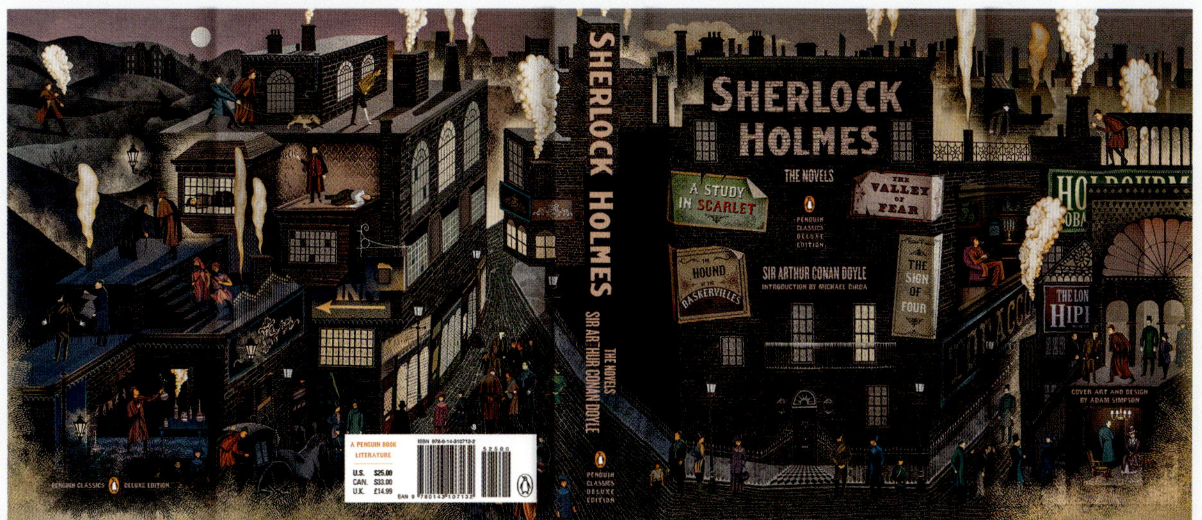

DELUXE CLASSICS

● Adam Simpson, ILLUSTRATOR

The main decision I made at the outset was to avoid the clichéd pipe and deerstalker combination as a central focus. I saw it as an opportunity to evoke the intriguing Victorian setting: a post–industrial revolution world of smoke, pea-soupers, and mystery, with atmosphere and texture, as opposed to the ubiquitous mono-dimensional silhouette. Holmes deserves better than that. Once I had found the bricks and mortar of Baker Street, the rest of the scene seemed to fall into place. I wanted to see him, in and amongst the chaos.

● Michael Dirda, INTRODUCER

Keeping to muted tonalities of brown and gray, Adam Simpson's brilliant wraparound cover for **SHERLOCK HOLMES: THE NOVELS** depicts an 1890s London of brick buildings and cobblestone streets, crowded with tiny figures. Peer closely and you soon realize that nearly every balcony, corner, or interior depicts a scene from one of the great detective's four novel-length adventures. Against a backdrop of smokestacks, one glimpses a man with a wooden leg, the word Rache scribbled on a wall, a woman bound and gagged, Sikh-like figures in turbans. Turn to the backflap and the hound of the Baskervilles springs out of the darkness. In nearly all these miniature tableaux one also observes an unmistakable figure sporting a deerstalker and inverness cloak.

In its overall impression, Simpson's cover calls to mind a toy theater cut out of cardboard. Appropriately, the titles of the four Holmes novels appear as wall posters, as if they were advertisements for the current attractions at the Lyceum or Hippodrome. A faintly Edward Gorey–like air adds to the atmospheric effectiveness of this wonderful and playful jacket art.

Persuasion and *Sense and Sensibility* JANE AUSTEN

ILLUSTRATOR: AUDREY NIFFENEGGER **CREATIVE DIRECTOR:** PAUL BUCKLEY **EDITOR:** JOHN SICILIANO

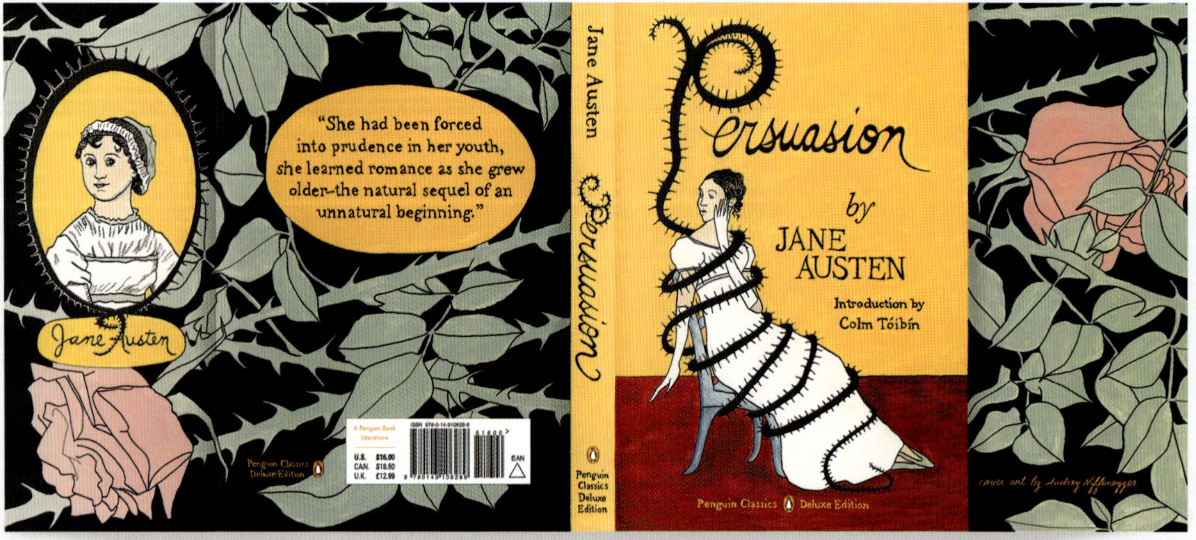

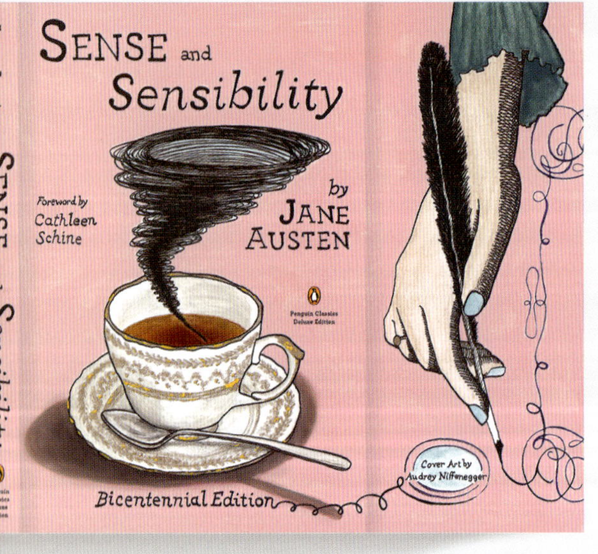

● **Audrey Niffenegger,** ILLUSTRATOR

I began by rereading **PERSUASION**, had an idea for the cover, made the sketch, got it approved, drew the final art, turned it in, and all was well. No muss, no fuss.

After that happy experience Paul and his editors kindly invited me to tackle **SENSE AND SENSIBILITY**. Piece of cake, I thought. But no. I began with a sketch that evoked Max Ernst's collage novels. *Too weird*, was the editorial response. *Austenites* won't like it. So then I veered off to the other extreme and drew Elinor and Marianne demurely strolling arm in arm. *Too boring*, quoth the editors. Then I ignored the project for a while and eventually, while drinking tea, realized that what I needed was an image that combined something tidy and something wild. *Voilà*, a tempest in a teacup.

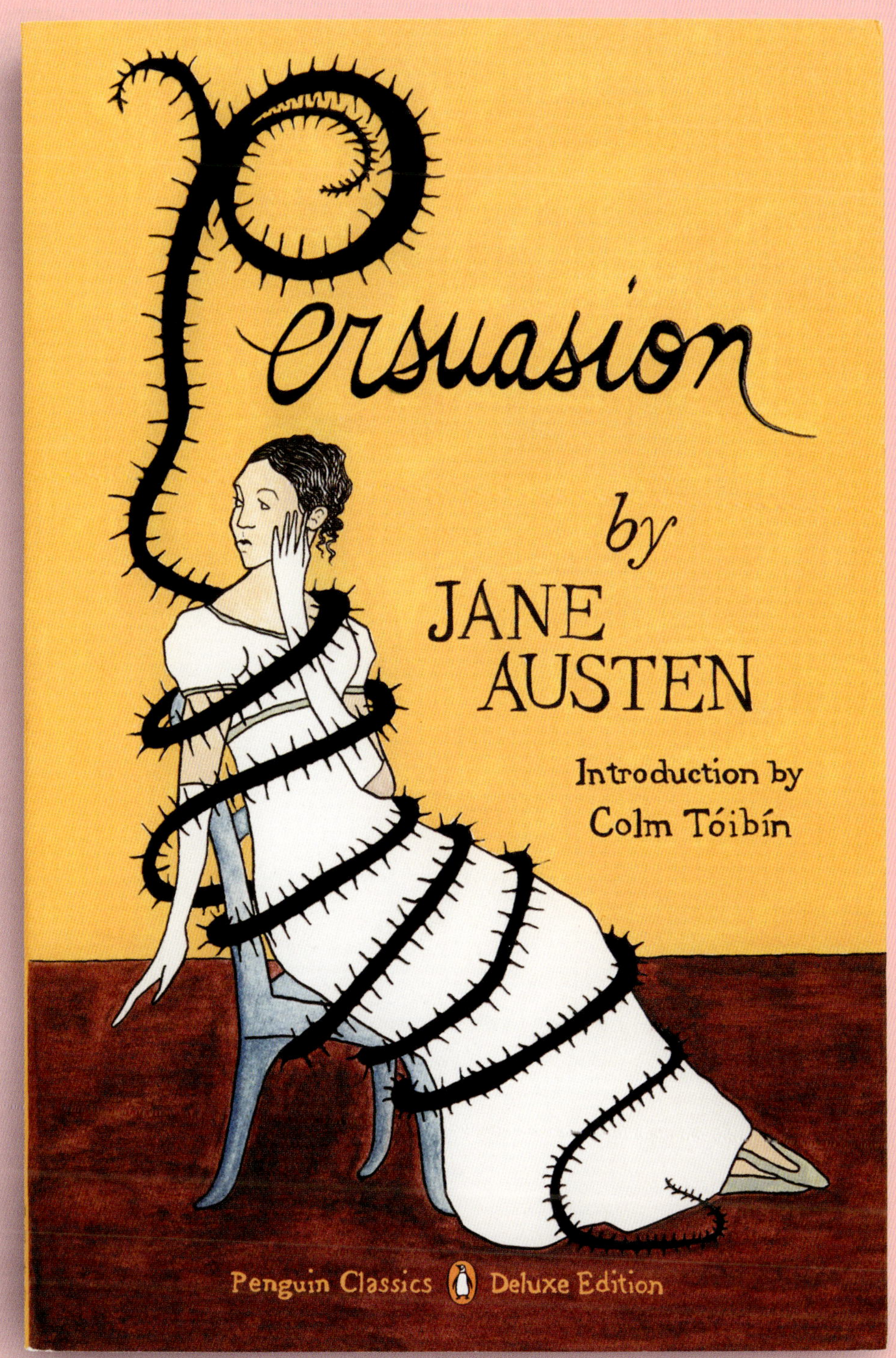
Persuasion
by
JANE
AUSTEN
Introduction by
Colm Tóibín
Penguin Classics Deluxe Edition

Heart of Darkness

JOSEPH CONRAD

ILLUSTRATOR: MIKE MIGNOLA **DESIGNER / CREATIVE DIRECTOR:** PAUL BUCKLEY **EDITOR:** ELDA ROTOR

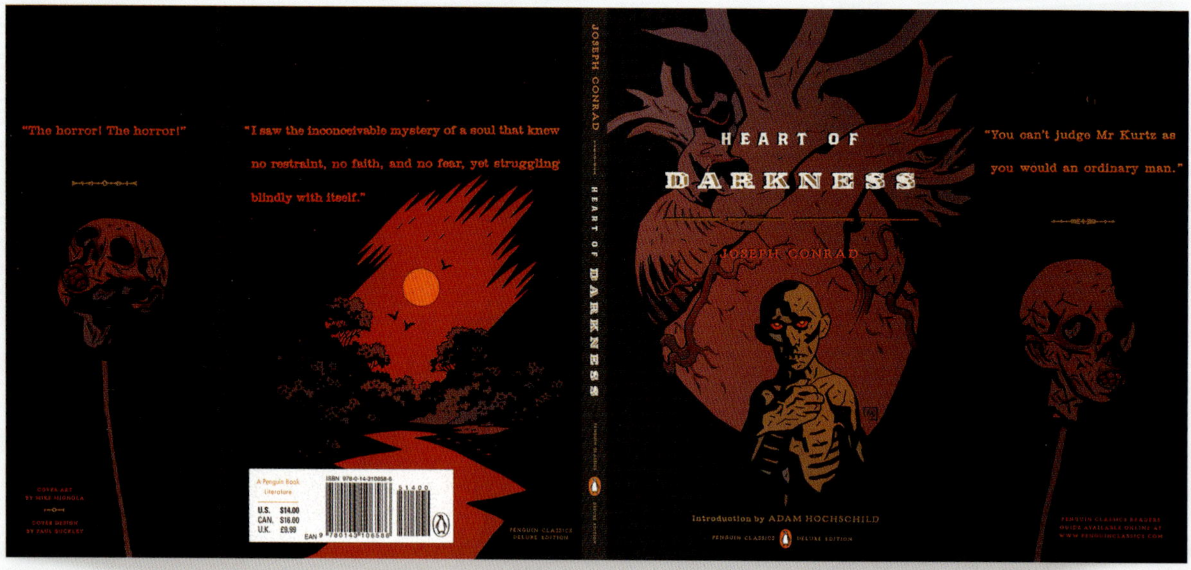

● **Mike Mignola,** ILLUSTRATOR

When I was asked to do the cover for **HEART OF DARKNESS**, my first thought (really my only thought) was "Why not *Dracula*? I love *Dracula*. I know *Dracula*. I've read *Dracula*."

I had tried reading **HEART OF DARKNESS** a couple times over the years and never got very far. I knew the basic plot and knew that I should really like it—but for whatever reason it had just never grabbed me. But I did like the idea of doing one of these covers and figured that if I turned this down they'd never ask again (guess I'll never know), so I said yes—and am very glad I did because it forced me to finally read the book. I loved how creepy Kurtz looked and thought he'd be fun to draw, but I knew I needed more than him for the cover. The idea of him in front of a giant heart leapt to mind right away—but was it going to be too obvious? A big dark heart for the cover of **HEART OF DARKNESS**? Would they let me get away with that? But I like drawing hearts. I don't think I ever had any other idea for the cover, so if they'd said no to that one I guess I would have been out—but they said okay and there it is.

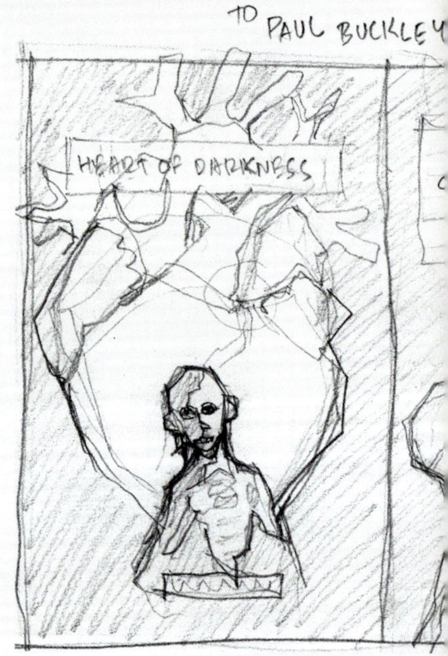

• SKETCH, MIKE MIGNOLA

HEART OF

DARKNESS

JOSEPH CONRAD

Introduction by ADAM HOCHSCHILD

PENGUIN CLASSICS  DELUXE EDITION

Faces of Love:

Hafez and the Poets of Shiraz HAFEZ JAHAN MALEK KHATUN & OBAYD-E ZAKANI

ILLUSTRATOR: NICK MISANI **CREATIVE DIRECTOR:** PAUL BUCKLEY **EDITOR:** ELDA ROTOR

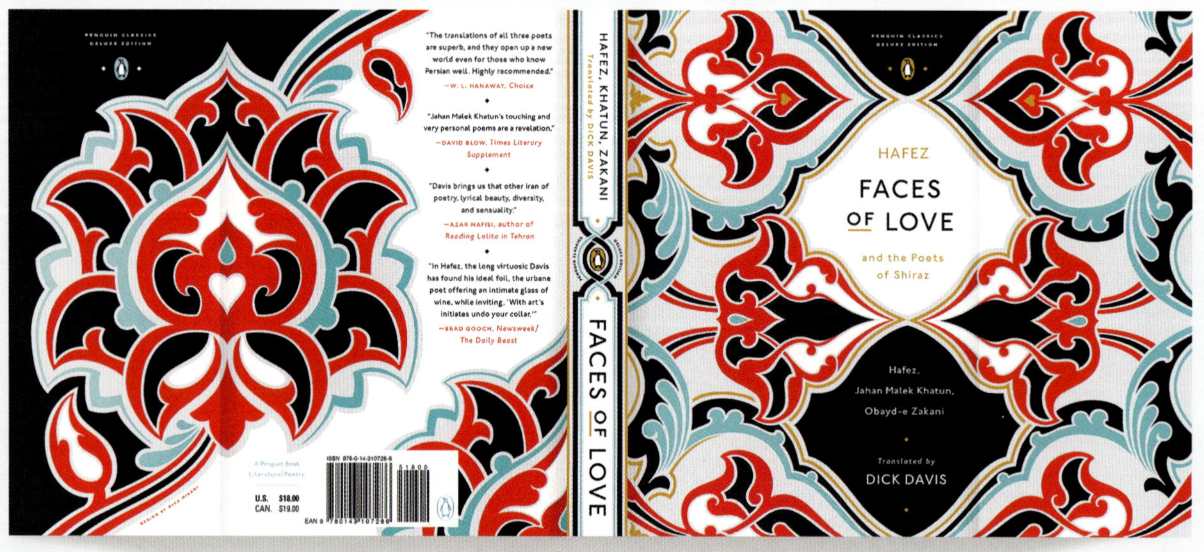

● **Nick Misani,** ILLUSTRATOR

I was thrilled to discover my first Deluxe Edition assignment was going to feature a collection of fourteenth-century Persian (and at times homoerotic) love poetry. I sought to mirror the language and theme of the verses—in equal parts spiritual, secular, and salacious—by creating something bold, graphic, and opulent. Inspired by photographs of stunning Arabic calligraphy embellished with lush ornamental borders and rosettes, I created something very referential that mimicked that evocative visual language. Initially, I loved the direction, but was quickly and forcefully told that by allowing myself to be seduced by the historical appeal of my reference, I eschewed any possible modern connection. Begrudgingly admitting to my mistake, I enlarged and abstracted the ornament and simplified the typography, to create a cover inspired—but not constrained—by the time and place in which the poems were composed.

• SKETCH, NICK MISANI

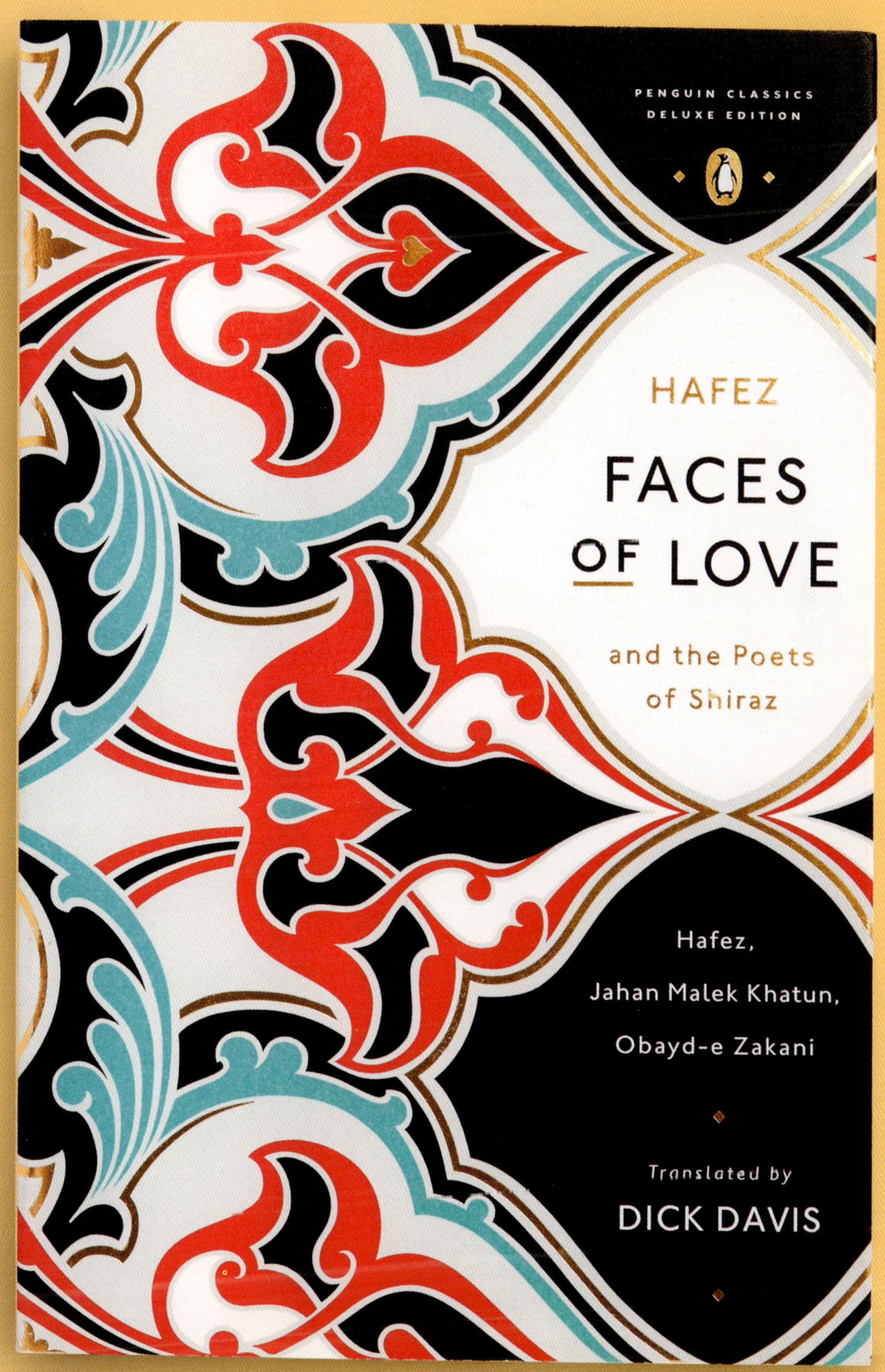
PENGUIN CLASSICS
DELUXE EDITION
HAFEZ
FACES OF LOVE
and the Poets of Shiraz
Hafez,
Jahan Malek Khatun,
Obayd-e Zakani
Translated by
DICK DAVIS

CAST OF CHARACTERS

VIOLET BEAUREGARDE
MASTICATING VULGARIAN

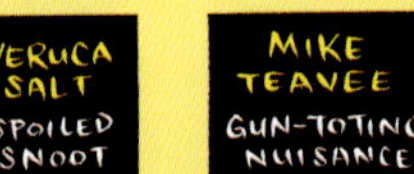

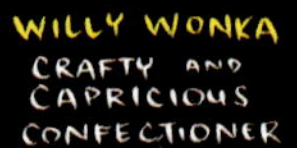

OOMPA-LOOMPAS
INDUSTRIOUS IMPS

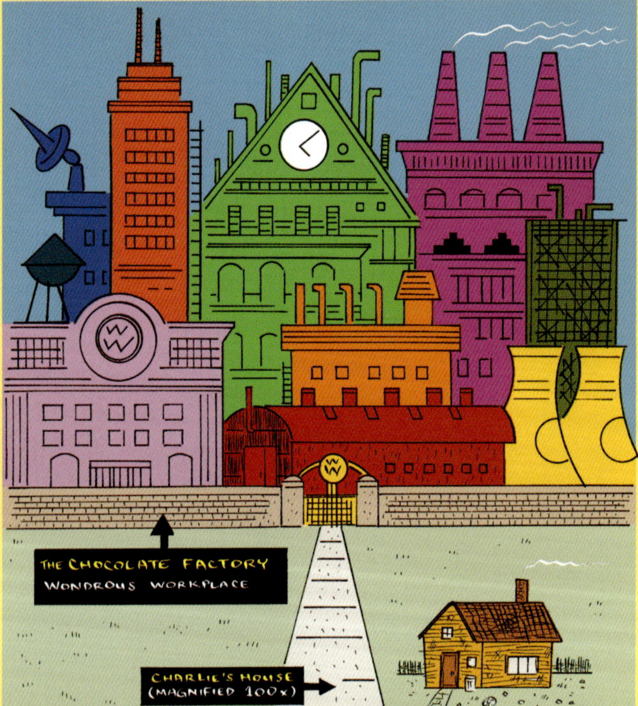

THE GREAT MOUSE PLOT OF 1924

ROALD DAHL

DELUXE CLASSICS

CHARLIE AND THE CHOCOLATE FACTORY

PENGUIN CLASSICS DELUXE EDITION

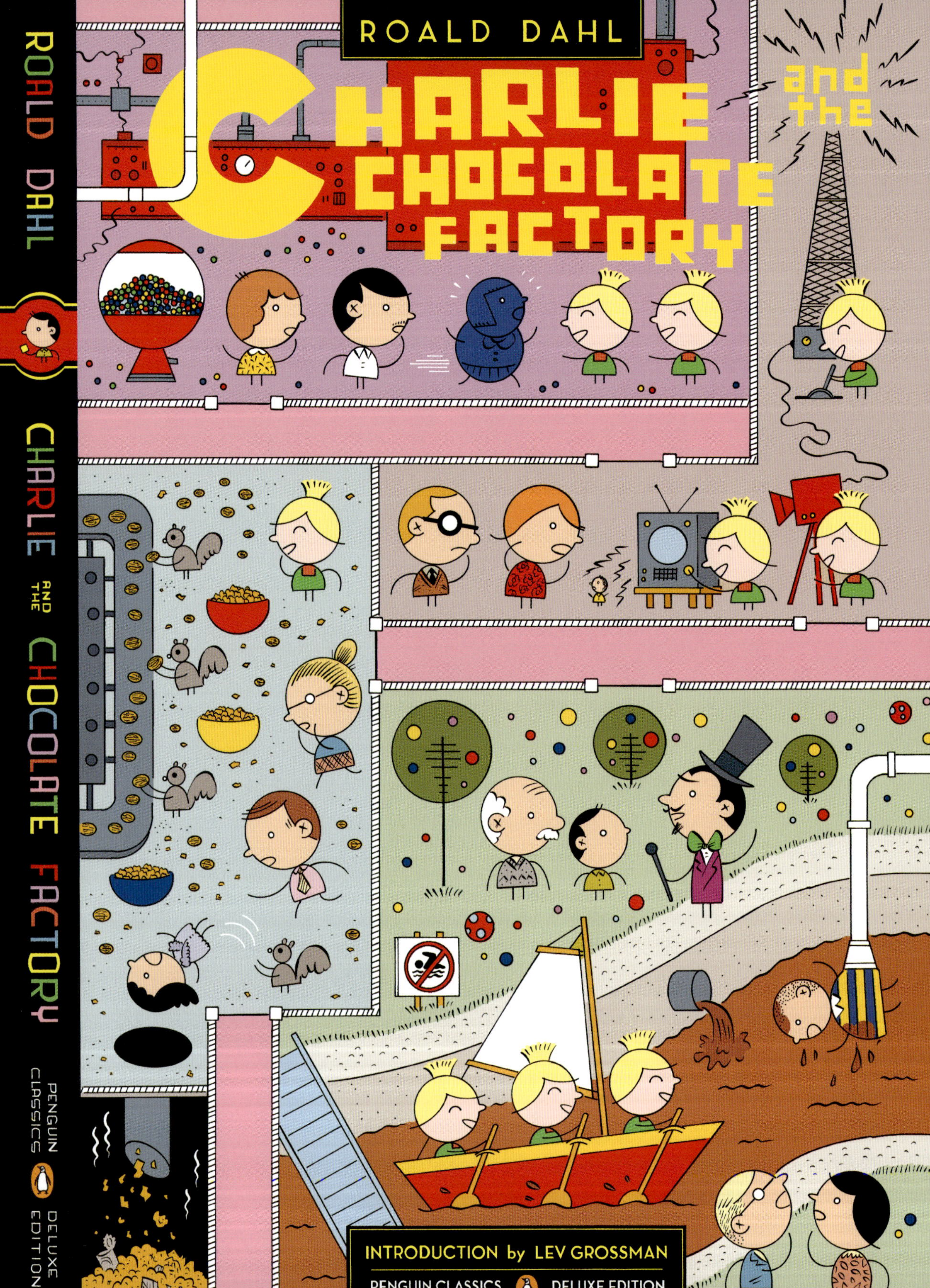
ROALD DAHL
CHARLIE and the CHOCOLATE FACTORY
INTRODUCTION by LEV GROSSMAN
PENGUIN CLASSICS
DELUXE EDITION
ROALD DAHL
CHARLIE AND THE CHOCOLATE FACTORY
PENGUIN CLASSICS
DELUXE EDITION

Charlie and the Chocolate Factory ROALD DAHL

ILLUSTRATOR: IVAN BRUNETTI **CREATIVE DIRECTOR:** PAUL BUCKLEY **EDITOR:** JOHN SICILIANO

DELUXE CLASSICS

● **Ivan Brunetti, ILLUSTRATOR**

I had always admired the Penguin Books series featuring cover designs and illustrations done by cartoonists, often quietly bemoaning the fact that I would never be part of the series, because, frankly, I really wasn't good enough. I'm sure I did a lot of whispered whining to some God I don't actually believe in. But then one day, out of nowhere, I was invited by Penguin to submit a cover for the series. Maybe the nonexistent God felt sorry for me or was simply tired of my droning self-pity. In any case, being asked to draw something, anything, for Penguin Books was the first surprise.

The second surprise was the book choice: **CHARLIE AND THE CHOCOLATE FACTORY**. Huh? I had never read the book, I'm ashamed to admit now; nor did I think my drawing approach would in any way be suitable for it. Frankly, I was a bit mystified, so I looked over some past work and tried to puzzle out why on earth they thought I should be the illustrator for this project. I did once draw a fictitious and not very realistic science laboratory, filled with little people running around in a non-Euclidean (or Newtonian, or Einsteinian) perspective, for *The New Yorker* magazine. Perhaps they saw that image and thought the laboratory might somehow translate for the chocolate factory. So I used that older image as a starting point, thinking maybe they wanted something along those lines. I finally read the book, liked it a lot, and decided to (a) avoid rewatching the Gene Wilder movie I'd seen as a kid, (b) avoid the more recent remake entirely, and (c) work up some sketches that used a superflattened perspective/projection system, so that I could fit as much narrative information as possible into the small space. Throughout, I fought a seeping, acrid feeling in my chest and stomach, worrying that my idea would be rejected outright.

(CONTINUED ON NEXT PAGE)

(CONTINUED FROM PREVIOUS PAGE)

The third surprise came when the sketches were approved both by Penguin and by the Roald Dahl estate. Huh? Well, it now felt like an intravenous antacid was flowing through my body. Then I realized that I, for real now, had to draw the actual cover (I always prefer the sketching process, which is much more organic than my final drawings). I began my usual procrastination process, succumbing to self-doubt, self-recrimination, self-loathing, and also pure laziness. At some point, the inevitable "Uh, when are you going to send us the final art?" e-mail arrived. The good Catholic boy inside me stepped up, and with my usual last-minute flurry of panic-stricken activity, I somehow finished on time. Or maybe it was slightly late. I don't remember, but I got the impression everyone hated me, and deservedly so. Dear Penguin Books: I hereby apologize for any inconvenience I may have caused.

As for the artwork, I decided to move my abstracted drawing style even further into geometry land, and my inking became even less free-handed during this project, a trend I have not been able to reverse, probably to my detriment. No one's exactly been beating down my door to produce yet more inexpressive, flat, antiperspectival drawings featuring nether spaces non-converging toward a zero point. But, you know, one can only make what one is capable of at any given time, and I think of drawing as a continuing unconscious document of the ebbs and flows of one's skill level and attendant mental state.

Since I have the floor here, I may as well use this opportunity to state that, for the record, I don't think the yellow foil stamping on the cover works. I wanted to use gold, to match the story, but I'm guessing there had been too much gold used already in the series. So we experimented. But the bright yellow foil came out a little too thin, I think. Oh, well. I can see why the designer chose it, as it does fit my simple, candy-colored drawings, while gold may have brought a little too much gravitas in this context. People tell me that I sometimes tend to focus on the negative, however, so take everything I say with a grain of salt.

The fourth surprise came when I went to a bookstore in search of the book, to see it in situ. I asked the clerk if he knew about a forthcoming new edition, and I was informed that it hadn't come out yet, but according to the computer, yes, there did seem to be a new version coming out in a few weeks, one featuring some sort of "psychedelic" cover. Well, I'm about as psychedelic as brown corduroy pants, but, what the heck, I'll take it as a compliment.

—**IB**

• SKETCH, IVAN BRUNETTI

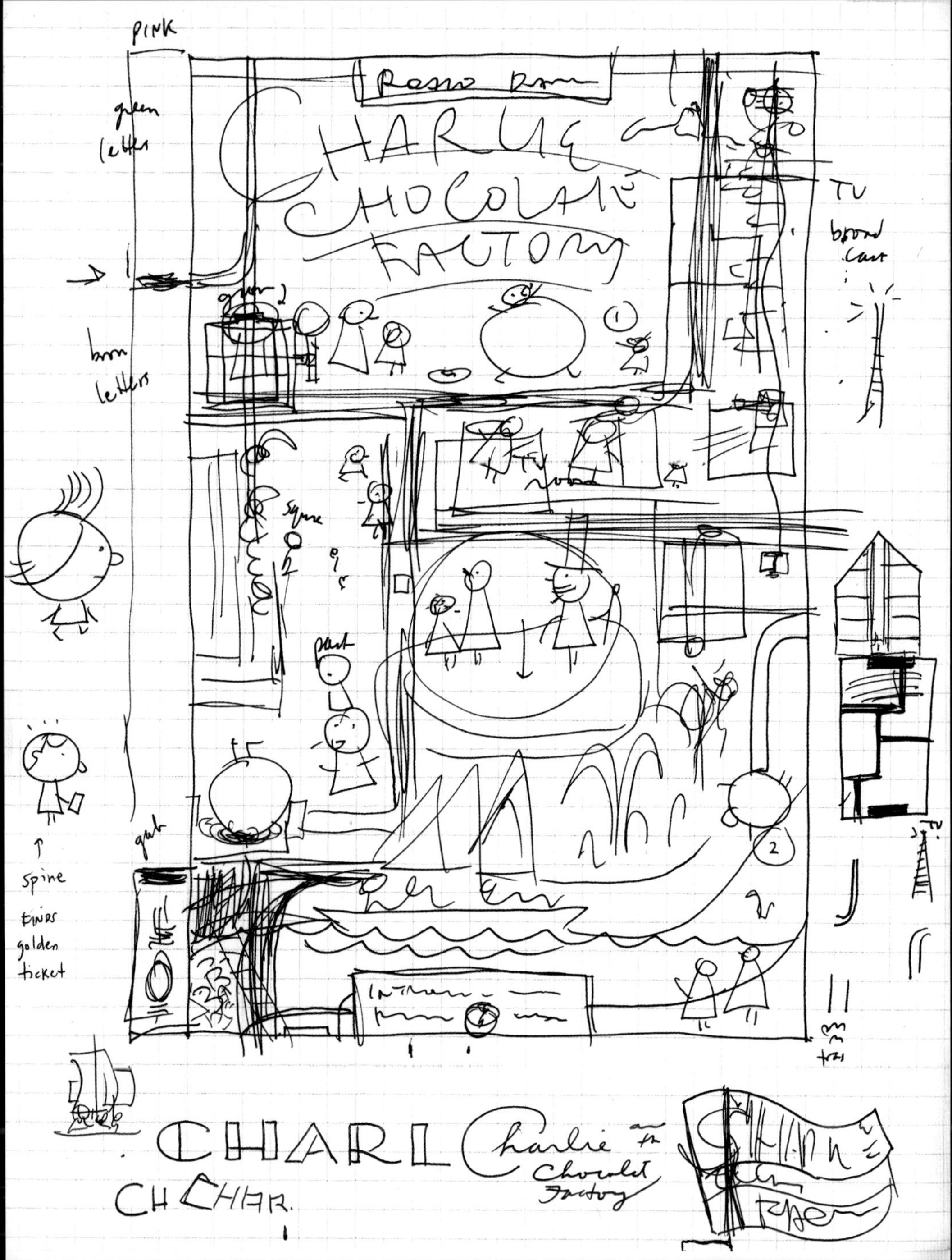

PINK

green letters

brown letters

TV broadcast

↑ spine

finds golden ticket

CHARLIE CHOCOLATE FACTORY

CHARL

Charlie and the Chocolate Factory

CH CHAR.

www.penguinclassics.com

Cover illustration: Alex Konahin
Cover art direction and design: Lynn Buckley

ANGELA CARTER
DELUXE CLASSICS
THE BLOODY CHAMBER
PENGUIN
CLASSICS
DELUXE
EDITION
A Penguin Book
Literature
U.S. $16.00
CAN. $18.00
ISBN 978-0-14-310761-3
51600
EAN 9 780143 107613

The Bloody Chamber
PENGUIN CLASSICS
DELUXE EDITION
Introduction by
Kelly Link
ANGELA CARTER
75th ANNIVERSARY
ANGELA CARTER
THE BLOODY CHAMBER
PENGUIN
CLASSICS
DELUXE
EDITION

The Bloody Chamber

ANGELA CARTER

ILLUSTRATOR: ALEX KONAHIN **ART DIRECTOR:** LYNN BUCKLEY **CREATIVE DIRECTOR:** PAUL BUCKLEY **EDITOR:** JOHN SICILIANO

• WORK IN PROGRESS, ALEX KONAHIN

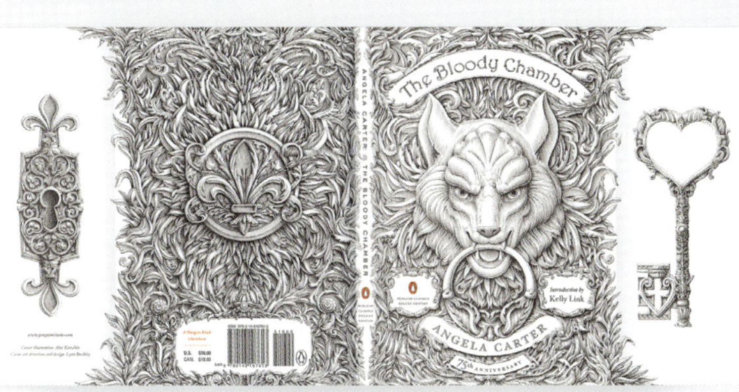

● Lynn Buckley, ART DIRECTOR

I asked Alex Konahin to illustrate this cover because his quirky, elaborate, Gothic style is perfect for Angela Carter.

The first sketches were too busy, incorporating too many images from the novel. We came back to what Alex is brilliant at: one iconic element with a lot of ornate detail surrounding it. We narrowed down the possible cover images to the door to the bloody chamber, a wolf, and a lily. Alex came up with the wolf as door knocker, with a lock and key on the flaps. This wonderfully suggests the castle door without showing it. I asked for the fleur-de-lis on back, which is a stylized lily—another important detail in the book.

The next challenge: integrating type and logos. Alex tends to fill up all the space with the ornate detail I hired him for—but we need type to read. I suggested cartouches. Alex very patiently reworked the cartouches multiple times, and kindly executed the title type as well. He even gave me a beautiful space for the bar code, and I love how ornament overflows organically onto the flaps.

We wanted to emulate Alex's detailed line work, so we printed it with a high-line screen for detail. One might assume you'd reproduce this sort of art in a single color, but seeing the warmth and depth of a black-and-gray duotone made it the clear winner.

Appointment in Samarra JOHN O'HARA

ILLUSTRATOR: NEIL GOWER **CREATIVE DIRECTOR:** PAUL BUCKLEY **EDITOR:** JOHN SICILIANO

● **Neil Gower, ILLUSTRATOR**

"Relishing every eloquently coarse and ...well, AMERICAN word of this!"—my tweet, on reading the opening chapters in preparation for this design.

I'd long been familiar with the striking 1934 cover,* but knew nothing of the story itself. It immediately became clear that O'Hara had a party going on in these pages; a dark party, deftly rendered and shot through with a carefully gauged humor that I hadn't anticipated.

The words I found myself writing in my sketchbook were "glamour/fracture/hurtling/headlong/menace." I decided to approach this jacket as if designing myself a shirt to break hearts—and highball glasses—at *the* most louche country club party ever.

*FOR FELLOW DESIGN OBSESSIVES, THE SPEEDING GREEN CAR ON THE FLYLEAF IS A DIRECT NOD TO ALFRED MAURER'S ORIGINAL COVER (SEE RIGHT).

• PHOTO, JAMES CUMMINS BOOKSELLER, NEW YORK, NY

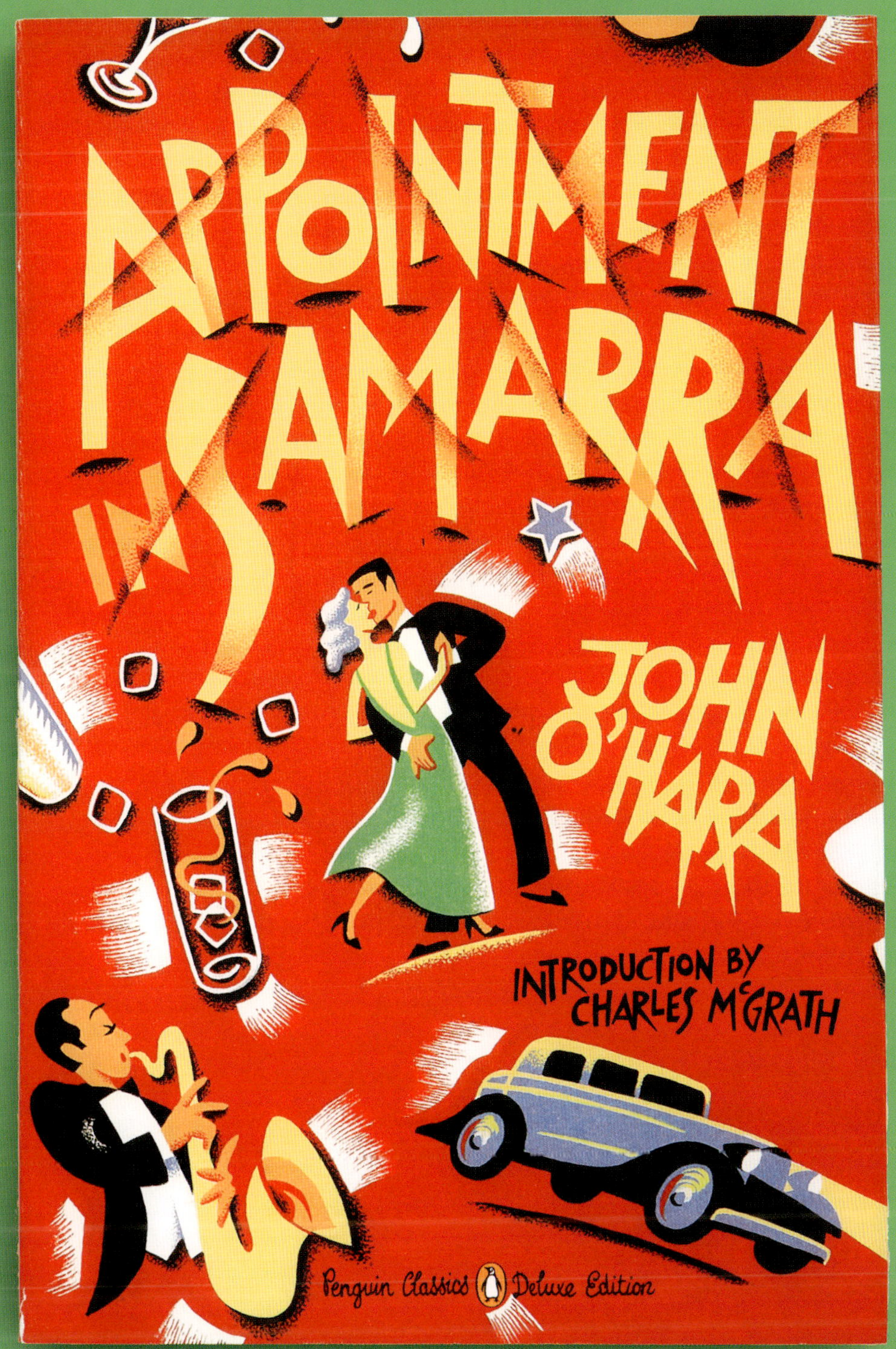
APPOINTMENT IN SAMARRA
JOHN O'HARA
INTRODUCTION BY CHARLES McGRATH
Penguin Classics Deluxe Edition

The Greek Myths

ROBERT GRAVES

ILLUSTRATOR: ROSS MACDONALD **CREATIVE DIRECTOR:** PAUL BUCKLEY **EDITOR:** JOHN SICILIANO

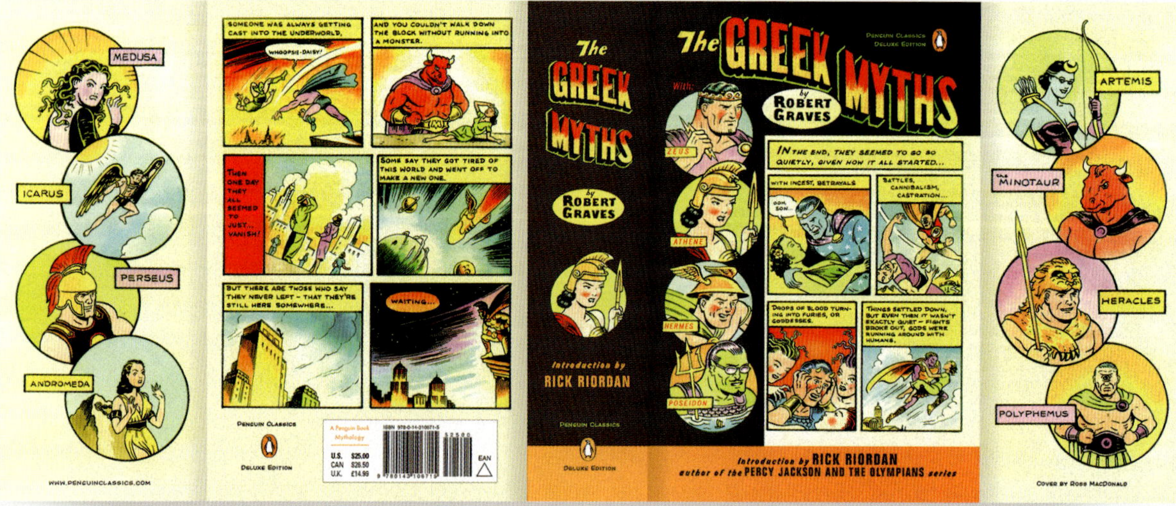

● **Ross MacDonald,** ILLUSTRATOR

When I first talked to Paul Buckley about this assignment, it seemed like one of those exciting "do anything you want" dream jobs. But my enthusiasm was dampened a bit when I got a follow-up e-mail from an assistant that said my cover image needed to reference a piece of back-cover copy that was included in the e-mail. The copy was the usual semi-bland book description. So my first sketch was pretty and tasteful and sedate—a series of gigantic ghostly gods stride through a classical Greek landscape with goatherd and temple. I sent it to Paul. To say that he was less than impressed would be an understatement. He made it clear, *in no uncertain terms*, that he would not stand for being given such a pedestrian idea. I explained about the note to reference the text and how I felt it was a bit limiting. "Oh," he said. "That was a mistake. You can ignore that. Write anything you want." So I tossed the copy and started reading the book. Pretty good stuff—lots of blood and magic and adventure. The story of the origin of the Greek gods almost reminded me of the classic Superman origin story from the golden age of comics. In fact, I thought, what were the Greek gods if not superheroes? When they had passed from this world, we had simply made up new superheroes. I looked at my first sketch, with the giant ghostly gods striding over the horizon to oblivion. What if they hadn't passed from this world, I thought. Maybe they're still here, waiting to start a new chapter....

• SKETCH, ROSS MACDONALD

The GREEK MYTHS
PENGUIN CLASSICS
DELUXE EDITION
With:
by ROBERT GRAVES
ZEUS
ATHENE
HERMES
POSEIDON
IN THE END, THEY SEEMED TO GO SO QUIETLY, GIVEN HOW IT ALL STARTED...
WITH INCEST, BETRAYALS
OOH, SON...
BATTLES, CANNIBALISM, CASTRATION...
DROPS OF BLOOD TURNING INTO FURIES, OR GODDESSES.
THINGS SETTLED DOWN, BUT EVEN THEN IT WASN'T EXACTLY QUIET – FIGHTS BROKE OUT, GODS WERE RUNNING AROUND WITH HUMANS,
Introduction by RICK RIORDAN
author of the PERCY JACKSON AND THE OLYMPIANS series

Jorge Luis Borges

SERIES

SELECTED POEMS, SELECTED NON-FICTIONS, COLLECTED FICTIONS

DESIGNER: PAUL BUCKLEY **EDITOR:** MICHAEL MILLMAN

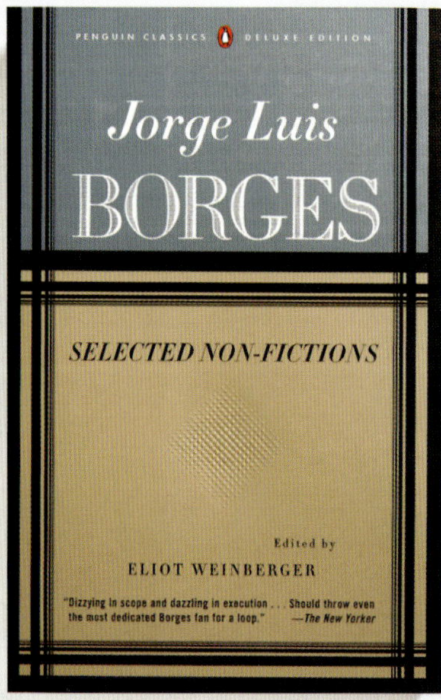

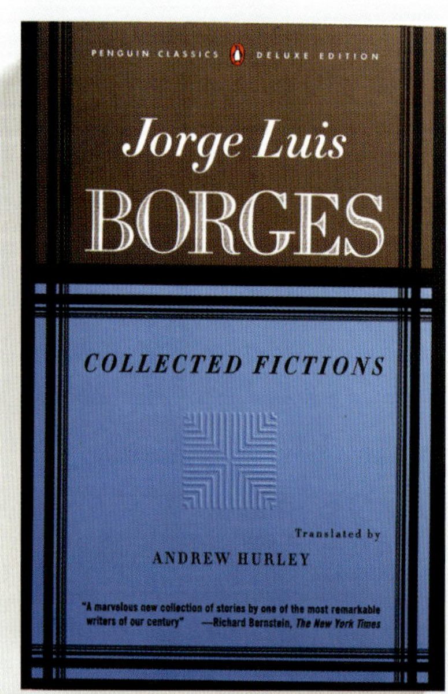

Paul Buckley, DESIGNER

The Borges series goes back a ways, but I still like the look of them. It's never not terrifying to be tasked to visually embody someone who is a hundred times brighter than yourself. Add to that, it's a three-book series that needs to be coordinated, spanning his nonfiction, his fiction, and his poetry, and now you're also tasked to find a common thread and to graphically create this essence of genius that runs through these diverse collections.

Borges was fascinated by intricacies both physical and metaphysical. He often incorporated complex structures into his writing, such as mazes, labyrinths, and libraries, whether of a physical nature or a mental construction, and they were usually wildly imaginative—this interest runs through these three books. With this in mind, my primary goal was to come up with an essence of this controlled complexity in a format that allowed these books to communicate what a major writer and powerful influence Borges was and still is. I also did not want to try and be overly clever with any of it, as I knew that would be a foolish undertaking, so I opted for a refined grid that hinted at some of this theme, but in a very restrained form paired with blind embossed shapes that signify his well-controlled abstract thinking. Borges became the director of the National Library of Argentina and went permanently blind soon after. He never learned to read braille.

In "Poem of the Gifts," he writes:

No one should read self-pity or reproach
into this statement of the majesty
of God; who with such splendid irony
granted me books and blindness at one touch.

Jorge Luis
BORGES
SELECTED
POEMS
PENGUIN CLASSICS
DELUXE EDITION
Jorge Luis
BORGES
SELECTED
NON-FICTIONS
PENGUIN CLASSICS
DELUXE EDITION
Jorge Luis
BORGES
COLLECTED
FICTIONS
PENGUIN CLASSICS
DELUXE EDITION

ED NON-FIC

TED POE

CTED FICT

EXANDER C

EW HUR

Paul Buckley, DESIGNER

Here is a blind self-portrait of Borges in New York City's famous Strand Bookstore that I just love. According to *The New York Times*, after drawing the portrait, Borges entered the main floor, where he paused to listen to the room and stated, "You have as many books as we have in our national library."

THE DEATH OF KIN
ARTHUR
THE IMMORTAL
LEGEND
SIR

The Death of King Arthur RETOLD BY PETER ACKROYD

ILLUSTRATOR: STUART KOLAKOVIC **CREATIVE DIRECTOR:** PAUL BUCKLEY **EDITOR:** ELDA ROTOR

Paul Buckley, CREATIVE DIRECTOR

Stuart specializes in ye-olde-hide-the-beautiful-wives-the-king-is-coming-to-town-type of imagery. Lots of skulls and monks and castles and horses, and all done with a mix of Bavaria meets English priory, yet rendered with a thoroughly modern edge and line quality. The results are startlingly singular. Each panel is exquisite and could stand on its own as a cover.

This is a retelling of these ancient stories, which fits the spirit and history of these tales so well, as even the original author—and like Shakespeare, not everyone agrees on exactly who the original author was—was writing down tales already centuries old, passed down by word of mouth, person to person, village to village; and more from France than England, making this original text a bit of a translation as well. Its authorship is debated because there were a number of men named Sir Thomas Malory during the timespan when the book is believed to have come into being. The particular Sir Thomas Malory who most scholars accept as the most likely author was quite the lifelong criminal—rape, murder, and plenty of thievery were on his résumé. So maybe you truly can't judge a book by its cover, because clearly the honor and virtue Malory was writing about were not part of the life he was living. He eventually died in prison, where it is believed he penned his book.

Every night as I gazed up at the window
I said softly to myself the word paralysis.
It had always sounded strangely in my ears,
like the word gnomon in the Euclid and the word simony in the Catechism.
But now it sounded to me like the name of some maleficent and sinful being.
It filled me with fear,
and yet I longed to be nearer to it
and to look upon its deadly work.
One by one they were all becoming shades.
Better pass boldly into that other world, in the full glory of some passion,
than fade and wither dismally with age.
The time had come for him to set out on his journey westward.
His soul swooned slowly
as he heard the snow falling faintly through the universe
and faintly falling, like the descent of their last end,
upon all the living and the dead.

JAMES JOYCE

PENGUIN CLASSICS

DELUXE EDITION

167

A Penguin Book / Literature

www.penguinclassics.com

Cover by Roman Muradov

U.S. $17.00
CAN. $19.00
U.K. £9.99

ISBN 978-0-14-310745-3

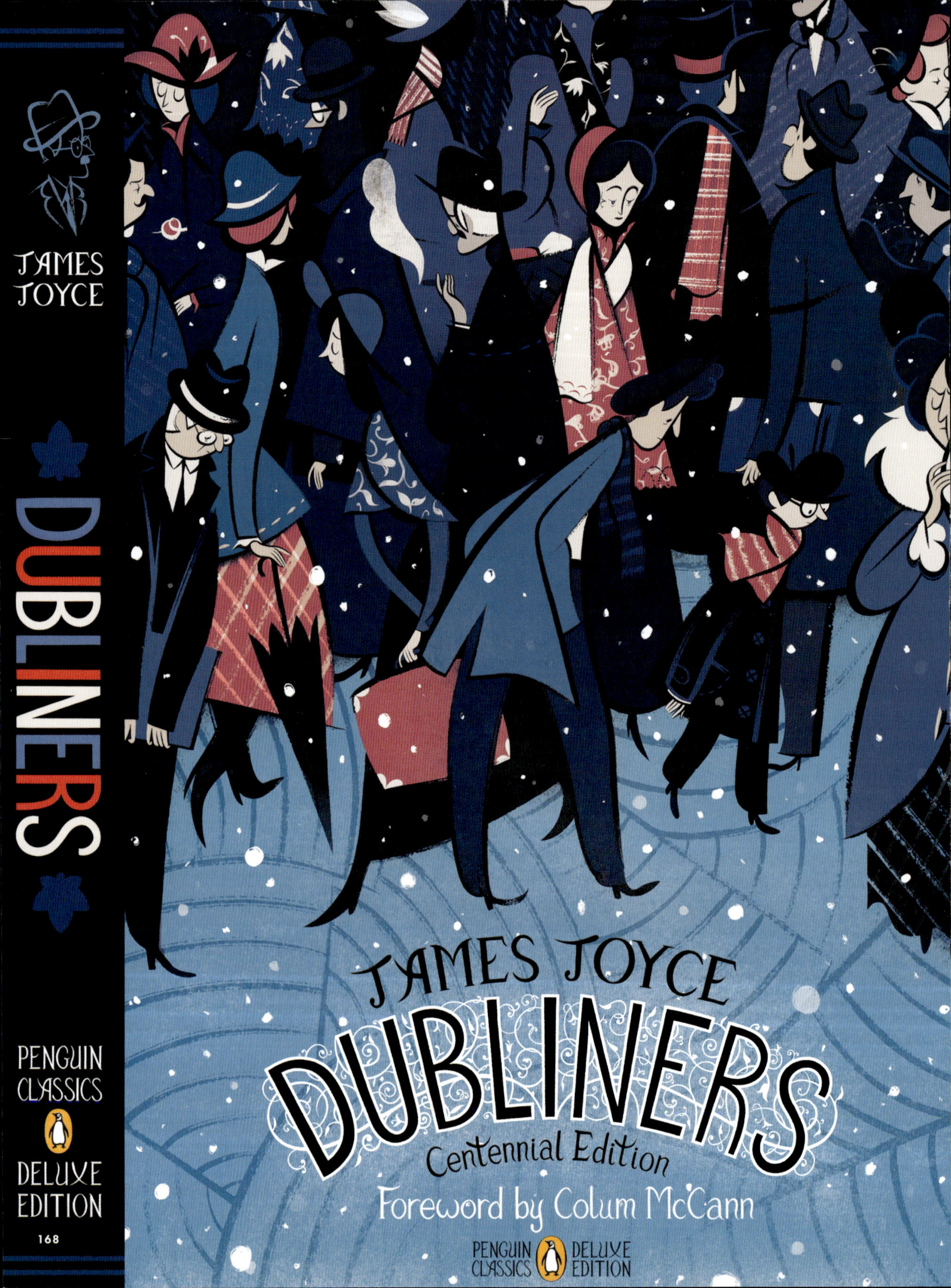

JAMES JOYCE

PENGUIN CLASSICS

DELUXE EDITION

168

JAMES JOYCE

DUBLINERS

Centennial Edition

Foreword by Colum McCann

PENGUIN CLASSICS DELUXE EDITION

Dubliners

JAMES JOYCE

ILLUSTRATOR: ROMAN MURADOV **CREATIVE DIRECTOR:** PAUL BUCKLEY **EDITOR:** JOHN SICILIANO

One by one they were all becoming shades.
Better pass boldly into that other world, in the full glory of some passion,
than fade and wither dismally with age.
The time had come for him to set out on his journey westward.
His soul swooned slowly
as he heard the snow falling faintly through the universe
and faintly falling, like the descent of their last end,
upon all the living and the dead.

A Penguin Book/Literature
www.penguinclassics.com
Cover by Roman Muradov
PENGUIN CLASSICS DELUXE EDITION
US $17.00
CAN $19.00
UK £9.99

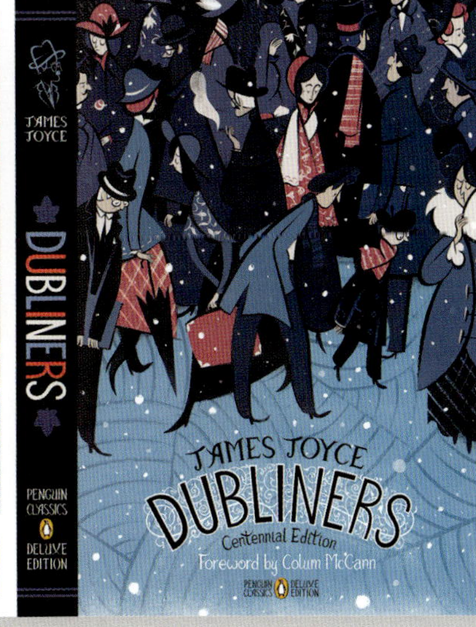

Every night as I gazed up at the window
I said softly to myself the word paralysis.
It had always sounded strangely in my ears,
like the word gnomon in the Euclid and the word simony in the Catechism.
But now it sounded to me like the name of some maleficent and sinful being.
It filled me with fear,
and yet I longed to be nearer to it
and to look upon its deadly work.

Paul Buckley, CREATIVE DIRECTOR

Roman has such a unique approach to his art and a skill level that is so flawless that all an art director need do is point his brilliance in a direction and sit back and wait for the home run to happen. This please-just-go-for-it-and-try-to-have-fun attitude is behind many a success in our classics line. I hate to sell any art director short, especially myself, as certainly there is skill in pairing the right artist to the right book or series, but if you do the matchup correctly from the beginning, not overdirecting someone is exactly how to get the best results. To illustrate that point, following is a snippet of our conversation showing how smooth it can be if you are lucky enough to work with the Roman Muradovs of the world.

PB: "**DUBLINERS** is a tale of turn-of-the-century middle-class Dublin folk. Many covers have focused on the architecture, the vista, the town of Dublin. We do not want that. We want this cover to be about the people. That's my art direction—have fun pls."

RM: "Thank you, Paul! I'd be honored to. James Joyce is one of my most beloved authors (*Ulysses* never leaves my desk), and I'm a huge fan of the Penguin Classics series. In fact, I'm a bit shocked to be honest, but I'll try to get over it! I love how each artist used the flaps and other parts of the design differently, and I think **DUBLINERS** really lends itself to this treatment thematically and structurally. Please let me know the details. Meanwhile, I'll start rereading the collection."

• DETAIL, ROMAN MURADOV

"To live,
to err,
to fall,
to triumph...
...to recreate
life
out of
life!"
PENGUIN CLASSICS
DELUXE EDITION

"I will try to express myself in some mode of life or art as freely as I can and as wholly as I can, using for my defence the only arms I allow myself to use— silence, exile, and cunning."

JAMES JOYCE

DELUXE CLASSICS

A PORTRAIT OF THE ARTIST AS A YOUNG MAN

A Penguin Book/Literature
www.penguinclassics.com

Cover by Roman Muradov

PENGUIN CLASSICS DELUXE EDITION

U.S. $17.00
CAN. $23.00
U.K. £11.99

ISBN 978-0-14-310824-5

PENGUIN CLASSICS DELUXE EDITION

PENGUIN CLASSICS DELUXE EDITION

A Portrait of the Artist as a Young Man

JAMES JOYCE

ILLUSTRATOR: ROMAN MURADOV **CREATIVE DIRECTOR:** PAUL BUCKLEY **EDITOR:** JOHN SICILIANO

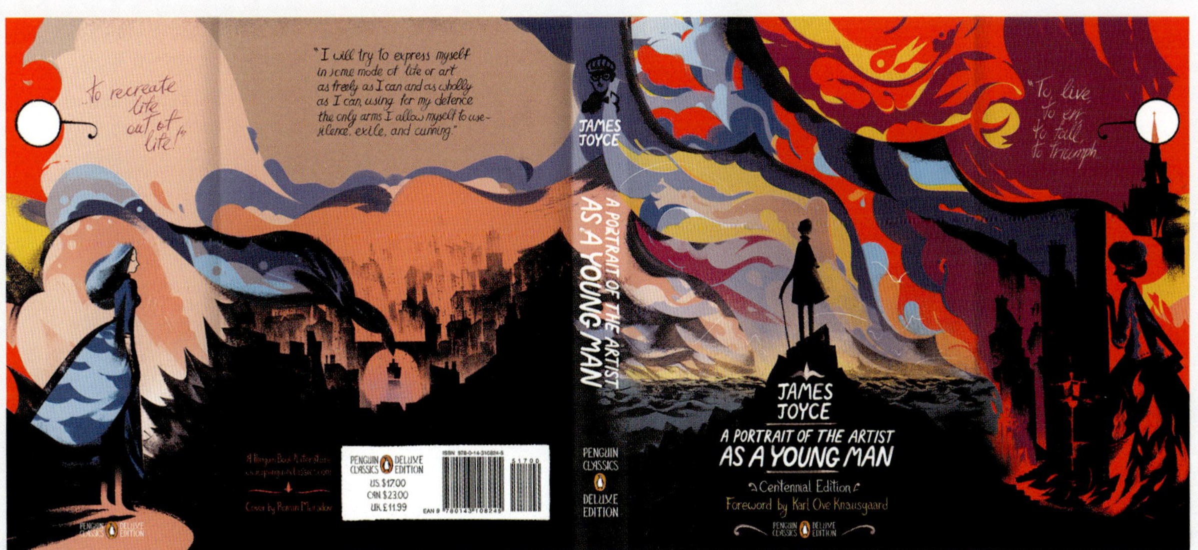

● **Roman Muradov,** ILLUSTRATOR

I first read the hellfire-sermon section of **PORTRAIT** during my torturously tedious graduation ceremony, so yes, James Joyce means a lot to me.

For both these covers I knew immediately what to draw. **DUBLINERS**: gaze firmly downward, a crowd frozen between movement and paralysis, "The Sisters" and "The Dead" joined flapward. **PORTRAIT**: color-coded in approximation of Joyce's techniques, infinitely flowing, the protagonist's poetic contractions dead center, black.

Between the two projects I met Paul at a dingy karaoke bar and markedly refused to sing a duet with him. I may or may not've mentioned my theory that "Ice Ice Baby" is superior to "Under Pressure." This opinion has severed many a tie, so I was surprised to receive another laconic prompt from Paul two years later: "PORTRAIT OF THE ARTIST OUI OUI?"

I sent a sketch, and he said it looks exactly like *Wanderer above the Sea of Fog*, a famous nineteenth-century painting that I'd somehow never seen. This delighted me to no end—my accidental plagiarism, Stephen's misquoted clouds, the opportunity to drown the romantic image in snot-green seas. I wrote all this and more, editing out excessive (four) references to "Ice Ice Baby," and got an approval.

Now let's hope we all survive till the centenary of *Ulysses* in 2022: myself, Paul Buckley, Penguin, the universe, and Joyce.

• *WANDERER ABOVE THE SEA OF FOG*, C. 1818. CASPAR DAVID FRIEDRICH.

Drop

CAPS

Drop CAPS

SERIES ILLUSTRATED BY JESSICA HISCHE

PRIDE AND PREJUDICE, JANE EYRE, MY ÁNTONIA, GREAT EXPECTATIONS, MIDDLEMARCH, MADAME BOVARY, LORD OF THE FLIES, SIDDHARTHA, AN ARTIST OF THE FLOATING WORLD, A PORTRAIT OF THE ARTIST AS A YOUNG MAN, THE SECRET LIFE OF BEES, NATIVE SPEAKER, MOBY-DICK, FIVE CHILDREN AND IT, BUTTERFIELD 8, SWANN'S WAY, THE GREEK COFFIN MYSTERY, HAROUN AND THE SEA OF STORIES, CANNERY ROW, THE JOY LUCK CLUB, KRISTIN LAVRANSDATTER, I: THE WREATH, CANDIDE, LEAVES OF GRASS AND SELECTED POEMS AND PROSE, SKY BURIAL, WHEN YOU ARE OLD, THE SHADOW OF THE WIND

DESIGNER / CREATIVE DIRECTOR: PAUL BUCKLEY **SERIES EDITOR:** ELDA ROTOR

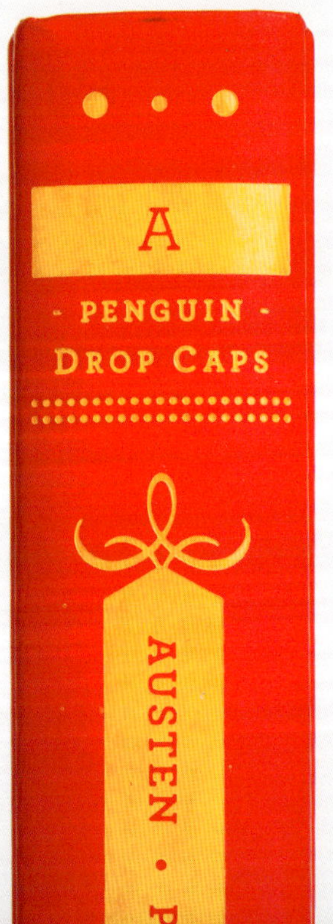

● **Jessica Hische,** ILLUSTRATOR

I think the biggest challenge with the Penguin **DROP CAPS** series was trying to not be so literal with the illustration and ornaments. Sure, there were times when it made sense to pluck a more obvious narrative element for the cover (like with Proust—how could we *not* include the infamous madeleine?), but with other covers, I wanted to allude to mood, tone, setting, etc., in a less obvious way. I'm sure so many people saw these and just assumed we'd appropriated some random Victorian ornamental letter for the cover, but every one was really agonized over and explored. Also, one of the most intimidating things about designing covers for classic books is that you know that many of the readers are already familiar (or really, really obsessed) with the book, so you have to appeal to them as well as all of the new readers coming to the content for the first time.

HERMAN MELVI
JANE AUSTEN
PRIDE AND PREJUDICE
ELLERY QU
ITMAN

PRIDE AND PREJUDICE

CHARLOTTE BRONTË
B
JANE EYRE

WILLA CATHER
C
MY ÁNTONIA

CHARLES DICKENS
D
GREAT EXPECTATIONS

GEORGE ELIOT
E
MIDDLEMARCH

WILLIAM GOLDING
LORD OF THE FLIES

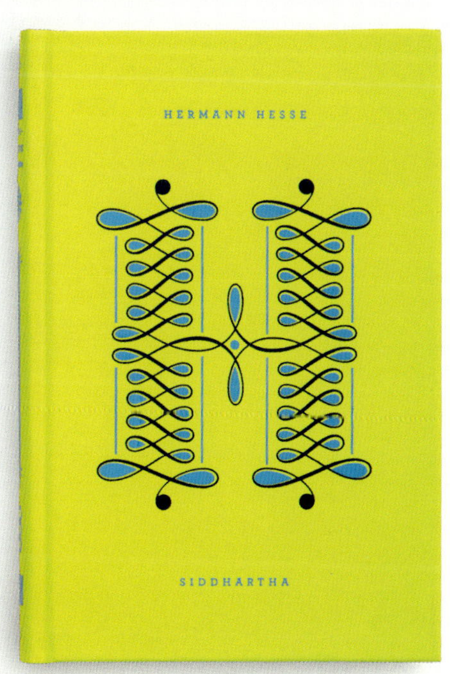
HERMANN HESSE
SIDDHARTHA

KAZUO ISHIGURO
AN ARTIST OF THE FLOATING WORLD

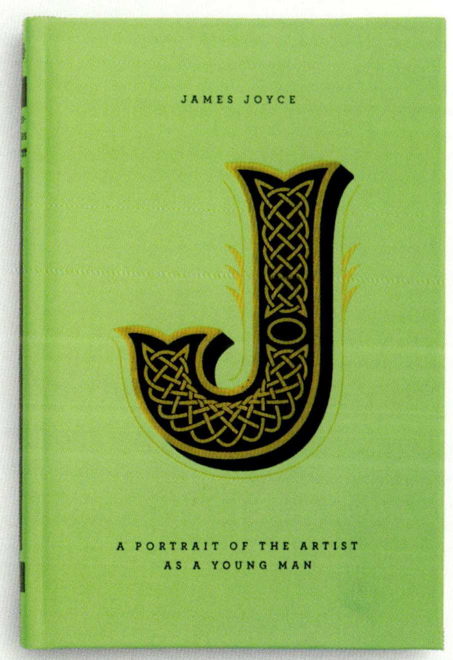
JAMES JOYCE
A PORTRAIT OF THE ARTIST
AS A YOUNG MAN

JOYCE
A PORTRAIT OF T
AS A YOU
RTIST AS A YOUNG MAN

SUE MONK KIDD

THE SECRET LIFE OF BEES

CHANG-RAE
SPEAKER

HERMAN MELVILLE
MOBY-DICK
OR, THE WHALE

E. NESBIT
FIVE CHILDREN AND I

N O'HARA
BUTTERF
TTERFIELD 8

MARCEL PROUST
SWANN'S WAY

ELLERY QUEEN
THE GREEK COFFIN MYSTERY

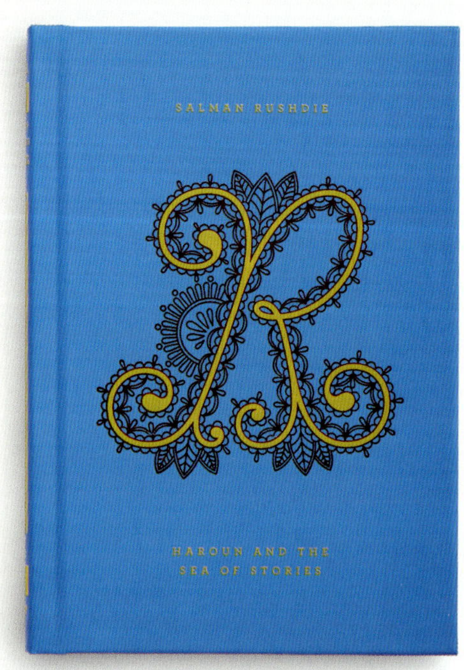
SALMAN RUSHDIE
HAROUN AND THE
SEA OF STORIES

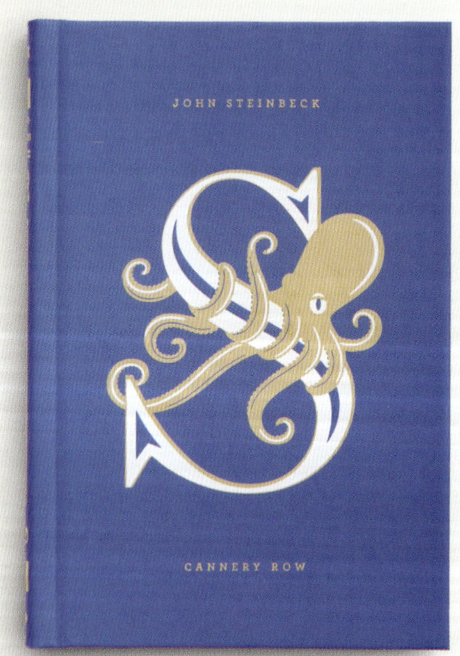
JOHN STEINBECK
CANNERY ROW

AMY TAN
THE JOY LUCK CLUB

SIGRID UNDSET
KRISTIN LAVRANSDATTER
THE WREATH

VOLTAIRE
CANDIDE
OR OPTIMISM

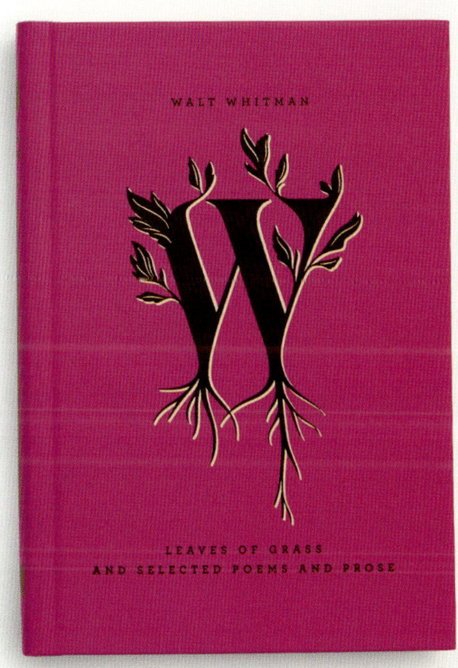
WALT WHITMAN
LEAVES OF GRASS
AND SELECTED POEMS AND PROSE

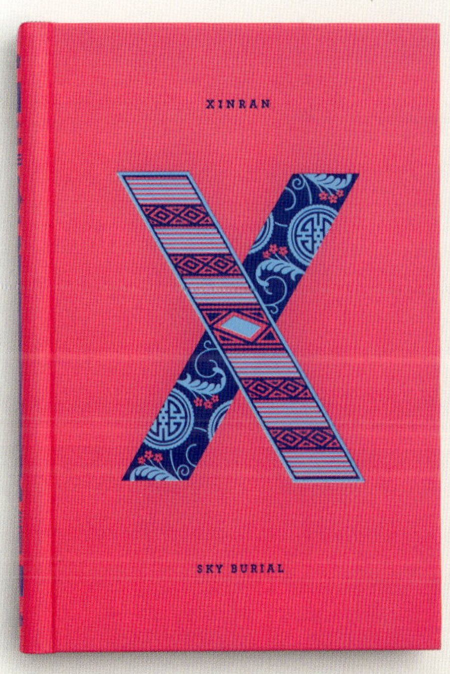
XINRAN
SKY BURIAL

XIN
SKY BURIAL

W. B.

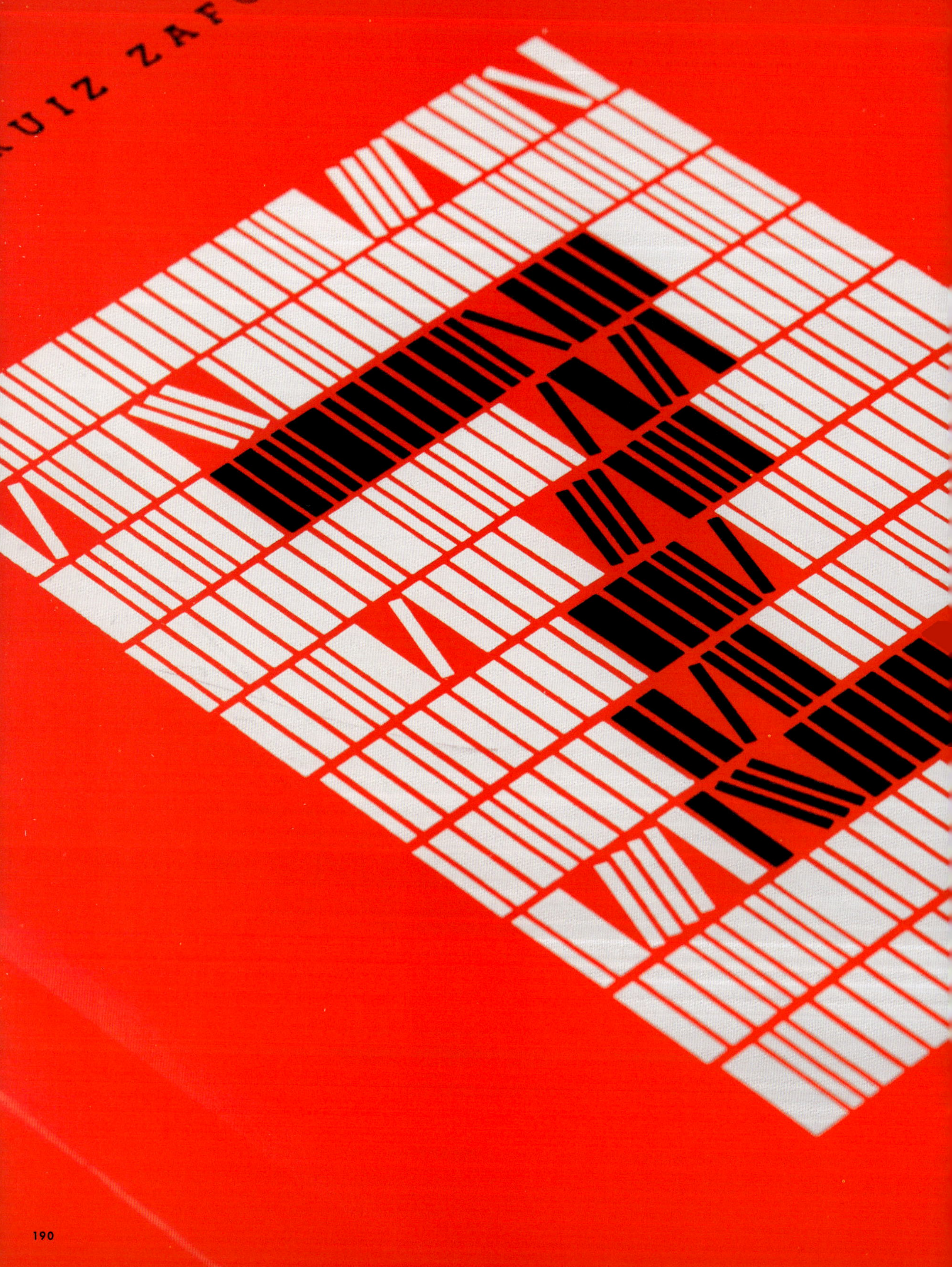

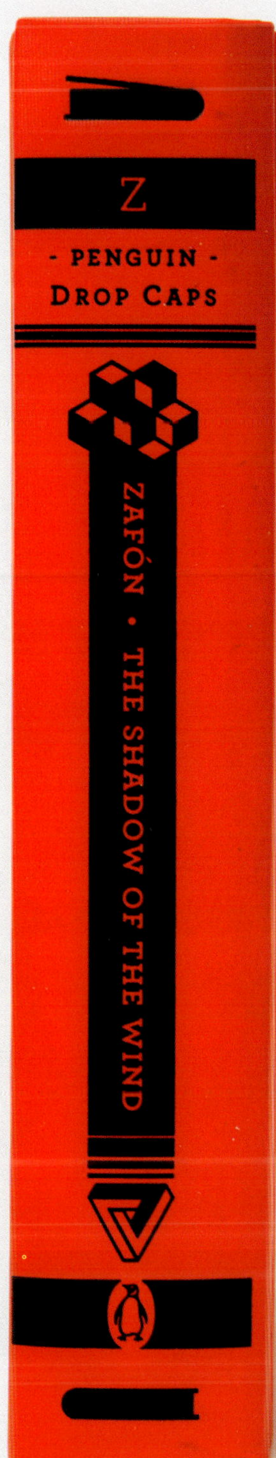

Paul Buckley, DESIGNER / CREATIVE DIRECTOR

I really enjoy working on series design, and series within the Penguin Classics imprint can be especially rewarding, creatively speaking. This series began with me going up to Elda Rotor's office to show her three ideas I had been ruminating on—two were idea driven and not driven by any specific artist, and the third was samples of Jessica Hische's drop caps that she had done for her site, dailydropcap.com, because I was convinced we could do a fabulous series with drop caps as the lead image. Of my three loose thoughts, Elda liked this concept the best. She immediately began thinking about twenty-six books, A through Z, which further got me excited. I came up with a spectrum idea, as with that many titles we could create a gorgeous, vibrant rainbow that would be a gem displayed on the shelves.

I get asked a lot, "Why give all these books to one person? Why not work with many different artists as we've done on most of our other series?" I did kick around that notion for all of five seconds—whether I wanted to work with twenty-six different hand letterers or to work solely with Jessica on the project. But it was her drop caps that excited us, so it simply had to all go to her; we just hoped she'd have the time and desire to take twenty-six titles, which fortunately she did.

Clearly these books fall into the collectible category—I am a physical book designer, so I do not compartmentalize "This book will be an object; this one will not." Some have a better opportunity and budget to be an object that looks more stunning on your tabletop than another—but the goal must always be to craft the most beautiful object you can, within the parameters you are given, whether you are building a loaf of bread or an art museum. That said, buyers have countless options for how they obtain classic reading material. If you are a student and just need a down-and-dirty copy of *The Iliad* for a class, there is a good chance you will buy the cheapest one you can get your hands on. For someone who is older and wants to own nice versions of things ...well, we have many gorgeous items that just happen to be amazing pieces of literature for the book buyer to consider.

(CONTINUED ON NEXT PAGE)

(CONTINUED FROM PREVIOUS PAGE)

Jessica is really thorough and easy to work with. She would send in four to six sketches for each letter, which I reviewed with the Penguin team. Once we decided on a direction, I would ask her to go to a finish; she'd then send me a black-and-white Illustrator file separated on two layers. We would then experiment with a series of printer drawdowns to find the two foil colors I'd want to work with on the particular color background we were at on the spectrum. Then I'd design the spine, the back, and the secondary type on the front. But pigmented foils are so damn tricky, they'd look opaque and then the drawdowns would come in and they'd be like a thin transparent film. It was easily the most challenging production job we've ever faced, and many of the colors I really wanted had to go into the scrap heap, as what would work on one paper color would do something completely different on another. It really was a bit of a nightmare, with many needed compromises to get through to the other side.

—PB

• PROCESS SCREENSHOT, PAUL BUCKLEY

• SCATTERED DROP CAPS COVERS, PAUL BUCKLEY

PB: This photo shows Brianna Harden (on the left) and Kristen Haff (Vanna White), both of whom helped me through this series.

A
- PENGUIN -
DROP CAPS
AUSTEN · PRIDE AND PREJUDICE
B
- PENGUIN -
DROP CAPS
BRONTË · JANE EYRE
C
- PENGUIN -
DROP CAPS
CATHER · MY ÁNTONIA
D
- PENGUIN -
DROP CAPS
DICKENS · GREAT EXPECTATIONS

F
- PENGUIN -
DROP CAPS
FLAUBERT · MADAME BOVARY
G
- PENGUIN -
DROP CAPS
GOLDING · LORD OF THE FLIES
H
- PENGUIN -
DROP CAPS
HESSE · SIDDHARTHA
I
- PENGUIN -
DROP CAPS
ISHIGURO · AN ARTIST OF THE FLOATING WORLD
J
- PENGUIN -
DROP CAPS
JOYCE · A PORTRAIT OF THE ARTIST AS A YOUNG MAN
K
- PENGUIN -
DROP CAPS
KIDD · THE SECRET LIFE OF BEES
L
- PENGUIN -
DROP CAPS
DROP CAPS
LEE · NATIVE SPEAKER

N
- PENGUIN -
DROP CAPS
NESBIT · FIVE CHILDREN AND IT
O
- PENGUIN -
DROP CAPS
O'HARA · BUTTERFIELD 8
P
- PENGUIN -
DROP CAPS
PROUST · SWANN'S WAY
Q
- PENGUIN -
DROP CAPS
QUEEN · THE GREEK COFFIN MYSTERY
R
- PENGUIN -
DROP CAPS
RUSHDIE · HAROUN AND THE SEA OF STORIES
S
- PENGUIN -
DROP CAPS
STEINBECK · CANNERY ROW

U
- PENGUIN -
DROP CAPS
UNDSET • KRISTIN LAVRANSDATTER
V
- PENGUIN -
DROP CAPS
VOLTAIRE • CANDIDE
W
- PENGUIN -
DROP CAPS
WHITMAN • LEAVES OF GRASS
X
- PENGUIN -
DROP CAPS
XINRAN • SKY BURIAL
Y
- PENGUIN -
DROP CAPS
YEATS • WHEN YOU ARE OLD
Z
- PENGUIN -
DROP CAPS
ZAFÓN • THE SHADOW OF THE WIND

"How much
sooner one tires
L
PENGUIN
DROP CAPS
LEE · NATIVE SPEAKER
M
PENGUIN
DROP CAPS
N
NESBIT · FIVE CHILDREN AND IT
O
PENGUIN
DROP CAPS
O'HARA · BUTTERFIELD 8
P
PENGUIN
DROP CAPS
PROUST · SWANN'S WAY
Q
PENGUIN
DROP CAPS
QUEEN · THE GREEK COFFIN MYSTERY

PRIDE AND PREJUDICE
JANE EYRE
MY ANTONIA
GREAT EXPECTATIONS
MIDDLEMARCH
WILLIAM GOLDING
LORD OF THE FLIES
HERMANN HESSE
SIDDHARTHA
KAZUO ISHIGURO
AN ARTIST OF THE FLOATING WORLD
JAMES JOYCE
A PORTRAIT OF THE ARTIST AS A YOUNG MAN
SUE MONK KIDD
THE SECRET LIFE OF BEES
CHANG-RAE LEE
NATIVE SPEAKER
HERMAN MELVILLE
MOBY-DICK OR, THE WHALE
E. NESBIT
FIVE CHILDREN AND IT
JOHN O'HARA
BUTTERFIELD 8
DROP CAPS
MARCEL PROUST
SWANN'S WAY
THE GREEN COFFIN MYSTERY
JOHN STEINBECK
CANNERY ROW
THE JOY LUCK CLUB
SIGRID UNDSET
WALT WHITMAN
XINRAN
W. B. YEATS

Civic

CLASSICS

INTRODUCTION BY RICHARD BEEMAN

Civic CLASSICS

SERIES DESIGNED BY GREGG KULICK

THE DECLARATION OF INDEPENDENCE AND THE UNITED STATES CONSTITUTION, COMMON SENSE, THE FEDERALIST PAPERS, LINCOLN SPEECHES, AMERICAN POLITICAL SPEECHES, SUPREME COURT DECISIONS

CREATIVE DIRECTOR: PAUL BUCKLEY **SERIES EDITOR:** RICHARD BEEMAN **EDITOR:** ELDA ROTOR

● **Gregg Kulick,** ILLUSTRATOR

I started working at Penguin Books in the winter of 2007 in Paul Buckley's art department. Each new season I would eagerly wait to see if Paul would finally let me work on a series cover, just one damn series! Winter would turn into spring, and the warmth of summer would fade into autumn. And my hopes, too, would fade with the onset of each cold and bleak new winter.

When the plan to publish a series of CIVIC CLASSICS was proposed, the original idea was to have Shepard Fairey design all the covers, and given his considerable fame after he created the *Hope* poster of Barack Obama, he seemed like the logical choice. But his legal problems with that poster made it difficult to reach an agreement for the series work, so he decided not to take on the commission. All the while, I had been pitching ideas to Paul every other week for different Classics series, so when Shepard dropped out of the CIVIC CLASSICS project, Paul rewarded my persistence (or perhaps decided to shut me up) by assigning the titles to me. Not only that, he insisted that I work on them myself. After five years of hard time in Warden Buckley's Penguin prison, I had finally been paroled. Score!

The CIVIC CLASSICS series was to include six books, each one important to our nation's history. I wanted each cover to be a mix of old and new in a way that would recall the historic nature of the writing but also look toward the future. The juxtaposition of old ephemeral images with new type, or vice versa, was working very well for me visually. The problem, of course, was that I decided to make them all red, white, and blue, which made them feel a bit too much—almost to the point of being cheesy. I accidentally made one cover black and white and suddenly what was maybe a little garish became sophisticated and clean. This is easily one of the projects that I am proudest of in my career.

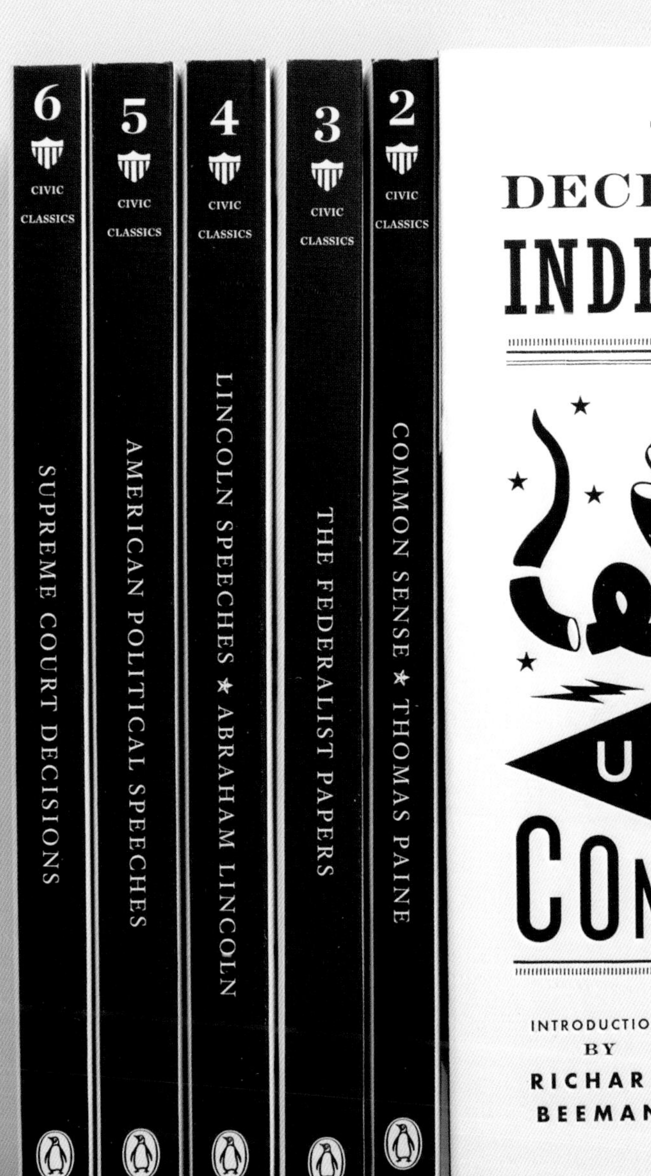
6
CIVIC
CLASSICS
SUPREME COURT DECISIONS
5
CIVIC
CLASSICS
AMERICAN POLITICAL SPEECHES
4
CIVIC
CLASSICS
LINCOLN SPEECHES ★ ABRAHAM LINCOLN
3
CIVIC
CLASSICS
THE FEDERALIST PAPERS
2
CIVIC
CLASSICS
COMMON SENSE ★ THOMAS PAINE

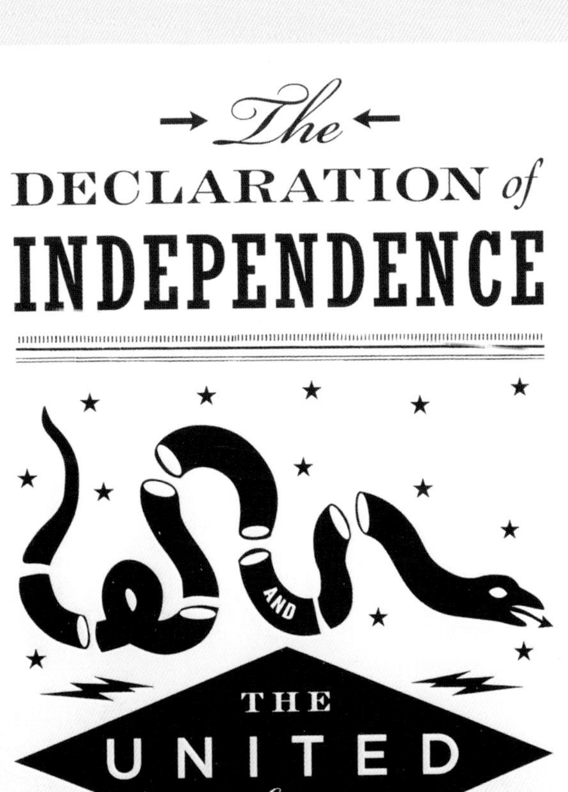
The
DECLARATION of
INDEPENDENCE
AND
THE
UNITED
States
CONSTITUTION

CIVIC
CLASSICS
INTRODUCTION
BY
RICHARD
BEEMAN
SERIES EDITOR
★
RICHARD
BEEMAN

COMMON

SENSE

THOMAS PAINE

CIVIC CLASSICS

INTRODUCTION BY RICHARD BEEMAN

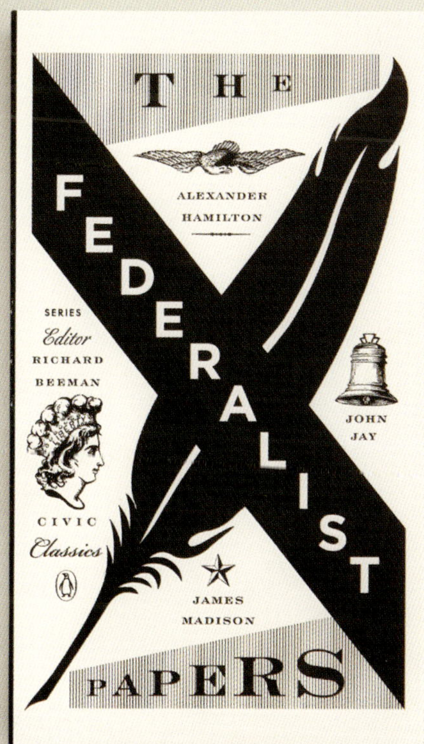
THE
FEDERALIST
PAPERS
ALEXANDER HAMILTON
JOHN JAY
JAMES MADISON
SERIES Editor RICHARD BEEMAN
CIVIC Classics

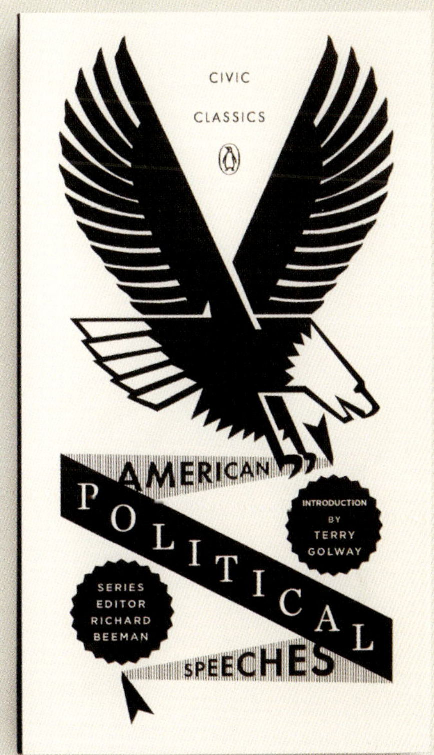
CIVIC
CLASSICS
AMERICAN
POLITICAL
SPEECHES
INTRODUCTION BY TERRY GOLWAY
SERIES EDITOR RICHARD BEEMAN

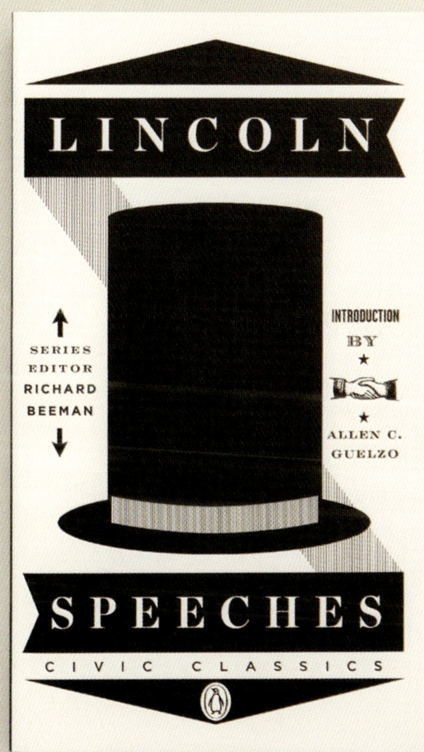
LINCOLN
SERIES EDITOR RICHARD BEEMAN
INTRODUCTION BY
ALLEN C. GUELZO
SPEECHES
CIVIC CLASSICS

SUPREME COURT
SERIES EDITOR
RICHARD BEEMAN
DECISIONS
INTRODUCTION BY
JAY M. FEINMAN
CIVIC CLASSICS

COMMON
SENSE
COMMON SENSE

INTRO
AMERICAN
POLIT
SERIES EDITOR RICHARD BEEMAN
CHES

AND
THE
UN
INTRODUC
JAY M. FEINMAN
DECISIONS
SERIES EDITOR
RICHARD BEEMAN
CIVIC CLASSICS

Penguin

HORROR
Title × Author
Introduction by Series Editor GUILLERMO DEL TORO
Penguin Horror

Penguin HORROR SERIES ILLUSTRATED BY PAUL BUCKLEY

HAUNTED CASTLES, THE THING ON THE DOORSTEP, THE HAUNTING OF HILL HOUSE, THE RAVEN, AMERICAN SUPERNATURAL TALES, FRANKENSTEIN

DESIGNER / ILLUSTRATOR: PAUL BUCKLEY **SERIES EDITOR:** GUILLERMO DEL TORO **EDITOR:** ELDA ROTOR

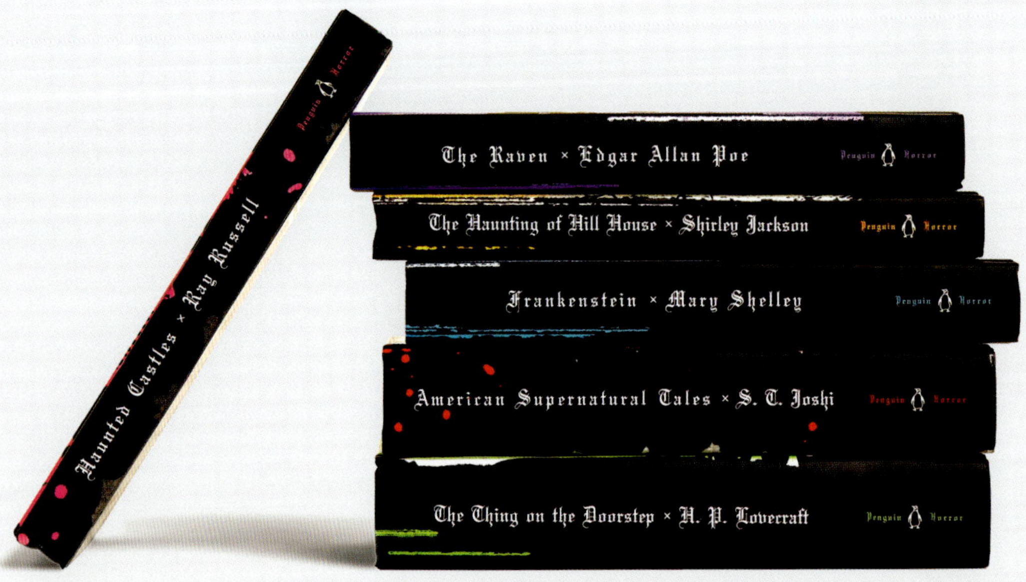

Haunted Castles × Ray Russell
The Raven × Edgar Allan Poe
The Haunting of Hill House × Shirley Jackson
Frankenstein × Mary Shelley
American Supernatural Tales × S. T. Joshi
The Thing on the Doorstep × H. P. Lovecraft

Paul Buckley, DESIGNER / ILLUSTRATOR

I designed and illustrated this series, and I worked insanely hard on every one of these covers—two I like; the others, not at all.

I went off the good path in a number of different ways. Most important, I should not have illustrated them myself—google Aaron Horkey or Aron Wiesenfeld and you will quickly see why. Matching the best artist to the material at hand should always be an art director's first priority.

Some history here will be needed: I attended School of Visual Arts NYC on an illustration scholarship. For my age and day, I was quite talented and I was insanely driven—when other children were being given Cat in the Hat books, my art director father was giving me that year's illustration annuals and books on every artist under the sun, and from a very young age, an illustrator was all I ever wanted to be. Obviously my love of the craft of illustration shows in the people I hire and in how our books look. A week after graduating high school in Pennsylvania, I was commuting five hours a day, five days a week, back and forth from Pennsylvania to New York City to work in a design and advertising studio. Once September hit, I went part time; a few days a week I'd go to college and the other days I'd work in that studio. I wanted to pass my young peers very, very badly, and for a while I did just that. They'd come into school with their charcoal drawings or whatever and I'd have these slick presentations that I'd worked thirty hours on in the studio utilizing its equipment and resources when I should have been doing the work they needed of me. Instead the professionals would propel me along rather than resort to "Paul, where is it?, I need that thing we pay you to be here to do." So, I had school teaching me, I had my father teaching me, and I had this entire NYC studio that took me under their wing, this seventeen-year-old mullet-headed kid from PA.

(CONTINUED ON PAGE 214)

THE COMPLETE GOTHIC STORIES
Haunted Castles × Ray Russell
Introduction by Series Editor GUILLERMO DEL TORO
Penguin Horror

(CONTINUED FROM PAGE 212)

Two years in, I moved to New York, graduated from SVA, and had a very good freelance illustration career going. Pieces were just starting to be commissioned by major magazines of the time, but I grew to dislike my own work, and as I grew older, the freelance lifestyle simply was not working out anymore. As well, at the studio I had begun to fall in love with the craft of design, and after graduation, my freelance design career started to take off as well. When I turned twenty-four I took a break from working and went on a three-month road trip to Belize and Guatemala. Once back, I had to pay my Brooklyn rent, and a friend alerted me to a job as a junior designer in a publishing art department. I thought, "I'll do this for a few months to bounce back." Twenty-six years later, I'm still here.

Long story short, book design fits me like a glove and I consider myself extremely lucky to have been found by publishing. Books matter. Print matters. This is the real discourse of our world—and on another path, I could have missed this opportunity entirely. And when I finally decided to throw myself entirely into the field of design, it was like a weight was taken off my shoulders. I became a far happier person.

But that illustration seed in me is so much a part of who I am and how I grew up—and every once in a while I feel the

(CONTINUED ON PAGE 216)

AND OTHER WEIRD STORIES
The Thing on the Doorstep × H. P. Love
Introduction by Series Editor GUILLERMO DEL TORO
Penguin Horror

The Haunting of Hill House × Shirley Jackson
Introduction by Series Editor GUILLERMO DEL TORO
Penguin Horror

TALES AND POEMS
The Raven × Edgar Allan Poe
Introduction by Series Editor GUILLERMO DEL TORO
Penguin Horror

American Supernatural Tales
Introduction by Series Editor GUILLERMO DEL TORO
Edited by S. T. Joshi
Penguin Horror

Frankenstein × Mary Shelley
Introduction by Series Editor GUILLERMO DEL TORO
Penguin Horror

(CONTINUED FROM PAGE 214)

need to illustrate something. It's not that often—I mean, I have been here twenty-six years and literally thousands of projects have passed through my hands without my saying, "I must illustrate this." I've been a fan of horror stories since childhood and I had a clear idea of the style of art I wanted, so these books sort of just grabbed me… and then I proceeded to create a series of decent yet not incredible covers. My whole you-gotta-come-at-the-classics-a-bit-out-of-left-field was nowhere to be seen and clearly most of these are pretty straightforward images for the titles. I'm told the series did well, so it's not like I went and sank the ship, but I should have remained the art director and brought these home in a way the material truly deserved.

The technique I felt compelled to do these with my father had taught me and is something you never see these days. I love the lost art of tempera resist, which utilizes water-soluble white paint, permanent ink, and a strong faucet. These are not woodcuts—far from it.

—PB

PB: My father, Gerald Buckley, did many pieces in this lost tempera-resist style and was a true master of it.

THE RAVEN
Tales and Poems
EDGAR ALLAN POE
Series Editor : GUILLERMO DEL TORO

HAUNTED CASTLES
The Complete Gothic Stories
RAY RUSSELL
Series Editor : GUILLERMO DEL TORO

FRANKENSTEIN
MARY SHELLEY
Series Editor : GUILLERMO DEL TORO

• TEMPERA-RESIST PROCESS: THE THING ON THE DOORSTEP, PAUL BUCKLEY

PB: There was a version of these covers that I liked much better but for reasons of my own did not fight for, thinking the bold neons would be a very cool departure for the material. They were a departure, but with these somewhat traditional drawings, maybe not a perfect match.

Christmas

CLASSICS
CHRISTMAS CLASSICS

Christmas CLASSICS

SERIES DESIGNED BY ROSEANNE SERRA

THE NUTCRACKER, THE LIFE AND ADVENTURES OF SANTA CLAUS, A CHRISTMAS CAROL, A MERRY CHRISTMAS, CHRISTMAS AT THOMPSON HALL, THE NIGHT BEFORE CHRISTMAS

ILLUSTRATOR: HAYA_P **DESIGNER / ART DIRECTOR:** ROSEANNE SERRA **SERIES EDITOR:** JOHN SICILIANO

• ROSEANNE'S FATHER'S HOME THE DAY AFTER THANKSGIVING FOR THE LAST 34 YEARS

● **Roseanne Serra, DESIGNER / ART DIRECTOR**

So I am the daughter of Christmas, and what better collection to get to design than the **CHRISTMAS CLASSICS**? I go up with all these books that have Christmas visuals to get the team inspired and talk direction, lots of vintage stuff. Paul Buckley surprises me with some of his own visuals too—kind of annoying, as this is my project; why is he getting involved? He does so many Classic Deluxe packages—can't he let go? I'm thinking of doing paper over board or linen with stamping on hardcovers. The group likes my idea, so I hire Jim Tierney to make my visions come to life.

I show two or three rounds of sketches and my editor comes back, not excited but gushing about some gift wrap packaging his sister bought in Target. This is what I am up against! Why didn't he say this at the outset? Kill fee, Jim.

OK, snow day, bad winter. I am home, no GoToMyPC set up yet, don't have my fonts. I hear Paul's working on creating wrapping paper! Pisses me off! Why is he getting involved? Give me a chance! He obviously has a secret love for Christmas. I feel like the Grinch right now. I come back and I see his work. Yes, it's nice, but I refuse to be competitive about wrapping paper!

So I lock myself in my office for three days. I scour the websites. I find vector art and I begin. At this point I want something different and fresh, something to last after Christmas and be something you could be proud to have on a table, sell on Etsy—something pretty and gifty. When I hit the cardinals, it hits home—they are personal to me; my dad has a cardinal on a bench with snow in his Christmas village. I find the artist but he's somewhere overseas, only responding at four a.m. with weird answers when I ask him to create new art. So instead I take all the art I've found at the stock site, rip it apart, and re-create some of it to fit my designs. I have other designs too, with different themes. We present all the comps: the wrapping paper, which is lovely, and my five other versions. Need I say more? Merry Christmas!

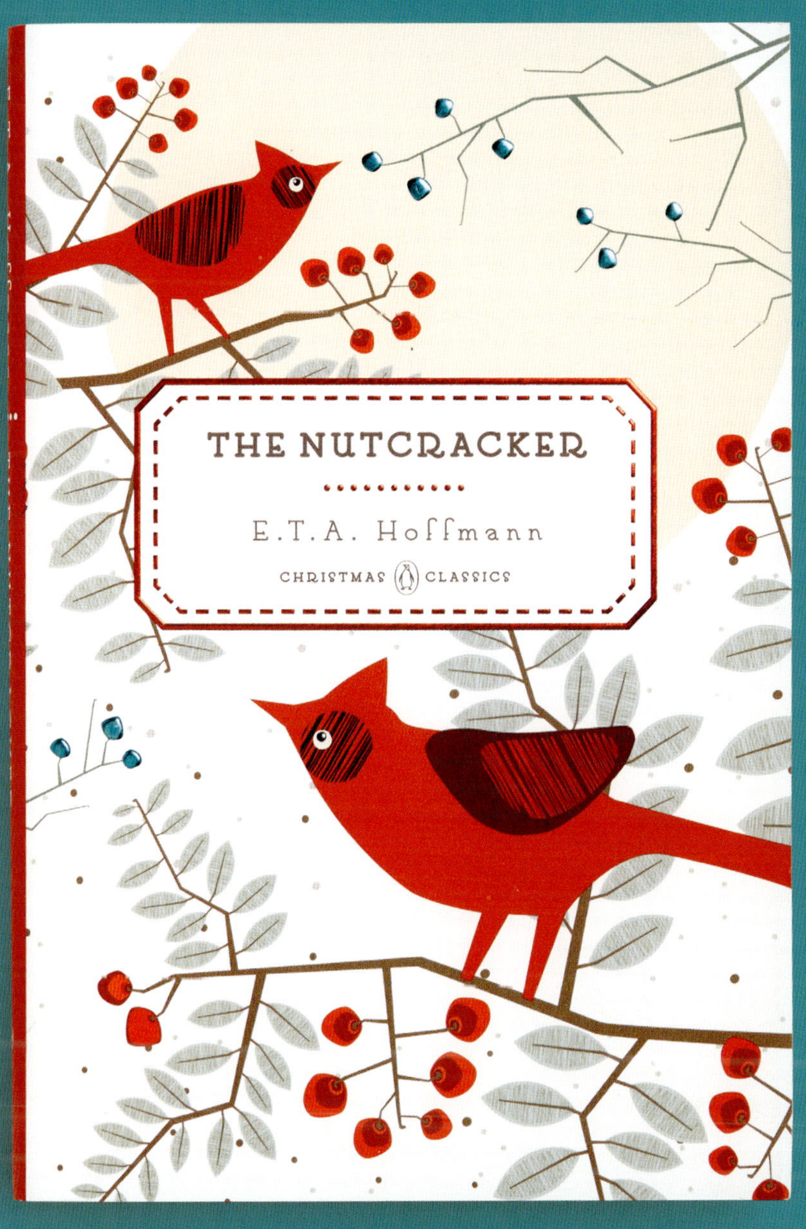
THE NUTCRACKER
E.T.A. Hoffmann
CHRISTMAS CLASSICS

THE LIFE
& ADVENTURES
OF SANTA CLAUS
L. Frank Baum
CHRISTMAS CLASSICS

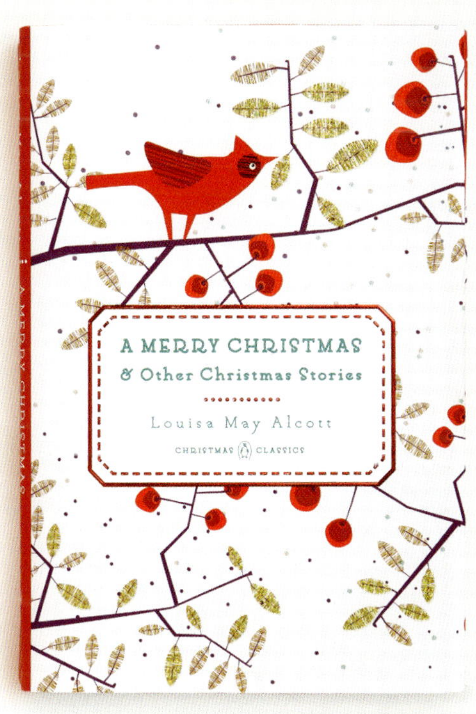
A MERRY CHRISTMAS
& Other Christmas Stories
Louisa May Alcott
CHRISTMAS CLASSICS

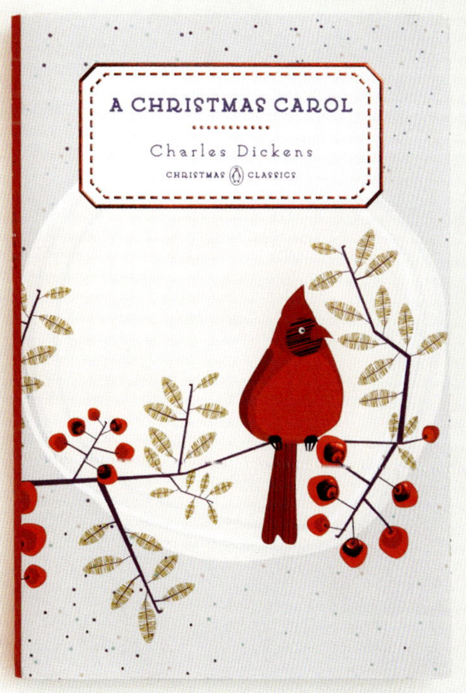
A CHRISTMAS CAROL
Charles Dickens
CHRISTMAS CLASSICS

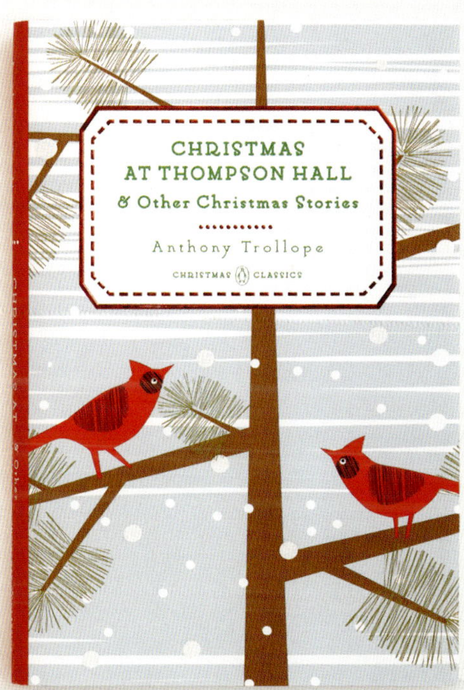
CHRISTMAS
AT THOMPSON HALL
& Other Christmas Stories
Anthony Trollope
CHRISTMAS CLASSICS

THE NIGHT
BEFORE CHRISTMAS
Nikolai Gogol
CHRISTMAS CLASSICS

THE NUTCRACKER
E.T.A. Hoffman
CHRISTMAS CLASSI

Paul Buckley, CREATIVE DIRECTOR

Roseanne is half-right about my encroaching behavior. I did almost, kind of, possibly to be if things go her way, sort of give her the project to work on. The thing was I had these amazing antique die-cut wrapping paper samples that I'd been holding on to for twenty years, so I discussed with Ro if I could show them and I definitely said something along the lines of "But if they like these, you gotta let me work on them." Hey, it's about what's best for the books, right? At least, that's how I sleep at night. I really love the look of old Christmas chromolithographs and specifically saw a unique opportunity here that may not ever present itself again.

That said, editorial said no to the antique papers, so I was out; Ro knew and I knew this was hers. But as we got to the end of the season (before the cardinals appeared) I was not loving the designs I was seeing, nor was editorial. Deadlines were looming and this was a six-book series that a lot of hopes were pinned on—so I stepped in. Again. This is a business and it is my job to make sure we are on track, so I can't always be all kumbaya in a situation where a deadline might be missed or we may accept something not as striking as the project deserves. My choice here was to leave Ro alone and have faith she'd bring this in at the last second or to show her what I think is being asked for (in which I was wrong and she was not). It should also be stated that Roseanne and I have worked together for over two decades and she never misses a deadline, nor does she ever not knock it out of the park, but here I was, panicking a bit. So I stayed late, hunkered down, and knocked out two designs. I really liked them but the softies upstairs went all gooey for those cardinals, pushing my covers to the side and saying things like "Oh-my-God Roseanne we looooooooove these," "These are just genius," "Talk about worth the wait," and other things that proved bruising to my sleazy, usurping soul.

Often at packing meetings when an editor is killing something I think is amazing, if applicable I often think to myself—and have said out loud on a number of occasions—"But you're not even the audience for this book. I am." This time I was the offender in that situation—if anyone knows Christmas, it's Roseanne.

Ro, I'm happy you got this off your chest!

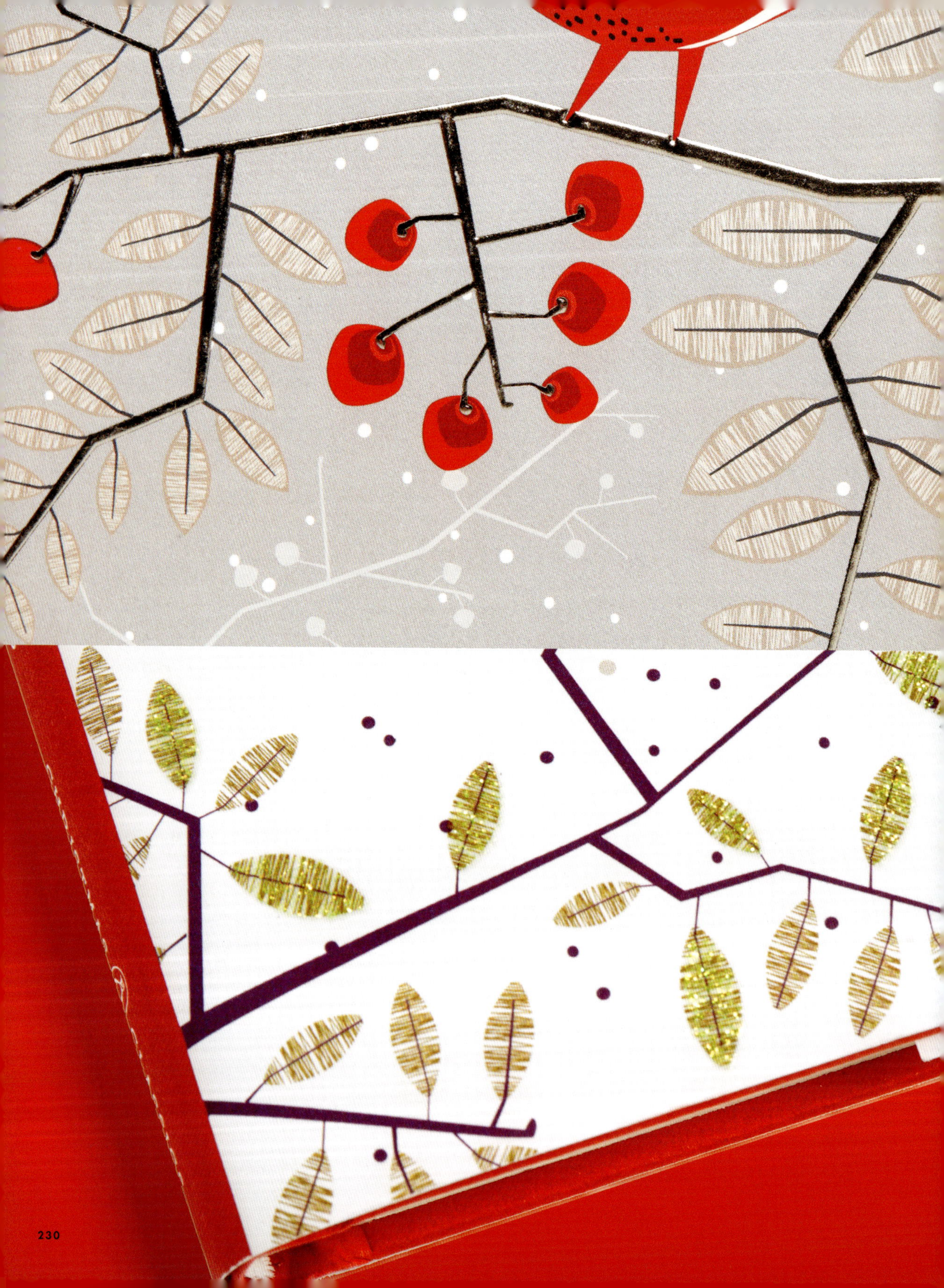

CHRISTMAS CLASSICS

Penguin

PENGUIN THREADS
THREADS

Penguin THREADS

ILLUSTRATED BY JILLIAN TAMAKI & RACHELL SUMPTER

JILLIAN TAMAKI: BLACK BEAUTY, EMMA, THE SECRET GARDEN

RACHELL SUMPTER: THE WIND IN THE WILLOWS, THE WIZARD OF OZ, LITTLE WOMEN

CREATIVE DIRECTOR: PAUL BUCKLEY **SERIES EDITOR:** ELDA ROTOR

• THE SECRET GARDEN WORK IN PROGRESS, PHOTO BY LYNN ROGAN

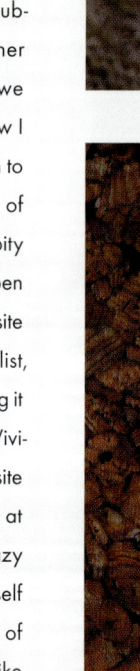

Paul Buckley, CREATIVE DIRECTOR

From time to time I pitch projects to my Penguin publishers, and I was just finishing up our Penguin Ink series. A fair percentage of the tattoo artists I tried to work with had proved more than challenging, which made us all walk away from that project. I was in search of something completely different to pitch and was looking around on Etsy and came across this cool little stitched portrait, which I promptly purchased and brought upstairs to Penguin Classics publisher Elda Rotor and Penguin publisher Kathryn Court, and we all agreed we should do a stitched-covers series. Now I just had to find someone insane enough to take on that amount of work. Thinking of Jillian Tamaki for this was pure serendipity (actually, many of my commissions happen through a found moment): I was on her site considering her for our Kerouac backlist, which I was redesigning. I was not feeling it for Kerouac (which eventually went to Vivienne Flesher) but I jumped from Jillian's site to her blog, just because. . . . And there at the very bottom of her blog was this crazy gorgeous quilt she had stitched for herself with a caption that was along the lines of "Please do not ask me to do anything like this, it just takes too long." Of course I did

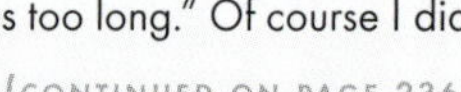

(CONTINUED ON PAGE 236)

• PORTRAIT BY ERIN PAISLEY, PURCHASED VIA ETSY

EMMA
JANE AUSTEN
PENGUIN THREADS

(CONTINUED FROM PAGE 234)

just that—I offered her any choice of the three books we were thinking of doing, waiting for the rejection e-mail. But in the morning was a glorious e-mail from her saying yes and please let me do all three. OK, problem solved; I hope she can pull it off.... And of course she did and then she went on to take a **GOLD MEDAL** that year from the Society of Illustrators, for **BLACK BEAUTY**.

I'm particularly proud of how we did the opposite sides of the covers. When I was looking at Jillian's embroideries, I noticed the backing she had on them. One was peeling back a little from the corner, so I peeked under it and saw that the backs were as gorgeous as the fronts, just in a different way. Seeing the behind-the-scenes process and aftermath was so amazing—so I suggested we print these inside to line up with the front, and got a resounding yes. On another day, it would have been, "Wait, how much will that cost?"

—PB

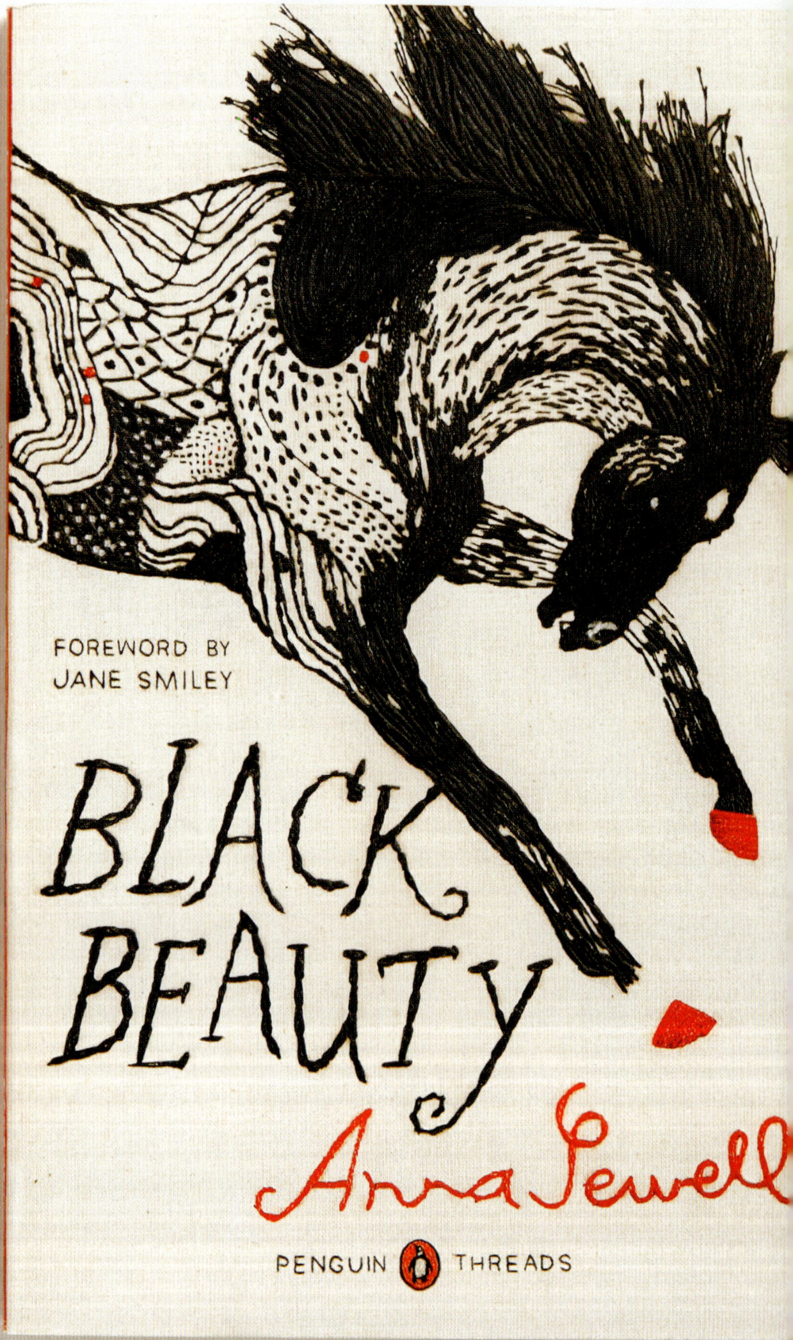

• GOLD MEDAL, SOCIETY OF ILLUSTRATORS. PHOTO BY MATT VEE

The Wind in the Willows
KENNETH GRAHAME
FOREWORD BY GREGORY MAGUIRE
PENGUIN THREADS

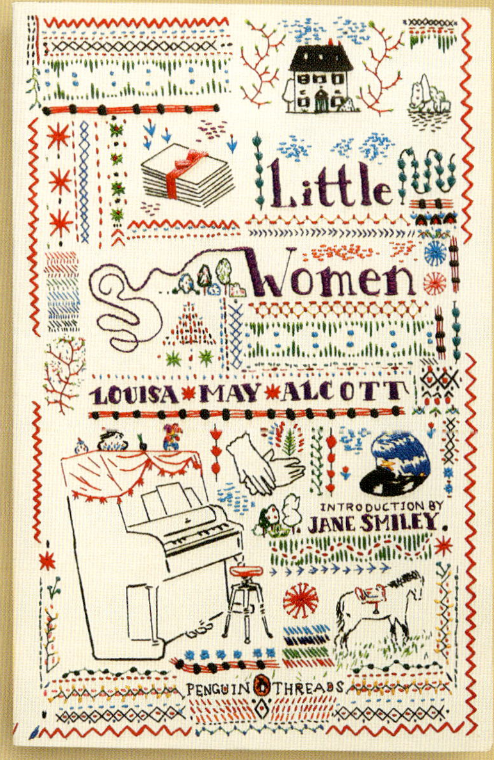
Little Women
LOUISA MAY ALCOTT
INTRODUCTION BY JANE SMILEY
PENGUIN THREADS

the Secret Garden
FRANCES HODGSON BURNETT
PENGUIN THREADS

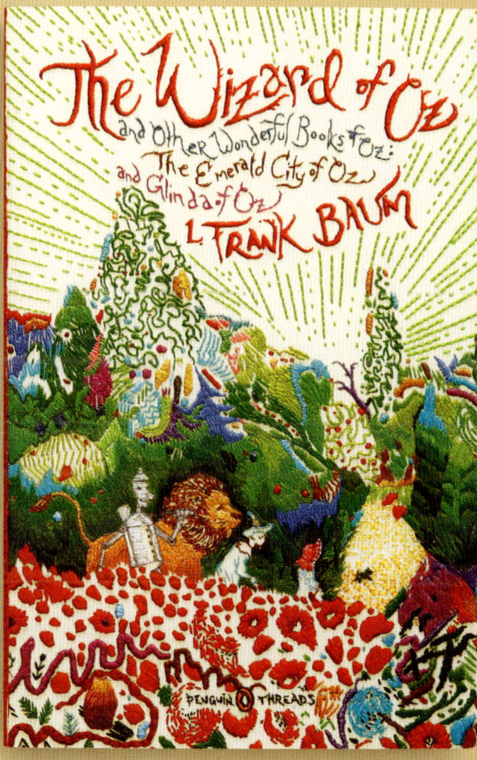
The Wizard of Oz
and Other Wonderful Books of Oz:
The Emerald City of Oz
and Glinda of Oz
L. FRANK BAUM
PENGUIN THREADS

HODGSON

Miller

● **Rachell Sumpter, ILLUSTRATOR**

I sort of tricked Penguin when Paul contacted me and asked if I would like to create the next set of Threads and if I embroidered. I said, "Yes, absolutely!"—though I had hardly embroidered in my life. He asked for test embroideries, which I had to create, quickly, and then the next step was for me to create extremely detailed sketches showing where every stitch was going to go. Someone who has never seen the covers could probably re-create them from the sketches, stitch by stitch. Jillian Tamaki was very helpful in recommending a book she uses and telling me to use stretcher bars. I learned quickly, but I also had a two-month-old nursing son and a show in Stockholm I was preparing for at the same time. It was nuts!

I had to create a test embroidery to prove my abilities—which was fine. I was a little unsure myself.

The deadlines were the same as a standard illustrated cover—two weeks for sketches, two weeks for final. (Is that correct? That's what I recall but I can hardly believe it.)

THE WIZARD OF OZ was first and of course the most detailed; I think I may have gone overboard. The poppies were my favorite part, and trying out the different stitches for pattern making on the flaps was interesting. (CONTINUED ON PAGE 241)

The Wind in the Willows
KENNETH GRAHAME
FOREWORD BY GREGORY MAGUIRE
PENGUIN THREADS

(CONTINUED FROM PAGE 239)

With **THE WIND IN THE WILLOWS**, I originally wanted to do the section where they are drifting down the river and encounter Pan—it felt very dreamy and surreal—but I also thought, "No, this is for young people—they want action!" Hence the obnoxious Mr. Toad. I did like the way the colors turned out; the complementary palette really sang. Plants and characters are my favorite things to draw and paint.

LITTLE WOMEN was challenging because it was last, which meant little leeway with deadlines. The big question was, Do I include the sisters? Or one—then which one? So I decided not to include any!

—RS

"O bliss!
O poop-poop!
O my!
O my!"

CLASSICS

Riccardo Vecchio, ILLUSTRATOR

4 ply, 4x5 cold pressed watercolor paper. Thin ink crusted nibs on a gray plastic holder dipped in walnut umber ink. The nib scratches and trembles on the porous uneven surface. The tension and elasticity of the thin nib catapults minuscule ink drops alongside a thin line. His gaze staring down. The hair combed back, his shoulders sloping forward. His left ear pointing high. Roher Calligraphy ink, green, lemon yellow ink, lavender, magenta, and pink. It smells musky. Wet brush strokes dissolve non-waterproof ink, bleeding outwards. Liquefied pigment spreads like thunderous clouds in water drops held together by surface tension. The sharp nib carves a small fiber booger out of porous paper, which grows like a snowball. As the cloth ball stuck to the nib grows, it absorbs ink, enlarging the surface area of the nib and the thickness of the line. The paper drawing lies head down on the flat bed. 300dpi, RGB, scan. In Photoshop the arrow cursor draws a perfect wave in the curve window, balancing luminosity and contrast. Let's go a bit more sour....The cursor pulls the hue level left, green and yellow and the saturation level slightly right, increasing the saturation. The input levels cursor, dragged towards the middle, brightens the white levels and cleans up the white background. The porous and imperfect paper structure disappears on the empty background but remains visible in the color washes. Perfect; Save as: Tiff - folder- Penguin, Arthur Miller Centennial folder - finals. Compress folder to zip, mail to Penguin Group (USA) INC; send.

THE PENGUIN
rthur Miller
THE MILLER CENTENNIAL | 2015
THE PENGUIN
rthur Miller
COLLECTED PLAYS
PENGUIN CLASSICS
DELUXE EDITION

Collected Plays

The Penguin Arthur Miller: Deluxe Edition

ILLUSTRATOR: RICCARDO VECCHIO **DESIGNER / CREATIVE DIRECTOR:** PAUL BUCKLEY **EDITOR:** ELDA ROTOR

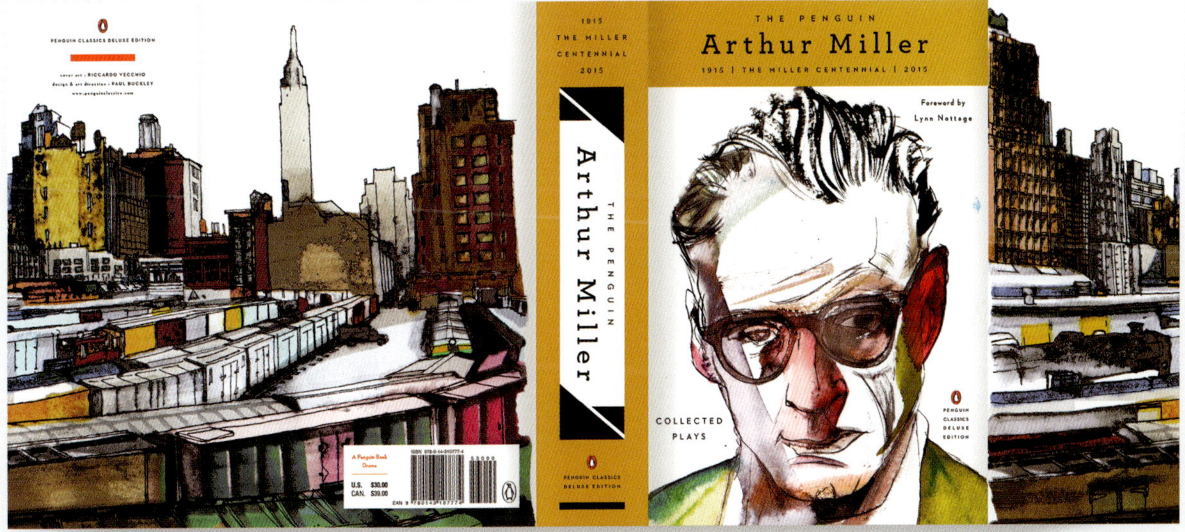

• ALTERNATIVE OPTION, UNUSED

Paul Buckley, DESIGNER / CREATIVE DIRECTOR

Riccardo can do no wrong; the man is always a home run, and works and works and works. He is very organic and very painterly, and experimentation is a core part of his process, so when you say, "Yes, we love this sketch, please go to a finish," he sends you not one but quite a few differently colored and rendered versions. He's also incredibly pleasant to work with, and all of this culminates in *This is going to go amazingly well*, before you've even seen the first sketch.

First we did **THE PENGUIN ARTHUR MILLER** Deluxe paperback. I asked Riccardo to do portraits of Miller and once we chose one of the many he did, I asked for an NYC street scene from the fifties, one that would create a continuous vista if you put both flaps together. (I really thought this was a brilliant idea and though simple enough, one I'd never seen before, and I've been doing this a long time—but then a month later Roman Muradov did the exact same thing with the flaps he conceived for *A Portrait of the Artist as a Young Man*. I do believe ideas accumulate in a time and place and really do sorta float out there ready to be picked up by people.... Is that too grand a statement for a mere flap art idea? Nonetheless...) Design-wise, my solution to play off the classic Broadway Playbill is only so-so, but it does nicely take a backseat and let Riccardo's art pop forth.

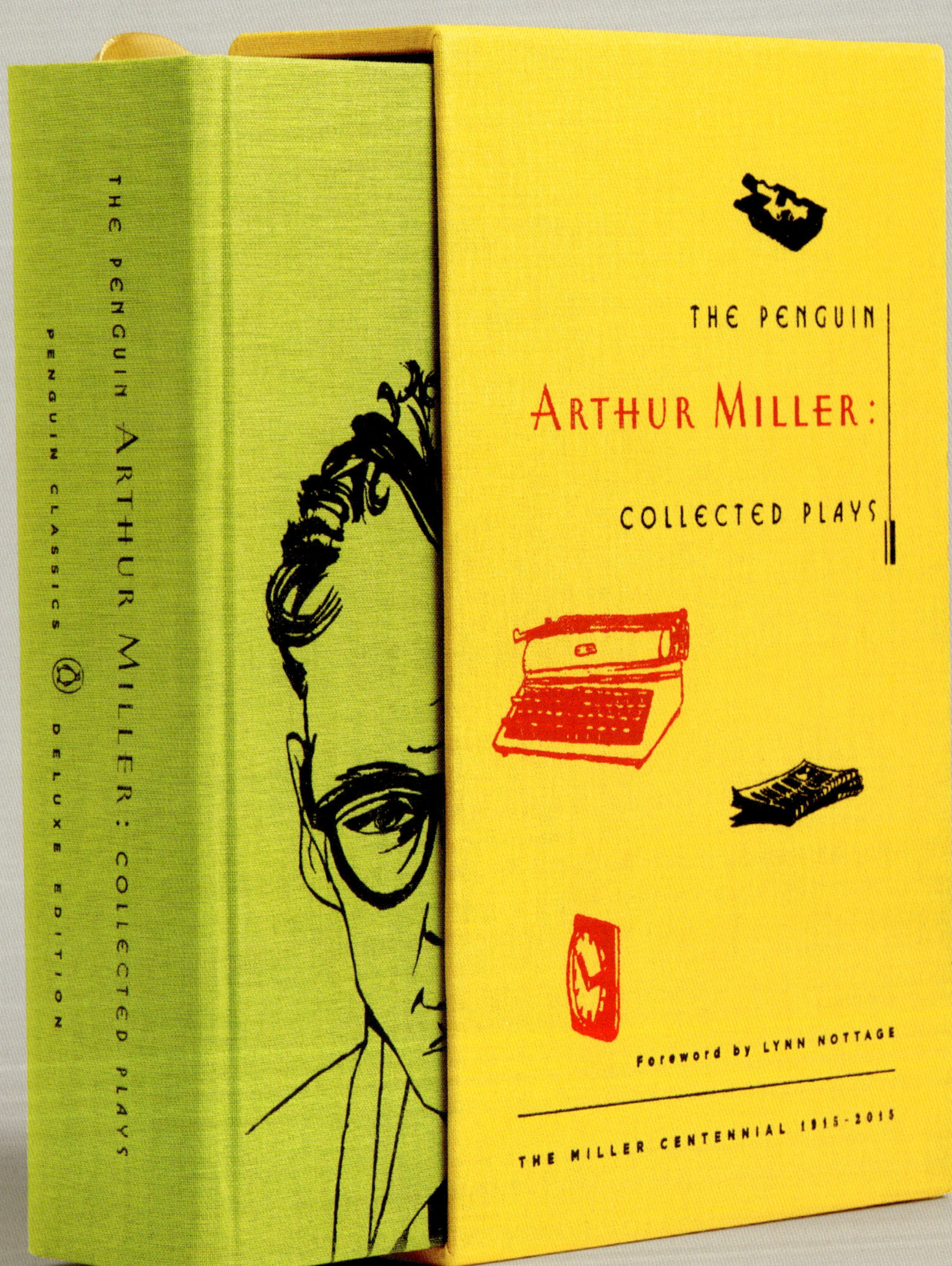
THE PENGUIN
ARTHUR MILLER:
COLLECTED PLAYS
Foreword by LYNN NOTTAGE
THE MILLER CENTENNIAL 1915-2015
THE PENGUIN ARTHUR MILLER: COLLECTED PLAYS
PENGUIN CLASSICS DELUXE EDITION

Collected Plays
The Penguin Arthur Miller: Box Set

ILLUSTRATOR: RICCARDO VECCHIO **DESIGNER & CREATIVE DIRECTOR:** PAUL BUCKLEY **EDITOR:** ELDA ROTOR

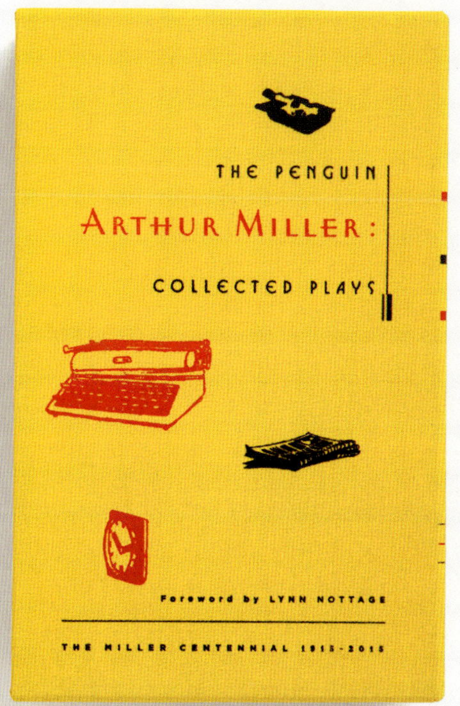

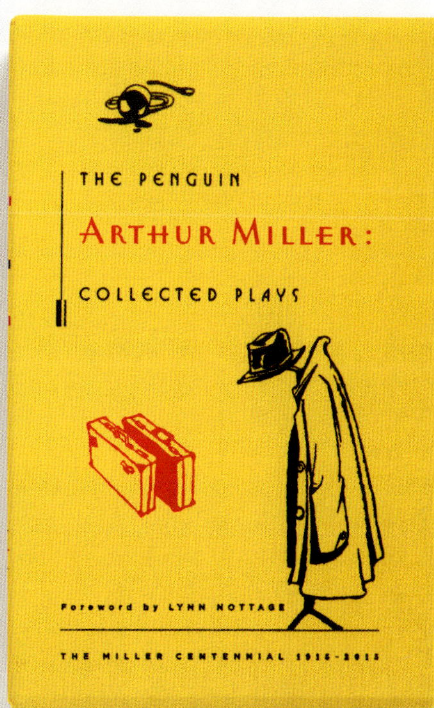

● Riccardo Vecchio, ILLUSTRATOR

I was on the subway doodling on my grocery list, heading home, when I started to think about this Arthur Miller job. And, you know, your mind wanders...Jules Dassin, *The Naked City*, 1950s NY, industrial, steam, raw, perfect! Bertolt Brecht, *Mother Courage and Her Children*, yes! Hmm, the theater. Oh, Marilyn, stage props, hmmm, Marilyn. Gee, how am I gonna please his daughter, she has to approve the work...isn't she married to Daniel Day-Lewis? "There will be blood," oil-black, lush, thick, powerful black ink drawings, small format 5"x7", better do lots of them, maybe 30–40. I hope one will work. My stop. Don't forget the milk.

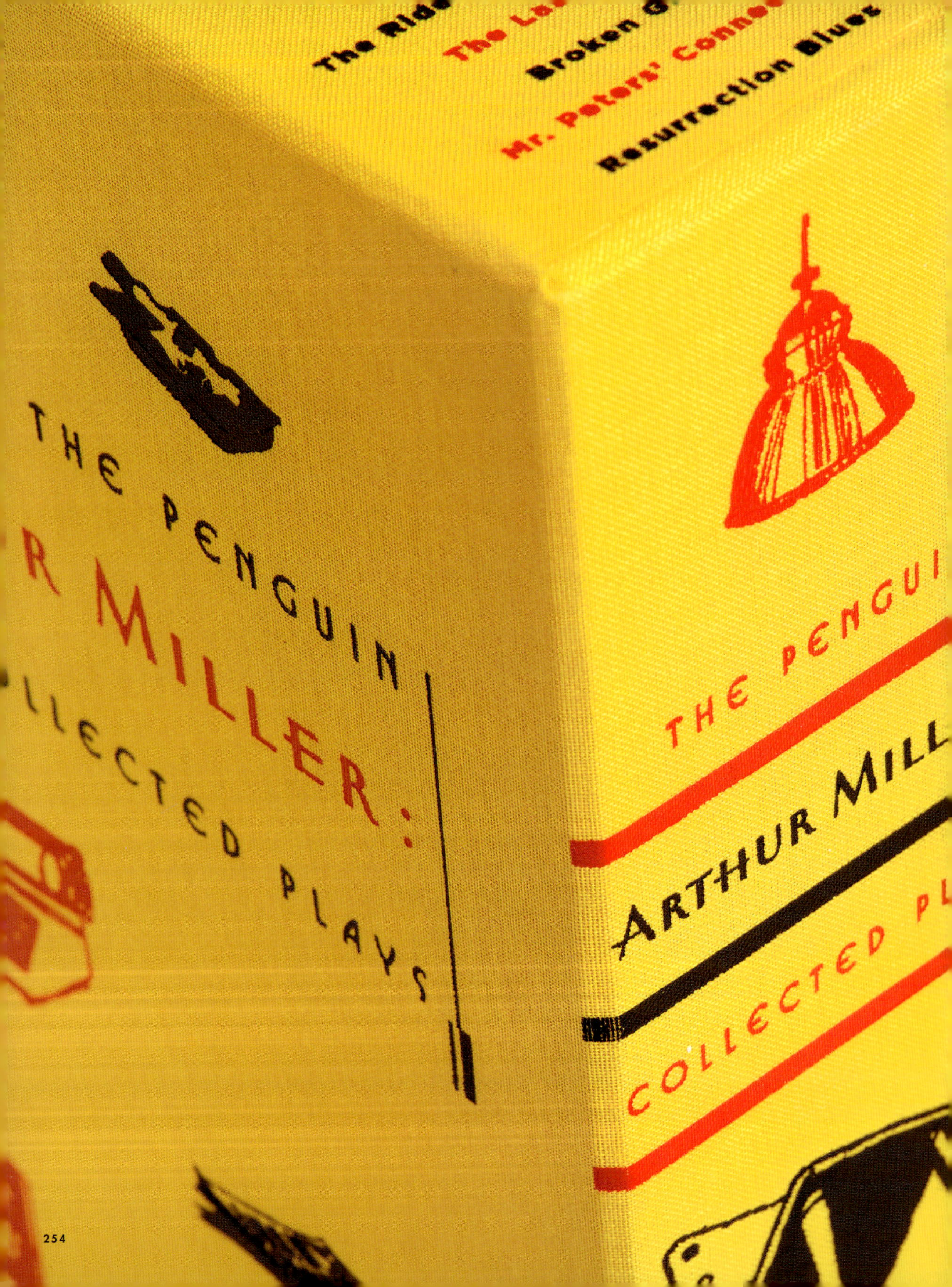
Resurrection Blues
THE PENGUIN
ARTHUR

COLLECTED PLAYS

THE PENGUIN ARTHUR MILLER: COLLECTED PLAYS
PENGUIN CLASSICS DELUXE EDITION

Paul Buckley, CREATIVE DIRECTOR

For the box set, I asked Roberto to do line art instead of painting, as I knew I'd want to be stamping his art on the linen. For the box, I asked for an empty stage scene, and Riccardo beautifully spun that off into drawing individual elements that I then placed around the box in a very simple manner. I like the lime-green books the best, for two reasons. First, that I got these colors approved for an entity as "male" as Miller; it was a way to modernize the work and to see him as we had not seen before, especially in combination with the yellow box. Second, I love the line art portraits Riccardo did of him. Many years back I did a similar box set for *The Tale of Genji* and did the exact same thing, except with portraits of Genji and Lady Kiritsubo.

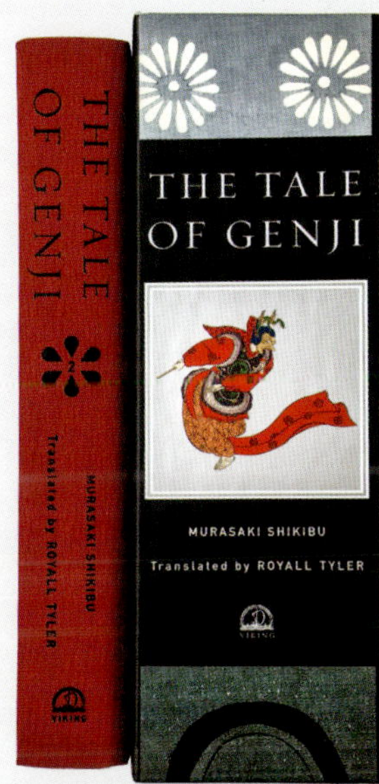

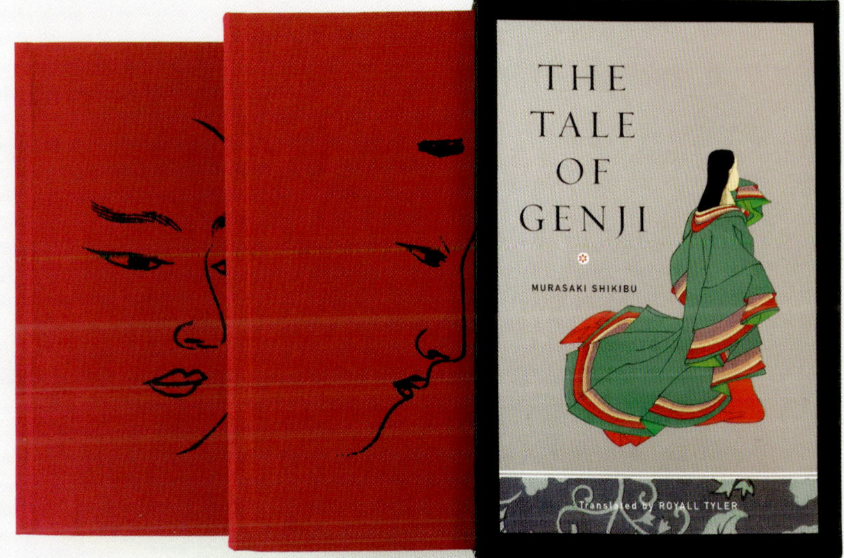

• GENJI BOX SET, PAUL BUCKLEY

Presence: Collected Stories ARTHUR MILLER

DESIGNER: MATT VEE **ILLUSTRATOR:** RICCARDO VECCHIO **CREATIVE DIRECTOR:** PAUL BUCKLEY **EDITOR:** ELDA ROTOR

Paul Buckley, CREATIVE DIRECTOR

All in all, we really pulled out all the stops for the Arthur Miller centennial: a deluxe paperback with French flaps; a bespoke hardcover edition in a linen slipcase; a slew of new packages to add into our already ongoing series of plays being done by Jim Tierney; and two repackages within our backlist titles. Jason Ramirez took over with Jim the series I had started with him years ago, Matt Vee took on the two backlist titles, and I had Riccardo Vecchio working with me on the deluxe paperback and the linen slipcase—five artists and designers all simultaneously working toward the same goal.

• APPROVED COVER

Collected Essays ARTHUR MILLER

DESIGNER: MATT VEE **ILLUSTRATOR:** RICCARDO VECCHIO **CREATIVE DIRECTOR:** PAUL BUCKLEY **EDITOR:** ELDA ROTOR

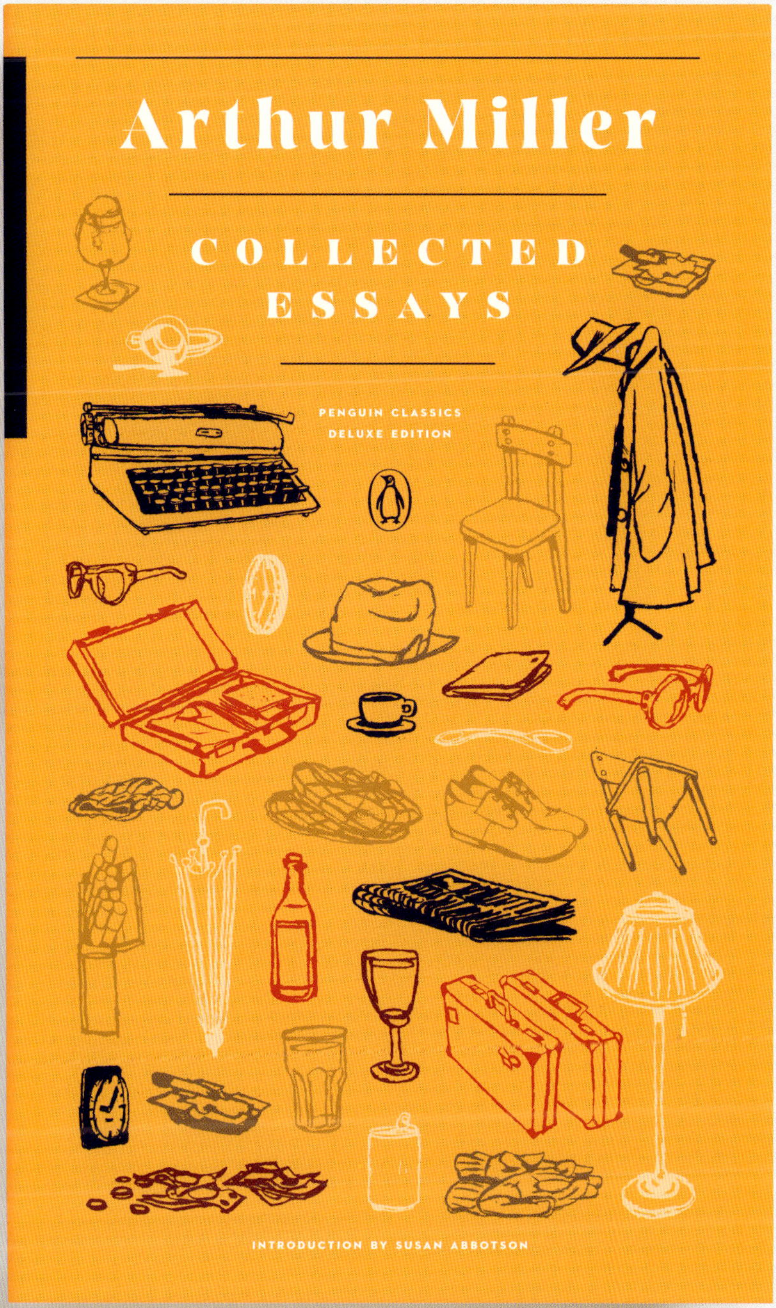

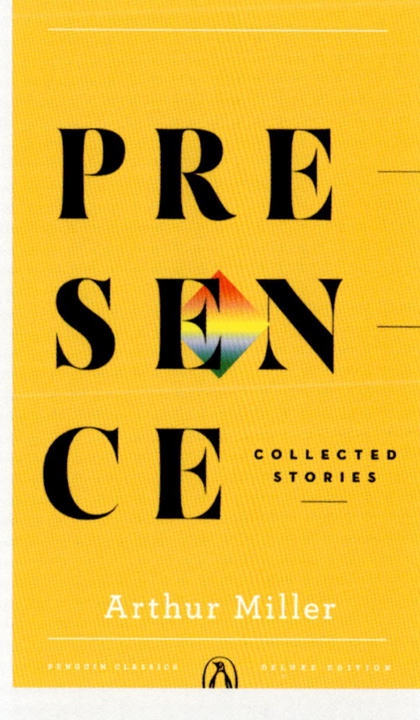

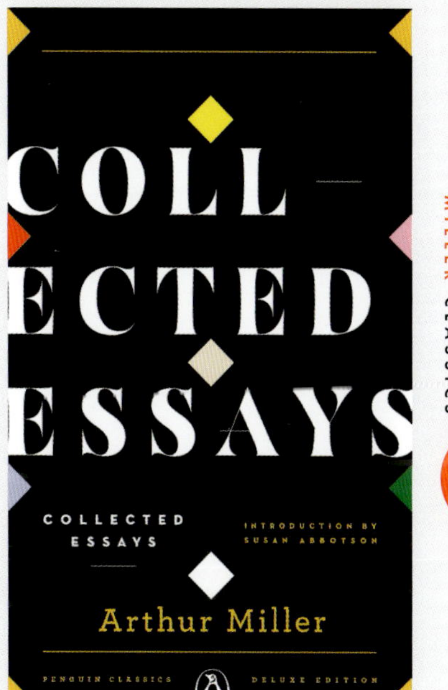

• APPROVED COVER

Penguin

PLAYS

Author

Title

PENGUIN PLAYS

Penguin PLAYS

ARTHUR MILLER SERIES ILLUSTRATED BY JIM TIERNEY

THE ARCHBISHOP'S CEILING, THE AMERICAN CLOCK, DEATH OF A SALESMAN, PLAYING FOR TIME, BROKEN GLASS, THE CRUCIBLE, AFTER THE FALL, A VIEW FROM THE BRIDGE, ALL MY SONS, AN ENEMY OF THE PEOPLE, THE PRICE, INCIDENT AT VICHY, THE MAN WHO HAD ALL THE LUCK, RESURRECTION BLUES, THE RIDE DOWN MT. MORGAN, THE CREATION OF THE WORLD AND OTHER BUSINESS

ART DIRECTORS: PAUL BUCKLEY & JASON RAMIREZ **SERIES EDITOR:** ELDA ROTOR

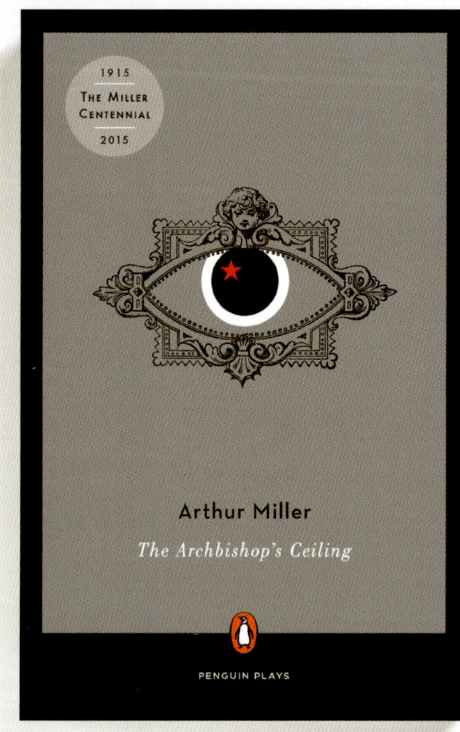

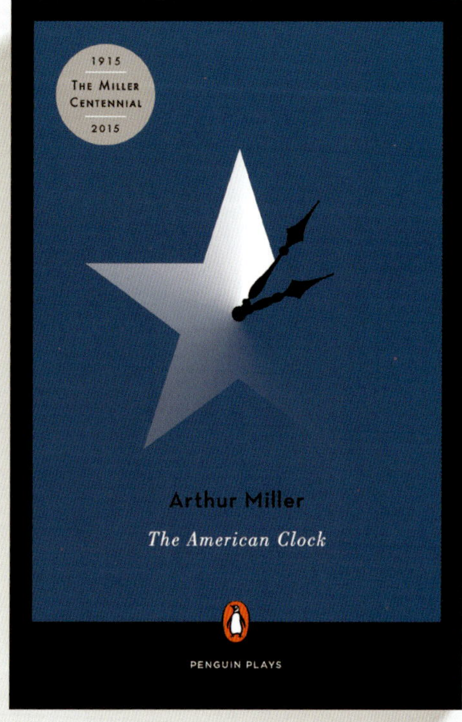

● **Jim Tierney,** ILLUSTRATOR

To be honest, the work of Arthur Miller had never quite appealed to me before I was asked to redesign his entire body of work for the **PENGUIN PLAYS** series. I was casually familiar with a few of his most famous plays, but had dismissed them as feeling too simple; heartbreaking and tragic, yes, but oppressively blunt in their sincerity.

Assigning this project to me must have been Paul's way of drop-kicking me out of the aesthetic comfort zone that I had created for myself as a young designer. I was a relatively new hire at the time, with a freshly earned degree in Illustration and a portfolio filled with decorative maximalism and European-inspired flourishes. None of this frilly nonsense, however, was going to save me from the stark gaze of America's most American playwright.

Finding a "look" for a story is a challenge. Finding a "look" for an author's entire body of work is another challenge. Finding a "look" that can be applied to seventeen unique stories without either becoming repetitive or fracturing the author's identity is yet another challenge, and one that I had never attempted before. Luckily for me, Arthur Miller's writing is nowhere near as simple or straightforward as I had previously assumed.

(CONTINUED ON PAGE 264)

PENGUIN PLAYS

(CONTINUED FROM PAGE 262)

If you look past the anguished dialogue of a Miller play, you'll nearly always find a few key objects, carefully chosen and crackling with symbolism. In Miller's hands, a shabby fedora, a broken briefcase, or an empty wheelchair can carry as much crystalized poignancy as a dramatic monologue, so I decided to isolate these metaphors and place them directly on the cover like artifacts in a museum display case. The thick black frame decisively contains the miniature world of each story, while the flat "stage" of color allows the graphically illustrated objects to speak for themselves. From first glance they invite the reader to discover their significance, and gather meaning and clarity as the narrative unfolds.

Striving for simplicity is deceptively difficult, and I struggled with deciding what not to show on these covers. Designing within the parameters of Arthur Miller's nuanced economy revealed a depth to his work that I had once completely underestimated, and I can't believe that it took me so long to appreciate not only what he was saying, but the immense skill with which he said it.

—JT

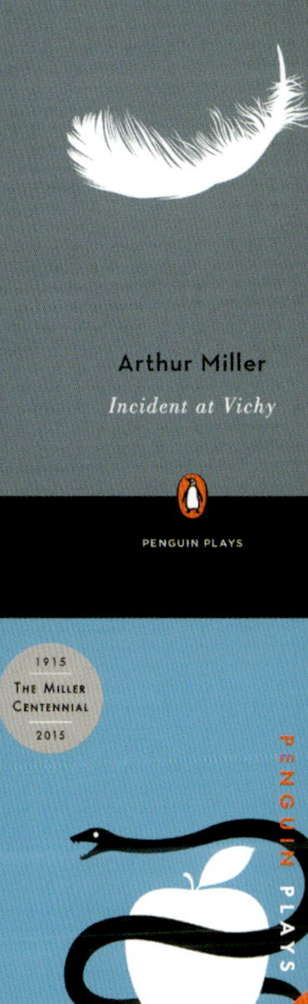

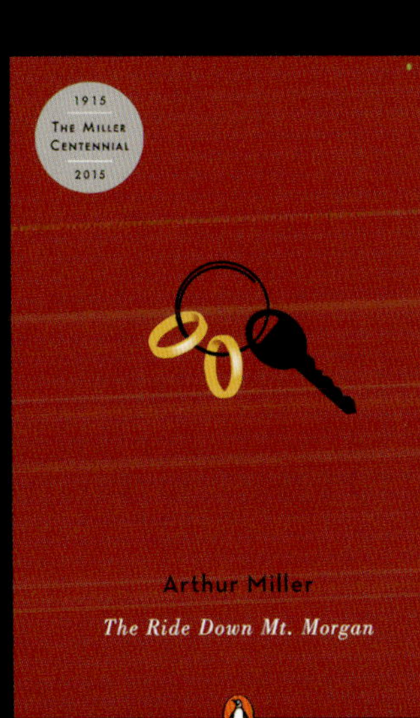

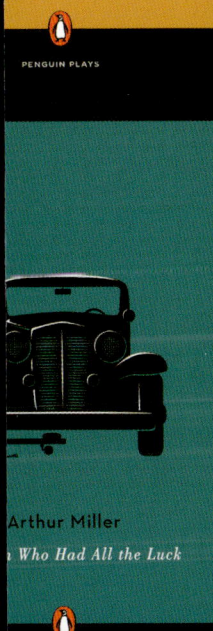

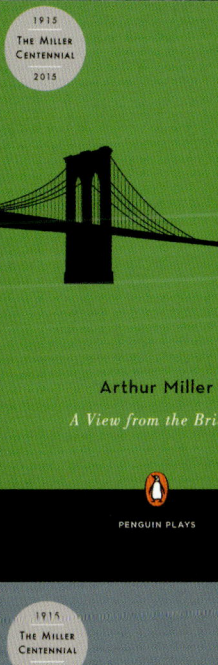

Arthur Miller
Broken Glass
PENGUIN PLAYS
1915 The Miller Centennial 2015
Arthur Miller
The Crucible
PENGUIN PLAYS
1915 The Miller Centennial 2015
Arthur Miller
After the Fall
PENGUIN PLAYS
1915 The Miller Centennial 2015
Arthur Miller
A View from the Bridge
PENGUIN PLAYS
Arthur Miller
All My Sons
PENGUIN PLAYS
1915 The Miller Centennial 2015
Arthur Miller
An Enemy of the People
An adaptation of the play by Henrik Ibsen
PENGUIN PLAYS
1915 The Miller Centennial 2015
Arthur Miller
The Price
PENGUIN PLAYS
1915 The Miller Centennial 2015
Arthur Miller
Incident at Vichy
PENGUIN PLAYS
Arthur Miller
Who Had All the Luck
1915 The Miller Centennial 2015
Arthur Miller
Resurrection Blues
1915 The Miller Centennial 2015
Arthur Miller
The Ride Down Mt. Morgan
1915 The Miller Centennial 2015
Arthur Miller
The Creation of the World and Other Business
PENGUIN PLAYS

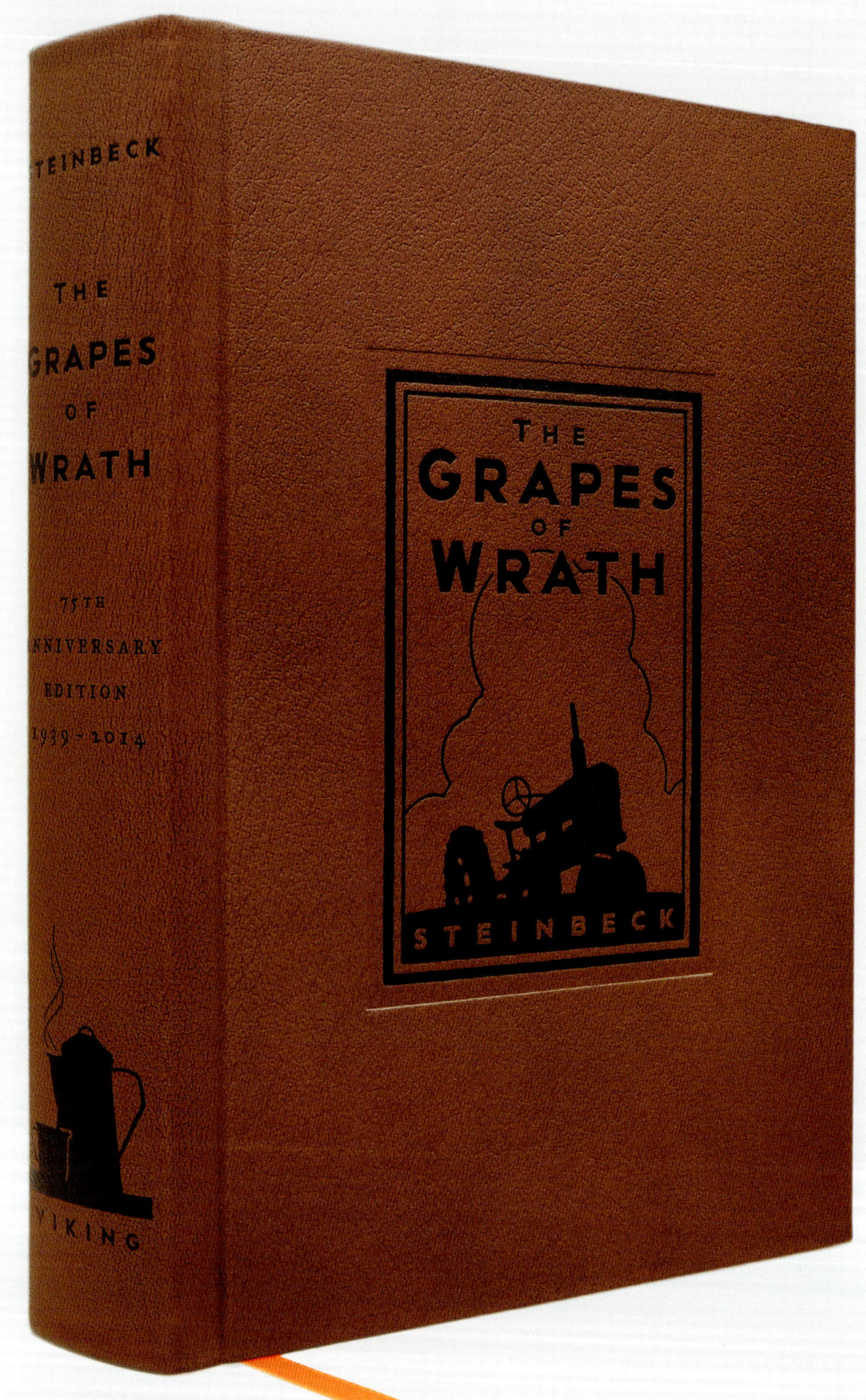
STEINBECK
THE
GRAPES
OF
WRATH
75TH
ANNIVERSARY
EDITION
1939–2014
VIKING
THE
GRAPES
OF
WRATH
STEINBECK

The Grapes of Wrath

JOHN STEINBECK

ILLUSTRATOR: MICHAEL SCHWAB **ART DIRECTOR:** JASON RAMIREZ **CREATIVE DIRECTOR:** PAUL BUCKLEY **EDITOR:** ELDA ROTOR

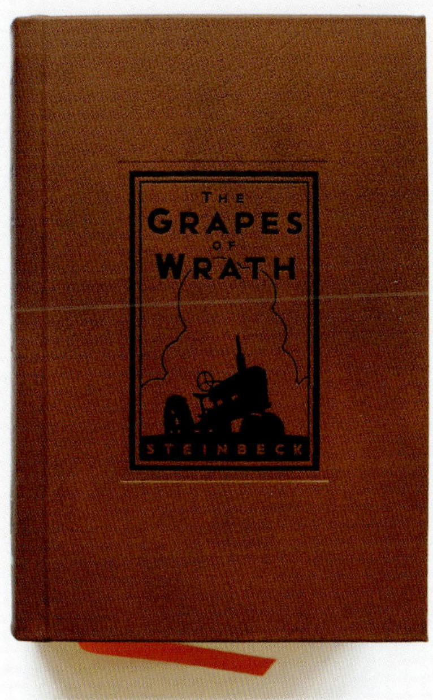

PHOTOS, JASON RAMIREZ

● **Michael Schwab,** ILLUSTRATOR

Born and raised in Oklahoma, I grew up with the distant ghosts of the Dust Bowl. As a twenty-one-year-old graphic artist, I too left Oklahoma for the romance and opportunities of California. Luckily, unlike the Joads, I was greeted by California with open arms: lapping waves, palm trees, exciting new ideas, food, glorious weather, and refreshing open-minded attitudes—clearly, a different era. Forty years later, I am still embracing California and all of her opportunities and natural beauty. Proud of my Oklahoman roots, I feel honored and grateful to contribute to this historic edition of Steinbeck's **THE GRAPES OF WRATH**.

I originally had three ideas for the cover art: a weathered barn and windmill silhouette, a tired old mule, and a broken-down tractor, all seemingly abandoned. The tractor—stuck and abandoned—seemed most appropriate for the Dust Bowl concept to both Jason, the art director, and me.

Other simple graphic images kept coming to me and, luckily, we found applications for them. The campfire coffeepot silhouette on the spine helped evoke the Joads' life on the road. I had found reference photos of old Route 66 highway signs. Fortunately, we were able to apply them as simple black-and-white icons to the endpapers.

It all worked for me; no creative horror stories. I'm very proud of the results—simple, bold, and dramatic.

The Prophecies NOSTRADAMUS

DESIGNER: ERIC WHITE **CREATIVE DIRECTOR:** PAUL BUCKLEY **EDITOR:** JOHN SICILIANO

● **Eric White, DESIGNER**

THE PROPHECIES – This is a puzzle to be solved. I wanted the viewer to be confused for a moment (ideally not much longer) and feel the need to re-assemble the letters and symbols into something coherent. I'm really happy that we kept the title, author, and "Penguin Classics" all at the same point size; that way it's even more difficult to read!

THE SOLITUDES – I presented this with the title only and the Penguin was perched on top of the mountain. It was quite powerful that way, but people of words like to see more words. Aren't there enough words inside? I'm still thrilled that it was approved in any form.

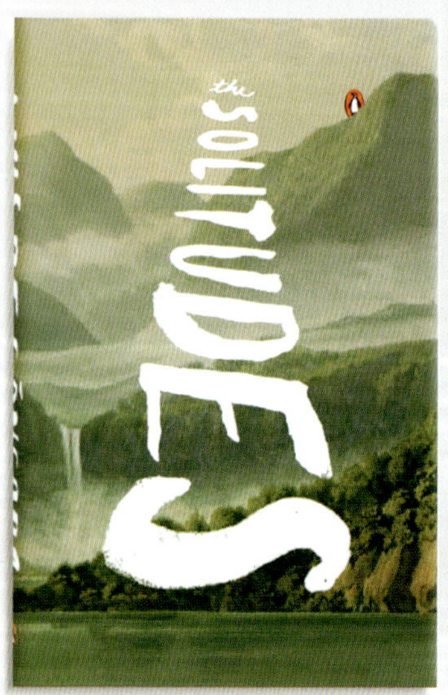

• ALTERNATIVE OPTION, UNUSED

The Solitudes LUIS DE GÓNGORA

DESIGNER: ERIC WHITE **CREATIVE DIRECTOR:** PAUL BUCKLEY **EDITOR:** JOHN SICILIANO

● **Edith Grossman,** TRANSLATOR

Góngora's THE SOLITUDES had intrigued me ever since I first read the poem years ago in graduate school. It is a famously difficult and utterly gorgeous piece of writing; over the years, the idea of translating it began to germinate, then finally blossomed into a book in 2011. Bringing that work over into English for Penguin was one of the most exhilarating experiences I've had as a translator.

This sense of excitement informed my first glimpse of the highly intuitive cover. The misty background is mysterious and quite beautiful, but the title is not easy to read, since your eye has to move from top to bottom instead of from left to right, and the letters are not all the same size. Well, I thought to myself, it's terrific: In a very subtle way the cover has captured the extremes of this poem. Nice!

● **Alberto Manguel,** INTRODUCER

The designer of the cover for Penguin Classics' edition of THE SOLITUDES has captured precisely the core of Góngora's art: the reconstruction of the physical world through words; the creation of a landscape in which the poem is both the thing described and its description, image and text transformed one into the other, conjuring up on the page a web of literal experience and textual reality which is the essence of the Baroque.

Pelican

The Pelican
SHAKESPEARE

TITLE

Edited by

Pelican SHAKESPEARE

SERIES DESIGNED & ILLUSTRATED BY MANUJA WALDIA

ROMEO AND JULIET, MACBETH, HAMLET, KING LEAR, OTHELLO, JULIUS CAESAR, THE TEMPEST, TWELFTH NIGHT, THE TAMING OF THE SHREW, A MIDSUMMER NIGHT'S DREAM

CREATIVE DIRECTOR: PAUL BUCKLEY   EDITOR: ELDA ROTOR

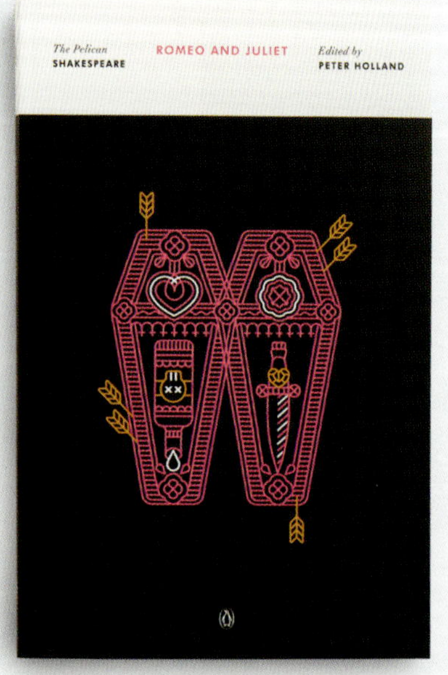

● **Manuja Waldia,** DESIGNER / ILLUSTRATOR

Shakespeare's work is quite old, while my illustration style is very modern. However, most of the broader themes that appear in the work are timeless, and it's genius of Paul to think of using this minimalistic approach to the cover art for these classics. Previous versions of cover art for other Shakespeare series were done by Milton Glaser and David Gentleman, which is intimidating, as those are some very large shoes to fill. I especially love Gentleman's because his covers are all woodcuts that took him more than a decade to finish. Even though my process is a lot quicker, his patient dedication inspires me to put my best foot forward for each title.

Being so iconic, every title has many existing artworks, and keeping these covers fresh is a challenge. While I don't want to reinvent the wheel just for the sake of it, I try to think of interesting concepts and execute the artwork in a unique manner. I strip away all frivolous plot details and try to condense the most interesting aspects into artwork made out of very basic shapes. Some titles have a lot of visual symbolism in the plot, while others have very abstract concepts, which are harder to translate into artwork.

Reading Shakespeare is always delightful; however, stumbling upon controversial aspects in some of the titles, like racist slurs and blatant misogyny, is never fun. You know it's bad when you're in favor of the shrew!

• THE TAMING OF THE SHREW SKETCH, MANUJA WALDIA

The Pelican
SHAKESPEARE

KING LEAR

Edited by
STEPHEN ORGEL

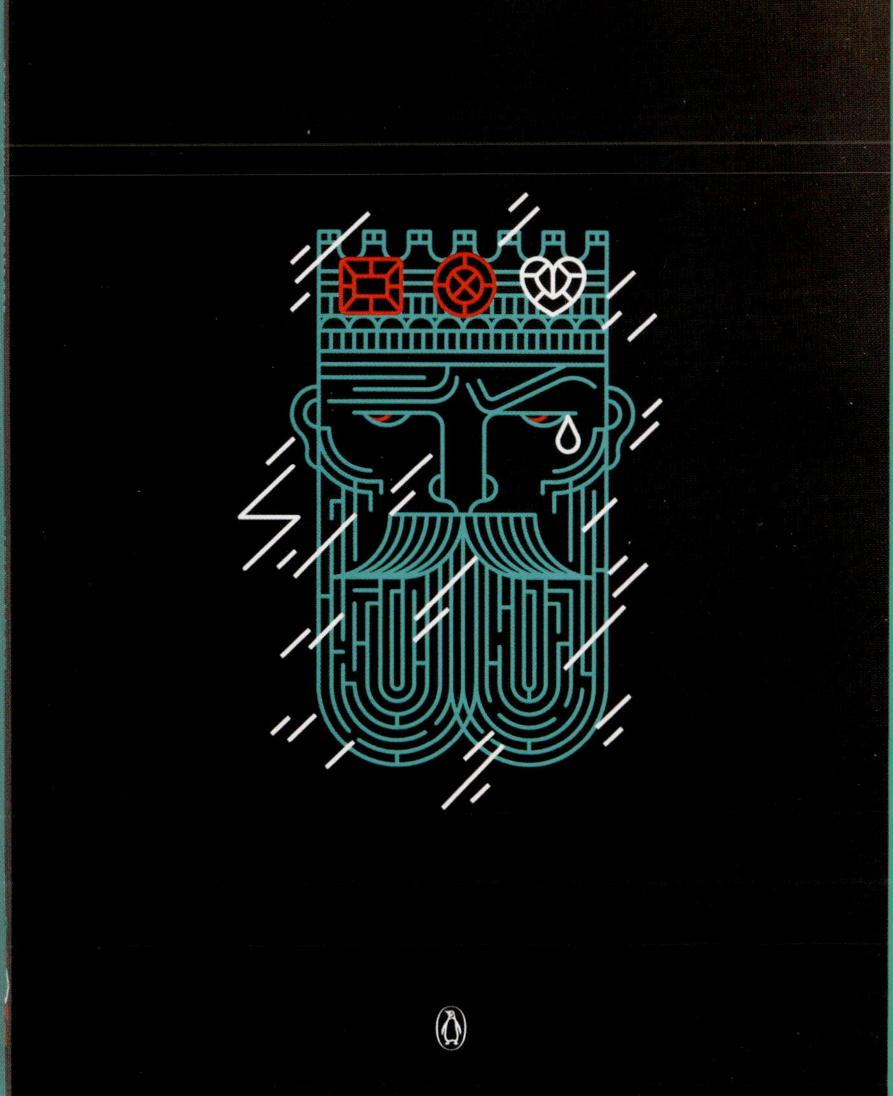

The Pelican
SHAKESPEARE

OTHELLO

Edited by
RUSS McDONALD

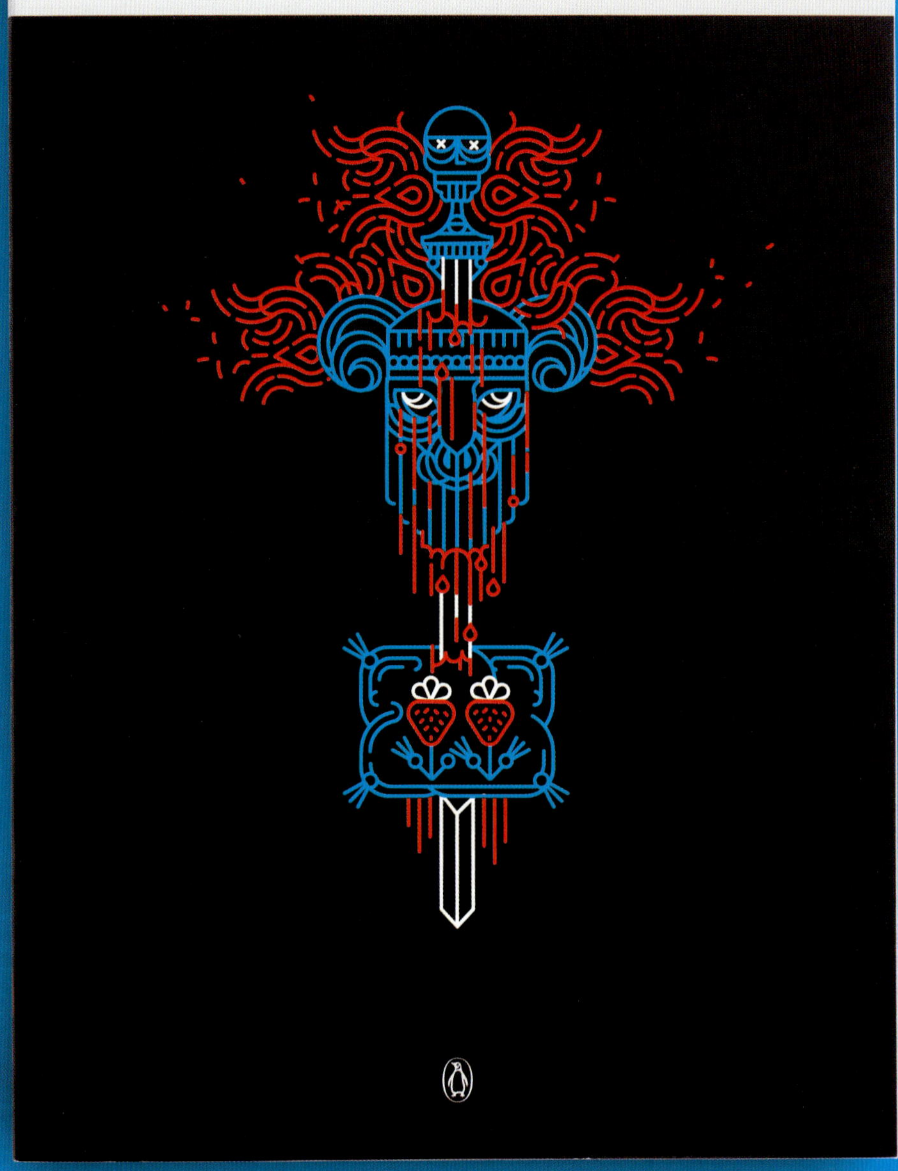

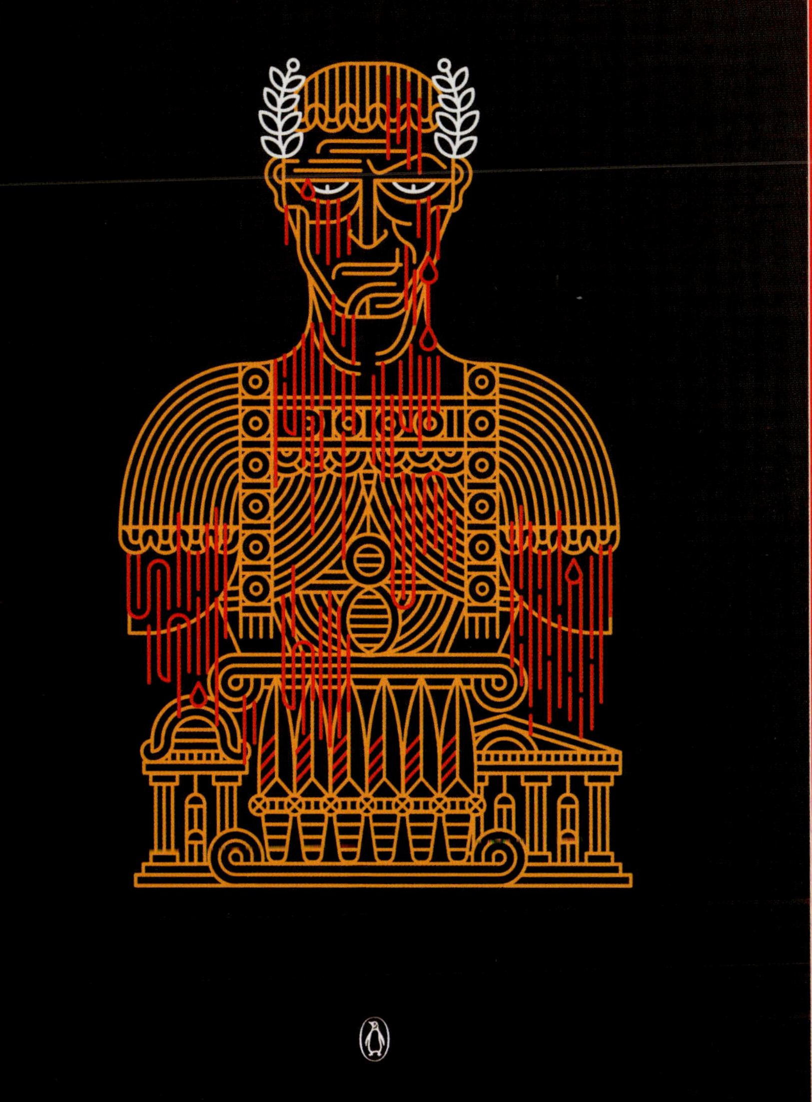
The Pelican
SHAKESPEARE
JULIUS CAESAR
Edited by
WILLIAM MONTGOMERY
With an Introduction by
DOUGLAS TREVOR

The Pelican
SHAKESPEARE

THE TEMPEST

Edited by
PETER HOLLAND

Paul Buckley, CREATIVE DIRECTOR

Serendipity plays a large role in the folks I work with, and the marriage of Manuja Waldia and William Shakespeare is a beautiful example of that. I'm thinking about so many projects at any one time, and while I don't believe the world is trying to talk to me, sometimes the world kinda sorta does talk to you—if you're panicked and fear heightened enough to be feeling like prey, knowing there's a deadline-induced predator right around the corner ready to pounce. In those moments, I pay attention to every artist submission in my office mailbox, every poster I walk by—every single manufactured image that flies by my eyeballs has me thinking, "Can this work? Would this work? If I did this? If I asked them to maybe come at it this way? Would they change their palette or style just a little to be a better fit?" You get the idea.

The **SHAKESPEARE** series is a *huge* commission. It's massive. Forty books, William F'in Shakespeare. Only giants have gone here—Milton Glaser, Riccardo Vecchio, David Gentleman—and I was thinking hard on which heavy hitter I was going to reach out to. I was quickly running out of time—forty books is not something I can make a mistake, any mistake, on. I can't be late; I can't hire someone who flakes out or becomes difficult in any way.

I was in full-on panic mode when I received an e-mail from someone I'd never heard of, Manuja Waldia. Anyway, 99 percent of that type of e-mail gets deleted, but hers was that rare 1 percent that demanded (politely) that I look. It was titled simply "Hello" and consisted of her introducing herself and saying nice things about my work. (C'mon, I'm just like you, reader—you like to hear nice things about yourself; don't you judge me.) She was recommended by Jessica Hische, which also made me pay attention, and she ended with a link to her website and asked that I take a look. No samples were attached, which is never a good idea, as a sample can mean the difference between "Oooh, that looks amazing" and "Crap, I gotta get this job out the door; I'll look later," then you forget it under a barrage of another hundred e-mails needing a few minutes of your time.

The Pelican SHAKESPEARE
THE TAMING OF THE SHREW
Edited by STEPHEN ORGEL

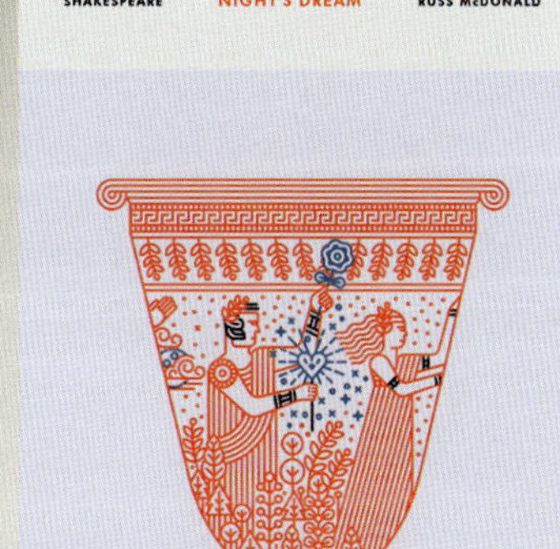

The Pelican SHAKESPEARE
A MIDSUMMER NIGHT'S DREAM
Edited by RUSS McDONALD

So I looked and was truly blown away. A very large percentage of highly vectorized work looks terrible, mostly because it tries to fool you and be something other than what it is. Manuja's vector work embraces its vector-ness like no other work I've ever seen, and it does so with perfect design precision. Every shape, every juncture, every single seemingly minor decision is flawless. The world lost something when Manuja chose not to be a brain surgeon or a city planner. Ornamental work of this caliber requires the illustrator be just as amazing a designer as she is an illustrator—this is all smartly designed combinations of shapes laid bare; there is no hiding mistakes in something like this.

So a lightbulb went off (cheap metaphor, I know, but there was an instant loud pop in my brain of "Something this vector would be so wrong for the topic of Shakespeare," followed instantly by "And that's why it's such a beautiful idea").

Shakespeare in our time brought to us by a then-twenty-two-year-old that my field had no real knowledge of yet. A dangerous idea that paid off forty times over.

MACBETH
KING LEAR
HAMLET
ROMEO AND JULIET

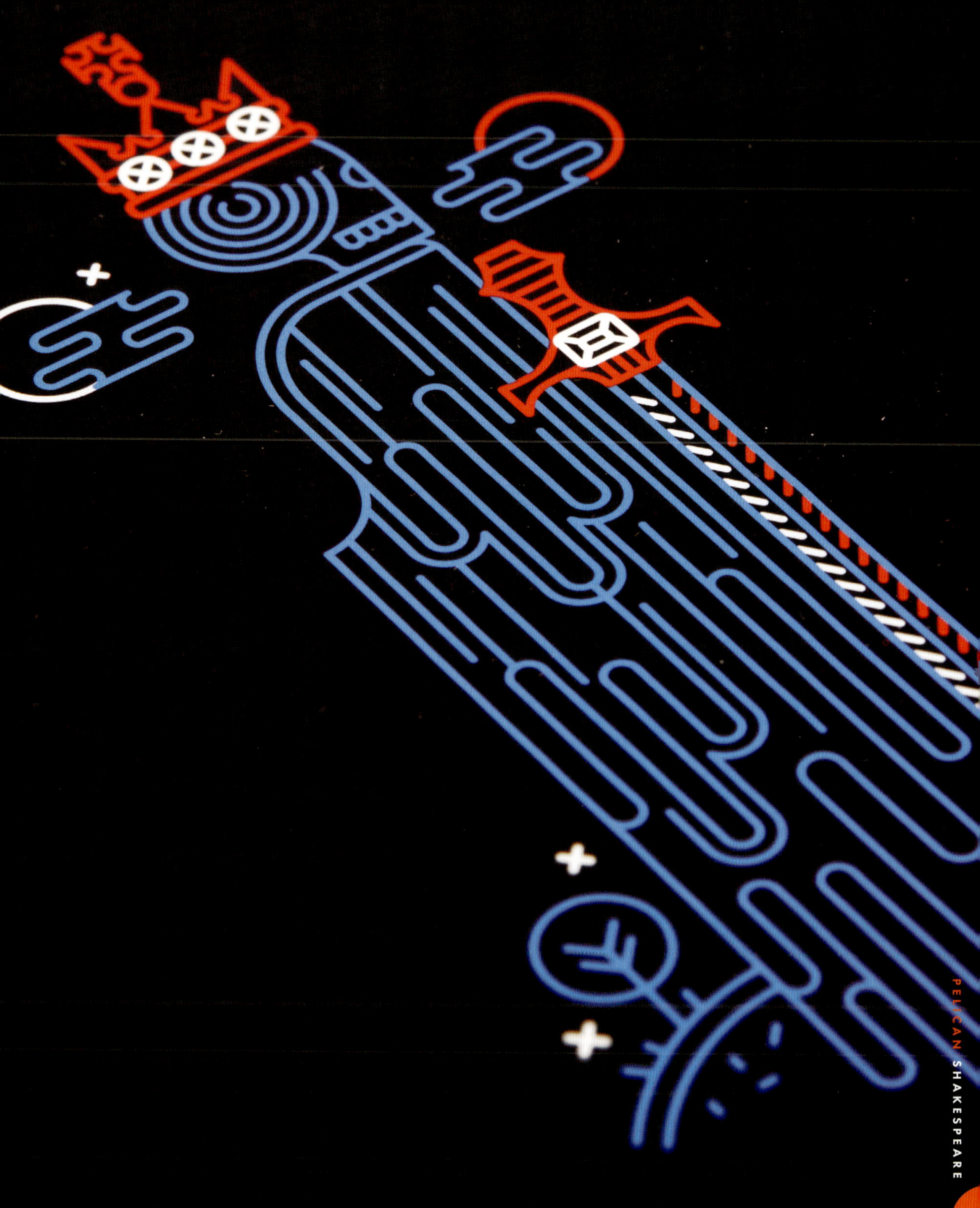

 • PHOTO, JAY LUU

Acknowledgments

These pages are dedicated to Elda Rotor and all the glorious artists who agree to collaborate with us. The visuals within illuminate the many reasons why, far better than any words I might summon forth.

My heartfelt thanks to all.

As well, I absolutely must thank the übertalented Matt Vee, who agreed to design this book. I wear many hats at Penguin Random House and oversee a daunting number of employees, imprints, and projects, and trying to get into my office to see me with armloads of layout proposals means four out of five times I'm going to say some version of *"I can't right now; I just can't. I'll come find you."* His dogged determination to see us through this project in the face of my taking on more than I probably should have often resulted in his being the true professional in the room.

Matt, thank you.

Index

PENGUIN BOOKS

An imprint of
Penguin Random House LLC
375 Hudson Street
New York, New York 10014
www.penguin.com

Library of Congress
Cataloging-in-Publication Data
Names: Buckley, Paul, 1965–
editor, writer of introduction.
Title: Classic Penguin :
cover to cover / edited with an
introduction by Paul Buckley.
Description: New York, New York :
Penguin Books, an imprint of
Penguin Random house LLC, [2016]
Identifiers: LCCN 2016016193 |
ISBN 9780143110132 (paperback)
Subjects: LCSH: Book cover art–
Collectibles. | Penguin classics.
| BISAC: DESIGN / Book. |
ANTIQUES & COLLECTIBLES /
Books. | DESIGN / Graphic Arts
/ General. Classification: LCC
NC1002.B65 C53 2016 | DDC
741.6/4075–dc23

Printed in China
3 5 7 9 10 8 6 4

Interior design by
Matt Vee (www.mattvee.me)

Cover design by
Paul Buckley & Matt Vee

Photography by George Baier IV,
unless noted otherwise
(www.georgebaier.com)

Production by
Matt Vee & Randy Reed

Cover Illustrations by
(front, left to right, top to bottom):
A. Wang, P. Killoffer, J. Tamaki,
J.C.P. Gomez (BAKEA), J. Tamaki,
C.C. Askew, Z. Lazar, M. Waldia,
R. Kikuo Johnson, R. MacDonald,
E. Kinsella III, B. Rea, W. Sweeney:
(front flap) R. Muradov,
R. MacDonald, C.C. Askew;
(back flap) R. Muradov

Page 160: Excerpt from "Poem of the Gifts" ("Poema de los dones") by Jorge Luis Borges, translated by Alastair Reid, from *Selected Poems* by Jorge Luis Borges, edited by Alexander Coleman (Viking Penguin, 1999).

• JILLIAN TAMAKI

01 14